The Interpretation of Archaeological Spatial Patterning

INTERDISCIPLINARY CONTRIBUTIONS TO ARCHAEOLOGY

ECOLOGY AND HUMAN ORGANIZATION ON THE GREAT PLAINS
Douglas B. Bamforth

HOLOCENE HUMAN ECOLOGY IN NORTHEASTERN NORTH AMERICA
Edited by George P. Nicholas

HUNTER-GATHERERS
Archaeological and Evolutionary Theory
Robert L. Bettinger

THE INTERPRETATION OF ARCHAEOLOGICAL SPATIAL PATTERNING
Edited by Ellen M. Kroll and T. Douglas Price

THE PLEISTOCENE OLD WORLD
Regional Perspectives
Edited by Olga Soffer

The Interpretation of Archaeological Spatial Patterning

Edited by

ELLEN M. KROLL and
T. DOUGLAS PRICE

University of Wisconsin
Madison, Wisconsin

Plenum Press • New York and London

Library of Congress Cataloging-in-Publication Data

The Interpretation of archaeological spatial patterning / edited by
Ellen M. Kroll and T. Douglas Price.
        p.   cm. -- (Interdisciplinary contributions to archaeology)
    Papers presented at a symposium organized at the 52nd Annual
Meeting of the Society for American Archaeology held in May 1987 in
Toronto, Ont.
    Includes bibliographical references and index.
    ISBN 0-306-43645-0
    1. Social archaeology--Congresses. 2. Excavations (Archaeology)-
-Congresses. 3. Spatial behavior--History--Congresses.
4. Ethnoarchaeology--Congresses.   I. Kroll, Ellen M. II. Price, T.
Douglas (Theron Douglas) III. Society for American Archaeology.
Meeting (52nd : 1987 : Toronto, Ont.) IV. Series.
CC72.4.I57 1991
930.1--dc20   90-19444
                                                                 CIP

ISBN 0-306-43645-0

© 1991 Plenum Press, New York
A Division of Plenum Publishing Corporation
233 Spring Street, New York, N.Y. 10013

Printed in the United States of America

Contributors

Laurence E. Bartram • Department of Anthropology, University of Wisconsin–Madison, Madison, Wisconsin 53706

Nicholas Blurton Jones • Graduate School of Education and Departments of Anthropology and Psychiatry, University of California at Los Angeles, Los Angeles, California 90024

Henry T. Bunn • Department of Anthropology, University of Wisconsin–Madison, Madison, Wisconsin 53706

Christopher Carr • Department of Anthropology, Arizona State University, Tempe, Arizona 85287

Rob Gargett • Department of Anthropology, University of California at Berkeley, Berkeley, California 94720

Susan A. Gregg • Center for Archaeological Investigations, Southern Illinois University, Carbondale, Illinois 62901

Kristen Hawkes • Department of Anthropology, University of Utah, Salt Lake City, Utah 84112

Brian Hayden • Department of Archaeology, Simon Fraser University, Burnaby, British Columbia V5A 1S6, Canada

Lawrence H. Keeley • Department of Anthropology, University of Illinois at Chicago, Chicago, Illinois 60680

Susan Kent • Anthropology Program, Old Dominion University, Norfolk, Virginia 23529

Keith W. Kintigh • Department of Anthropology, Arizona State University, Tempe, Arizona 85287

Ellen M. Kroll • Department of Anthropology, University of Wisconsin–Madison, Madison, Wisconsin 53706

James F. O'Connell • Department of Anthropology, University of Utah, Salt Lake City, Utah 84112

T. Douglas Price • Department of Anthropology, University of Wisconsin–Madison, Madison, Wisconsin 53706

Jean-Philippe Rigaud • Direction des Antiquites Préhistoriques d'Aquitaine, 6 bis Cours de Gourgue, 33074 Bordeaux, France

Jan F. Simek • Department of Anthropology, University of Tennessee, Knoxville, Tennessee 37996-0720

Marc G. Stevenson • Department of Anthropology, University of Alberta, Edmonton, Alberta T6G 2H4, Canada

Robert Whallon • Museum of Anthropology, University of Michigan, Ann Arbor, Michigan 48109

Preface

Investigations of archaeological intrasite spatial patterns have generally taken one of two directions: studies that introduced and explored methods for the analysis of archaeological spatial patterns or those that described and analyzed the formation of spatial patterns in actualistic—ethnographic, experimental, or natural—contexts. The archaeological studies were largely quantitative in nature, concerned with the recognition and definition of patterns; the actualistic efforts were often oriented more toward interpretation, dealing with how patterns formed and what they meant. Our research group on archaeological spatial analysis at the University of Wisconsin–Madison has been working for several years on both quantitative and interpretive problems. Both lines of investigation are closely related and are important complements.

In order to demonstrate the convergence of archaeological and actualistic studies for the understanding of intrasite spatial patterns, we organized a symposium at the 52nd Annual Meeting of the Society of American Archaeology in Toronto, Canada, in May 1987. The symposium, titled "The Interpretation of Stone Age Archaeological Spatial Patterns," was organized into two sessions. The six papers presented in the morning session, five of which comprise Part I of this volume, focused on ethnoarchaeological and experimental research. Michael Schiffer was the discussant for this half of the symposium. Our intention for the ethnoarchaeological contributions to the symposium and volume was the delineation of some of the significant accomplishments achieved thus far by actualistic studies regarding the formation of spatial patterns. The eight papers in the afternoon session, of which four comprise Part II of this volume, largely examined the strengths and weaknesses of current interpretations of spatial patterns at particular archaeological sites. Robert Whallon was the discussant. Our goal for the afternoon session at the symposium and Part II of this volume was to examine the extent to which studies of archaeological spatial patterns have employed and benefited from the results of actualistic research.

We believe that these papers clearly identify the important, current trends in archaeological research on the distribution of artifacts and other refuse at prehistoric sites. In compiling this volume, our intention is not to emphasize particular interpretations or directions of research regarding spatial patterning in the ethnographic or archaeological record. We hope rather to encourage the ongoing interplay between studies oriented at identifying spatial patterns and interpreting them in both present and prehistoric contexts—whether the patterns involve cultural and/or natural processes or formation. Both directions contribute to the growth of our understanding of the past.

The final versions of the papers that appear in this volume have been revised and expanded since Toronto. We wish to thank the contributors to the volume for both their participation in the symposium and their punctual response to our requests for papers and subsequent revisions. We and the other contributors to the volume would like to thank the discussants at the symposium and the staff at Plenum Press—especially Eliot Werner, Senior Editor, and Michael Jochim, Series Editor—for the comments and suggestions on the organization of the volume and on the individual papers.

Contents

The Interpretation of
Archaeological
Spatial Patterning

Introduction

ELLEN M. KROLL AND T. DOUGLAS PRICE

The interpretation of archaeological spatial patterns, in a sense, is as old an endeavor as Paleolithic archaeology itself. Since the earliest findings of prehistoric artifacts, prehistorians have tried to interpret the spatial associations and arrangements of materials in their depositional context. A major concern in the last century—the establishment of human antiquity—relied on the analysis of spatial relationships, specifically the co-occurrence of ancient bones and stone artifacts in stratified deposits.

Almost a century has passed since archaeologists began recording the precise location of items that were uncovered in Paleolithic excavations. It is only since the 1950s, however, that the quantity of such information has greatly increased. In the last 30 years, significant strides have been made in the analysis and interpretation of intrasite spatial data. This 30-year period can be considered in three stages of development.

In the initial stage, a site map was typically scrutinized, sometimes to confirm the absence of natural disturbances, but more often to ascertain the presence of an overall structure or pattern to the distribution of artifacts that could be used to substantiate the archaeological site as a camp or habitation. Classic monographs on the Mesolithic site of Star Carr by Grahame Clark (1954) and on the Oldowan sites at Olduvai Gorge in Tanzania by Mary Leakey (1971) are exemplary and document the use of spatial data at either ends of the Pleistocene. In the former study, Clark reported the distribution of a variety of bone and stone objects and their implications for understanding the nature of the habitation area. In the latter, Leakey considered the distributions of broken bones and technologically simple stone artifacts—their vertical concentration, their horizontal spatial associations, and their specific horizontal configurations at several sites (e.g., DK, FLK *Zinjanthropus*, FLK North Levels 1 and 2)—as evidence of the "living floors" or "occupation sites" of ancient hominids.

ELLEN M. KROLL and T. DOUGLAS PRICE • Department of Anthropology, University of Wisconsin–Madison, Madison, Wisconsin 53706.

1

In the second stage of research, beginning in the late 1960s and early 1970s, approaches to intrasite spatial data diverged in three directions. First, the visual analysis of archaeological sites benefited from the dissolution of composite maps into multiple overlay plans, showing selected features and categories of refuse, which could be compared and contrasted. These plans were also enhanced by detailed distributions of refitted artifacts and bones. Studies at the Upper Paleolithic site of Pincevent in France by Leroi-Gourhan and his colleagues (Leroi-Gourhan and Brézillon 1966, 1972) and the Mesolithic site of Meer by Van Noten *et al.* (1978, 1980) are outstanding examples of such research. It is reasonable to say that Pincevent set the standard toward which most subsequent work has been aimed.

Second, emerging largely in an attempt to find new ways to resolve the question of variability in Mousterian assemblages, archaeologists adopted quantitative techniques for spatial analysis, largely from fields such as plant ecology and geography. Robert Whallon (1973a, b, 1974) was primarily responsible for this work, recommending the use of several different quantitative techniques, including the dimensional analysis of variance and nearest neighbor analysis. These more objective [and less visual] methods involved a search for nonrandom spatial associations of various categories of artifacts and other refuse. The objective was to identify Paleolithic "tool kits" and activity areas. Common in the archaeological literature and in symposia at academic meetings at that time were studies concerned primarily with the development of statistical methods for pattern recognition.

Third, and perhaps in part as a reaction to the assumptions of both visual and statistical approaches to spatial data, yet another direction sought new insights into the factors involved in the formation of archaeological sites and the distribution of artifacts. This work involved ethnoarchaeological observations of the camps of modern hunter–gatherers, experimental observations of simulated archaeological distributions, and taphonomic observations of naturally formed spatial patterns of bones or stones. Studies by Ascher (1968), Binford (1978), Gifford (1978), Gould (1968), Hayden (1980), O'Connell (1987), Schiffer (1972, 1976), and Yellen (1977) are well-known examples. Some of the basic problems, inherent in the assumptions and methods of archaeological intrasite spatial analysis, became readily apparent in these "actualistic" studies. It was no longer a viable research goal to search archaeological spatial data exclusively for nonrandom distributions and associations of particular categories of stone artifacts. Quantitative methods that crammed spatial distributions into a limited template of *a priori* patterns were outmoded. New methods were needed that considered spatial patterns as variable in size, shape, density, composition, and spacing.

The recent emergence of the third stage of intrasite spatial analysis has involved the convergence of the three previously distinct paths that were pursued during the second developmental stage. Essentially, the assumptions of the 1970s have become the questions and working hypotheses of the 1980s. For example, where the presence of "activity areas" was previously an underlying assumption of many studies, now the demonstration of the existence and preservation of such areas is a major focus of research. Earlier studies, particularly during the second developmental stage described above, have emphasized *methods* for the identification of spatial patterns, rather than the interpretation of the information gained from such methods. The present volume is intended to bring together the work of various individuals who are concerned with the *interpretation* of spatial patterns, as well as with methods of pattern recognition. The focus of the volume is also on the camps of hunter–gatherers, both contemporary groups and prehistoric groups of the Stone Age. Sites formed by hunter–gatherers comprise the baseline data for the enquiry into 99% of past human behavior. Farming and village settlements introduce major changes in the human use of space and the disposal of refuse that are best considered in another volume.

This volume has two major sections that share important themes. Chapters in the first part of the book are concerned with the spatial patterning of archaeological materials, formed by cultural and/or natural processes in the present day—the ethnoarchaeological evidence of archaeological patterning. The authors consider hunter–gatherer groups from Africa and Australia in this discussion, as well as human and nonhuman factors in the use of living space. James O'Connell, Kristen Hawkes, and Nicholas Blurton Jones report on recent work among the Hadza of East Africa. Their ethnographic overview provides important new data on the relationship of time, various daily activities by males and females, and the production and location of refuse among these contemporary hunter–gatherers. Laurence Bartram, Ellen Kroll, and Henry Bunn provide a similar perspective on the variability in camp structure at camps of the Kua San hunter–gatherers of Botswana in southern Africa. They examine some of the factors affecting the composition and distribution of bone food refuse. Both of these field studies were conducted within the last several years. Susan Kent considers the relationship between the intended length of stay and the resulting site structure, also using data from contemporary groups of Botswana. Rob Gargett and Brian Hayden share the view from Australia in a discussion of spatial structuring at Aborigine campsites. Intriguing differences can be seen in the camp size and the organization of activities among the Hadza, San, and Aborigine hunter–gatherers.

The final chapter in Part I deals with the myriad factors affecting the spatial patterning of archaeological materials, both human and nonhuman. Susan Gregg, Keith Kintigh, and Robert Whallon take a fascinating look at what might happen to material remains at a contemporary hunter–gatherer camp, given the vagaries of preservation in the archaeological record. The spatial data reported in John Yellen's (1977) earlier work among the !Kung San are used as the baseline data for this computer simulation. Refuse is moved or destroyed by the computer to recreate postdepositional disturbance and to determine how much of the original patterning remains subsequent to such movement and disappearance.

The second part of the volume offers a survey of the archaeological evidence from a series of Stone Age sites. One chapter focuses on a Middle Paleolithic site (Rigaud and Simek), and two chapters examine Upper Paleolithic sites (Carr; Keeley). Jean-Philippe Rigaud and Jan Simek report on the processes of site formation at the Vaufrey Cave (Grotte XV, Couche VIII, Dordogne, France) and the difficulties of interpreting spatial patterning among prehistoric stone artifacts and bones in cave and rockshelter deposits. Interpretations of prehistoric site use are enhanced through the use of several methods of spatial analysis, including visual impressions, k-means cluster analysis, and refitting. Christopher Carr reexamines the classic data from Pincevent Habitation No. 1. He stresses the importance of testing multiple alternative models of the formation of spatial patterns and argues for the convergence of multiple lines of evidence. He demonstrates his plea by contrasting Leroi-Gourhan's and Binford's alternative interpretations of the hearth-associated stone and bone distributions that are well known from Pincevent. Lawrence Keeley examines the effects of the manufacture and use of stone tools on the spatial patterning of materials at the site of Verberie in the Paris Basin of France. He confronts the problem of incorporating relatively new microwear evidence on stone artifacts into analyses aimed at distinguishing the locations of use, retooling, and discard of hafted and unhafted artifacts.

Stone artifacts are the predominant material remains for 99% of human prehistory. Patterns of production and discard of lithic tools and waste products are the source of much of our information on the Paleolithic. Because modern hunter–gatherers generally discontinued the use of such materials decades or more ago, there have been few contemporary opportunities to investigate their importance as indicators of past human activities. Extrapolations from experimental stone knapping and stone using and from ethnographic observations of the production, use, and discard of artifacts of various raw materials provide important clues for the analysis and interpretation of lithic distributions from the past.

In the final chapter of Part II, Marc Stevenson discusses several conclusions from ethnoarchaeological research about the universal size sorting of refuse around outdoor hearths in short-term hunter–gatherer camps. He develops two models, one for interpreting the sequential formation of hearth-associated artifact assemblages at archaeological sites based on artifact size sorting and the other for linking gender to particular lithic concentrations.

The volume concludes with a commentary by Douglas Price in the Postscript forming Part III on the interplay between "actualistic" and archaeological studies in the analysis and interpretation of intrasite spatial patterns.

The volume emphasizes the value of examining a diverse set of spatial data and considering multiple alternative interpretations of particular spatial patterns. The chapters touch on current problems facing spatial analysts and on ones to be resolved in future research, including methods for determining the contemporaneity of materials and features that constitute a spatial pattern, for distinguishing whether particular hearths were used as foci for domestic or other maintenance or special-purpose activities (e.g., in hunting blinds), and for attributing gender to refuse from predominantly male or female activities.

Although the methods for the identification of intrasite spatial patterns are not the focus of the volume, several of the chapters summarize the recent developments in pattern-recognition methods and demonstrate the use of several techniques, including dissected maps, density countour diagrams, k-means analysis, and unconstrained cluster analysis (e.g., those by Carr; Gregg *et al.*; Rigaud and Simek; Stevenson). The results obtained from a variety of analytical methods emphasize the necessary and fruitful relationship among actualistic observations and archaeological research for defining interpretive goals and developing relevant methods of pattern recognition.

As attested by the studies herein, quantitative spatial methods are no longer expected to find masked or invisible spatial patterns; rather, such methods are being used to confirm and to explore further the bolder patterns within archaeological sites. All archaeological sites do not share an equal potential for spatial analysis; those with a structure that is clear to the naked eye provide the best opportunity for interpreting the natural and artificial processes of formation, and, where appropriate, for reconstructing the spatial distribution of hominid activities.

There is an unavoidable lag time between the revelations of actualistic studies and the exploration of their implications for archaeological studies. The chapters in this volume bridge that gap and pose new problems for future research. Spatial analysis is clearly a subject of major and continuing interest in archaeology.

1. REFERENCES

Ascher, R., 1968, Time's Arrow and the Archaeology of a Contemporary Community. In *Settlement Archaeology* (K. C. Chang, ed.), National Press Books, Palo Alto, pp. 43–52.

Binford, L. R., 1978, Dimensional Analysis of Behavior and Site Structure: Learning from an Eskimo Hunting Stand, *American Antiquity* 43:330–361.

Gifford, D. P., 1978, *Observations of Modern Human Settlements as an Aid to Archaeological Interpretation*, Ph.D. dissertation, Department of Anthropology, University of California.

Gould, R. A., 1968, Living Archaeology: The Ngatatjara of Western Australia, *Southwestern Journal of Anthropology* 24:101–122.

Hayden, B., 1979, *Palaeolithic Reflections*, Australian Institute of Aboriginal Studies, Canberra.

Leroi-Gourhan, A., and Brézillon, M., 1966, L'habitation Magdalénienne No. 1 de Pincevent près Montereau (Seine-et-Marne), *Gallia Préhistoire* 9:263–385.

Leroi-Gourhan, A., and Brézillon, M., 1972, Fouilles de Pincevent, Essai d'Analyse Ethnographique d'un Habitat Magdalénien. (la section 36), *Gallia Préhistoire*, 7th supplement, CNRS, Paris.

O'Connell, J. F., 1987, Alyawara Site Structure and Its Archaeological Implications, *American Antiquity* 52:74–108.

Schiffer, M., 1972, Archaeological Context and Systemic Context, *American Antiquity* 37:156–165.

Schiffer, M., 1976, *Behavioral Archeology*, Academic Press, New York.

Van Noten, F., Cahen, D., Keeley, L. H., and Moeyersons, J., 1978, *Les Chasseurs de Meer*, de Temple, Brugge.

Van Noten, F., Keeley, L., and Cahen, D., 1980, A Paleolithic Campsite in Belgium, *Scientific American* 242(4):48–55.

Whallon, R., 1973a, Spatial Analysis of Occupation Floors I: Application of Dimensional Analysis of Variance, *American Antiquity* 38:266–278.

Whallon, R., 1973b, Spatial Analysis of Paleolithic Occupation Areas. In *The Explanation of Culture Change: Models in Prehistory* (C. Renfrew, ed.), University of Pittsburgh Press, pp. 115–130.

Whallon, R., 1974, Spatial Analysis of Occupation floors II: The Application of Nearest Neighbor analysis, *American Antiquity* 39:16–34.

Yellen, J., 1977, *Archaeological Approaches to the Present: Models for Reconstructing the Past*, Academic Press, New York.

Part I

Spatial Analysis of Ethnoarchaeological Sites

Many of the initial reports and analyses of spatially oriented ethnoarchaeological and actualistic observations were aimed at assessing the accuracy of archeological assumptions about activity areas in sites—was it indeed legitimate to search for single-activity areas in which the association or co-occurrence of particular artifact types and/or other categories of refuse indicated what activity had occurred? The revelations of such studies were enlightening and showed that the basic assumptions of the initial quantitative analyses of archaeological intrasite spatial patterns needed revision; the spatial relationships and distribution patterns that were being rigorously sought through the use of quantitative analyses were not necessarily meaningful for interpretations of past human behavior. That direction of actualistic research—focused on an understanding of the relationship between the distribution of dynamic activities in the camps of modern hunter–gatherers and the static refuse that would become the archaeological record of those activities—is considered in three chapters in this part.

O'Connell, Hawkes, and Blurton Jones investigate the distribution of male and female activities relative to the overall camp structure of contemporary Hadza hunter–gatherers of Tanzania and the implications for comparable archaeological studies. A prerequisite to applying their ethnographic findings to Stone Age sites is the methodology for attributing particular archaeological materials to male or female activities.

Moving from the Hadza to the Kua San hunter–gatherers of Botswana, the chapter by Bartram, Kroll, and Bunn reports on the distribution of activities involving the butchery, cooking, and consumption of carcasses relative to the distribution of bone refuse and overall camp structure as a guideline for interpreting comparable patterning in prehistoric sites. The archaeological invisibility of some of the structures that affect the distributions of activities and bone refuse in contemporary camps—for example, brush windbreaks, bushes, and shade trees—make difficult the interpretation of Stone Age distributions of bones, especially in the absence of hearths, as is so for much of the Pleistocene.

Both of these chapters offer useful guidelines for interpreting the archaeological record as well as presenting previously unpublished and spatially relevant ethnographic data. These chapters challenge archaeologists to examine spatial patterns in new ways. Exemplary archaeological counterparts to these ethnographic studies are presented in the volume in Part II; for example, Stevenson pursues the identification of male and female activity areas at archaeological sites.

In their chapter, Gregg, Kintigh, and Whallon analyze the arrangement of structures, features, and refuse in an ethnographic camp of the !Kung San, which was previously published by John Yellen (*Archaeological Approaches to the Present*), to make two important observations for archaeological spatial studies. First, they demonstrate that two of the currently available methods for the quantitative analysis of archaeological intrasite distributions, *K*-means analysis and unconstrained cluster analysis, are each successful in identifying the spatial patterns that were reported as significant from ethnographic interviews. Second, despite the computer-simulated disturbance of the spatial patterns at the same camp, including the movement and destruction of refuse, the original spatial patterns reported by Yellen could still be discriminated by quantitative analyses. Both of these conclusions provide optimism regarding the efficacy of spatial studies in archaeology. The challenge remains, nevertheless, for archaeologists to attach meaning, both cultural and natural, to the patterns that are identified at prehistoric sites.

A different direction of inquiry, also based on previously published ethnoarchaeological observations, is developed in two other chapters in this part. They converge on the issues of camp size and the spacing of household clusters within the camps of contemporary hunter–gatherers in Africa and Australia. The chapter by Gargett and Hayden examines ethnographic evidence from Australia in support of a socially rooted explanation of camp size and structure. The chapter by Susan Kent considers ethnographic evidence from southern Africa to argue that anticipated mobility has a significant effect on the arrangement and organization of camps. These chapters join several other recently published examinations of site size and structure (e.g., Whitelaw 1983; Gould and Yellen 1987; O'Connell 1987) aimed at answering the following questions. Why is there cross-cultural and intracultural variability in the dimensions of hunter–gatherer camps? Is this variability related to population size, length of occupation (actual or intended), social relationships and sharing among the occupants, the intensity and kind of activities, environmental contexts including the abundance of potentially threatening predators, or a combination of these factors?

Using ethnographic information on variability in site size for the interpretation of archaeological observations, however, will encounter several obstacles. These involve the interpretation of multiple hearths in an archaeological site, specifically the demonstration of their contemporaneity and domestic function and of food sharing among the occupants of the hearths. These obstacles also are addressed in the chapter by Bartram *et al.* The documentation of anticipated mobility further involves both ethnographic and archaeological problems. How does one measure the intangible concept of anticipated mobility in an ethnographic context, let alone in an archaeological context?

The following five studies should stimulate new questions to be pursued by actualistic research. Their final contribution, however, will become apparent only after their implications and usefulness for archaeological spatial analyses are further explored and assessed in future archaeological research.

Chapter 1

Site Structure, Kinship, and Sharing in Aboriginal Australia
Implications for Archaeology

ROB GARGETT AND BRIAN HAYDEN

1. INTRODUCTION

Interactions between and among individuals in hunter–gatherer societies contribute fundamentally to the adaptiveness of the culture. Through the analysis of
site structure (the distribution on the landscape of habitations, activity areas,
refuse areas, and other features), it is possible to make inferences about past social
interaction, thus enabling archaeology to make a significant contribution to the
study of prehistoric cultural adaptations and dynamics.

The determinants of site structure are not well known. However, one important dimension that needs to be understood is the reason for the distribution
of habitations on the landscape. Decisions about where to live and how close to
live to others may not be made consciously, but their importance in shaping a site
makes understanding them imperative. The variables that influence such decisions must be explicitly identified before the correlates of site structure, as a
mirror of the cultural system, can be clearly understood. The translation of this

ROB GARGETT • Department of Anthropology, University of California at Berkeley, Berkeley,
California 94720.   BRIAN HAYDEN • Department of Archaeology, Simon Fraser University,
Burnaby, British Columbia V5A 1S6, Canada.

understanding to the archaeological situation requires a model or a set of models that will enable inferences to be made. Although some researchers may question the utility of such models for archaeology, given the limited areas exposed in most excavations, we are confident that the models we deal with in this chapter will help in interpreting the past, at least in some instances. For example, a number of contemporaneous habitations have been identified at the Paleo-Indian site of Vail in Maine (Speiss 1982), the Magdalenian site of Pincevent in France (Leroi-Gourhan and Brézillon 1966, 1972), and at the Mesolithic site of Meer in Belgium (Cahen, Keeley, and Van Noten 1979), and others. Given current trends in archaeology, many more comparable sites are likely to be excavated in the future.

This study seeks to clarify one aspect of site structure, namely the spacing between households. It has been argued that interhousehold spacing is a good indicator of social distance between occupants (Whitelaw 1983:55). By comparing an index of kin affiliation to the physical separation of huts at !Kung encampments, Whitelaw was able to demonstrate the existence of a relationship between these two variables. The more closely two households were related to one another, the more likely it was that they would be relatively close together in space. O'Connell (1987:86) perceived a similar situation at the Alyawara camps he studied. He found that 64% of nearest neighbors showed some "primary" genealogical links between them. A further 19% displayed close classificatory equivalents. His observations, however, only included nearest neighbors and did not take into account the fact that in aboriginal society one is always related by blood to a large portion of the inhabitants of the camp, which makes it difficult to avoid living next to kin.

Following Whitelaw's (1983) suggestion, our study examines the relationship between kinship distance and physical distance at a Pintupi encampment in the Western Desert of Australia. It examines a variety of kin relationships and identifies kinship links associated with the most pronounced spatial patterning. We argue that kinship and economic interdependence provide the best insights into the reasons for observable habitation patterning in a site. By building on original models like those of Whitelaw, a better understanding of a variety of determinants of hunter–gatherer site structure should emerge, enabling archaeologists to establish general statements about hunter–gatherers. The study of traditional groups offers the only chance for us to apprehend the determinants of spatial patterning.

From what we have learned about the !Kung and the Alyawara, it is possible to generate hypotheses to be applied to the Pintupi data and to test Whitelaw's hypothesis. Notably,

1. If sharing is heavily emphasized in certain social relationships in the Pintupi adaptation, we should see closer spacing between those household pairs that are expected to share resources between them more often than with other households in the group.

2. If interhousehold spacing is a sensitive indicator of social distance, we should see results similar to those of Whitelaw (1983) in an overall comparison of kin distance and physical separation.

If these hypotheses are borne out, we can then begin to ask questions about more specific relationships and affiliations that govern site structure and hope that they lead to conclusions that can be applied to other hunter–gatherer adaptations.

2. DATA COLLECTION AND MANIPULATION

The observations that form the basis of this study were made during an ethnographic reconaissance by Hayden in 1971 at Papunya, in the Western Desert of Australia. There, he encountered a group of about 300 Pintupi, most of whom had become acquainted with settlement life in the previous 10 to 25 years. They live near a permanent government housing project, in traditional or quasi-traditional shelters constructed of branches and various covering materials. Although a significant portion of their diet consists of hunted and gathered foods, which are shared according to traditional expectations, much of the food consumed is bought at the Papunya store with money obtained from occasional wage labor and pensions. This food, too, is often shared.

Within the larger settlement, several clusters of residences are discernible, which correspond roughly, in terms of kin group representation and geographical distribution, to four traditional bands and their estates (Hayden 1979:9). The clusters are similar to the extended family camps reported by Howitt (1904) for Southeast Australia. Spatial arrangements along kinship lines have also been observed among hunter–gatherers in northern North America and elsewhere in Australia (Honigmann 1961:56; Gould 1968:109; Burch 1975:250 ff).

Sixty structures comprise the main Pintupi camp at Papunya. Thirty-seven are shelters, which we will refer to as households, in which the occupants sleep, eat, and store possessions. The locations of all structures, including day-time sun shelters, were mapped, but in the site plan that appears in Figure 1, only the structures representing households are illustrated for simplicity's sake. Each shelter is associated with one or more hearths, an activity area, a day-time sun shelter, and a refuse area. These closely resemble the description for homologous features in the Alyawara camps studied by O'Connell (1987). The total area of these constellated features varies according to the number of occupants and the duration of occupation, but it is relatively predictable. Including refuse areas, these can be up to 20 meters in diameter per household (O'Connell 1987:78).

These communities are by no means permanent encampments. They vary constantly in response to the viscissitudes of personal relationships, maturation, availability of resources, marriage, and death. These same processes appear to operate among most generalized hunter–gatherers, whether following traditional susbistence strategies or living near industrial outposts (e.g., Lee 1979). In light of the well-documented tendency for households to change locations, any principles governing residence location must accommodate many acceptable possibilities. Nevertheless, although habitation locations are in a constant state of flux under traditional and settlement conditions, *the structure of each succeeding permutation should be determined by the same principles of association and affiliation.* Thus, even though the pattern of households is constantly changing, the data gathered at Papunya should enable us to monitor the principles at work in structuring sites, whether traditional or contact in nature.

At Papunya, and most other hunter–gatherer communities, households consist of three types of occupants: (1) married couples living with their dependent offspring; (2) unmarried males residing together (with older men usually living in different households from adolescents); (3) unmarried females living together. Unmarried males are quite mobile, whereas the households of married couples and the residences of unmarried women are more stable. In the households of unmarried men and women, close filial or sibling relationships usually obtain.

The Pintupi at Papunya retain, quite naturally, memories of pre- or pericontact lifeways, and many of the traditional organizing social behaviors are still observable. The eight-section kinship system, affiliation with ritual lodges, and other cross-cutting ties are still extant and active. Traditional rituals are performed, and gerontocratic polygyny is still practiced, often involving sisters. Rules governing postnuptial residence also seem to follow traditional lines: that is, for a period following the first marriage of a man, he is obliged to reside near the parents of his wife. This occurs for reasons discussed later but is, roughly speaking, the price paid for having received the woman from her parents (for an overview of these aspects of social organization, see Peterson 1970; Shapiro 1979).

With the help of a native interpreter, the genealogical relations of each person were recorded. It was not always possible to collect complete information due to taboos on referring to deceased persons and those living at different locations, but most of the relations within the camp were enumerated. From these observations, a table was constructed, and data concerning interhousehold distance, relationships, and sex and marital status were compiled. Because of the nature of the aboriginal kinship system, each of the people within one of the kin group clusters is related in a primary consanguineal sense to one or more others in the same cluster. As mentioned previously, similar observations were made by O'Connell (1987:78) for the Alyawara. In order to avoid the unenlightening conclusion that everyone in a cluster is related, we decided to restrict our study of spatial variability to primary genealogical links. And, rather than look only at nearest neighbors, we endeavored to monitor all of the related household pairs to see if there was any more interesting patterning.

The technique employed in this study to monitor the variability in household spacing is that of the simple bivariate plot of kinship distance against physical distance in related household pairs. Kinship distance is measured by assessing the number of primary genealogical links between each household. Primary kinship links are defined as those existing between parents and their natural children and between natural offspring of the same parents. (This definition is as precise as it is to preclude confusion with classificatory equivalents.) Thus, for example, a husband, wife, and child live in one structure, their daughter and her husband live in another. There are three primary links observed between the two households.

Various other aspects of kinship relationships were also studied. For example, marital status and sex were included to see if they were related in some way to the structure of the site. These subsets of the primary relationship were chosen for examination on the basis of ethnographic indications of social and economic importance and also on the basis of preliminary results indicative of strongly patterned relationships. Some of our expectations, given what is known of Pintupi social organization, follow:

1. Primary family relationships will be the most important economic and social relationships, and close spacing should be the result.
2. Daughters should reside close to their parents before and for a time after marriage.
3. Unmarried males should reside in a variety of places, showing little if any patterning.
4. Weaker relations should exist between classificatory, subsection relatives.
5. Close relations should obtain between brothers.

It will be seen that most relationships that we expect to result in close spacing do, in fact, manifest predictable spatial configurations.

3. RESULTS

As Figure 1 illustrates, the Pintupi households are arranged in four relatively coherent clusters. We view the within-cluster pattern of habitations as most closely representative of traditional encampment relationships. Indeed, when the parent/child relationship is highlighted, as in Figure 1, it is possible to see the rayed crescent arrangement observed by Howitt (1904:774). An informant described to Howitt a hypothetical camp whose structure was governed by the social relationships of the families comprising it. The traditional pattern installs an important person at the focus of the groups of households. At Papunya, the important person was usually a widow living in an unmarried women's residence. In the modern Pintupi camp, however, the pattern is more spread out than in the

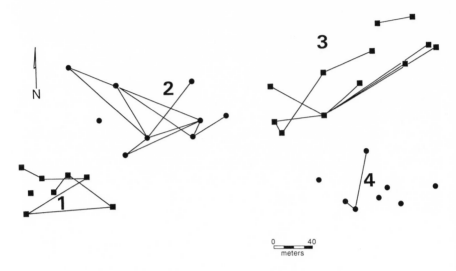

Figure 1. Plan of households at Pintupi encampment, Papunya 1971.

traditional context, probably due to factors accompanying long-term aggregation near an industrial outpost, some of which will be discussed later.

The crescent arrangement is less visible in clusters 1 and 4 (Figure 1). Their structure is somewhat confused by the presence in Cluster 1 of the mother of several of the women in Cluster 4. It would appear tht she is "visiting" her son, who is living near his wife's parents. The mechanisms governing the relative positions of habitations are, of course, the subject of this chapter and will be dealt with presently. Nevertheless, it is clear that the "ideal" of spatial organization is not always perceptible in reality. The ever-changing nature of hunter–gatherer sites can complicate the pattern. As clusters 2 and 3 demonstrate, however, the traditional structure is still coherent, and we are encouraged to think that our models will be generally applicable.

All of the distance values for household pairs related by primary links are represented in Figure 2. Curves for mean values, both at the site and the cluster level, have been superimposed to show trends. Clearly, there is a tendency for households related by several links to be more closely spaced. This is similar to the results obtained by Whitelaw (1983:51). Both site and cluster curves for mean values are flat at 40 meters and four links. Admittedly, the number of values for more than three links is small. However, the absence of any observations greater than 100 meters for these categories is probably significant, and we expect that the close spacing where many links exist is a nonrandom occurrence.

The household pair at eight links and 110 meters exemplifies the difficulty of dealing with anything as complex as site structure using small samples for

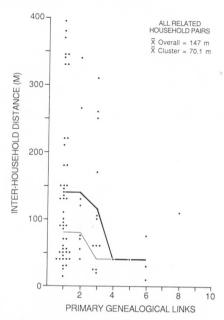

Figure 2. Scatterplot of interhousehold distance and primary genealogical links using all related household pairs.

some categories. This unusual case is primarily due to the presence of, once again, a household of "visitors" in Cluster 2 having no parental links in the cluster. The distance between this household and those closely related to it should probably be closer to 40 meters than 110 meters (the observed distance). We do not think that households related by so many kin ties would always be separated by 110 m; it is much more likely that most of the time they would be on the order of 20 to 40 m apart.

Figure 3 illustrates the distances between households related by classificatory relationships only. It is a much more nebulous array, displaying higher mean values and an erratic slope to both curves. This accords with our expectation that primary links should be more important and show more consistent patterning than the less important classificatory relationships. Consistent with our expectations, the proportion of households related by classificatory links within 50 m of each other is among the lowest. Only 21% of the classificatory household pairs, against 29% for the primary relations, are within 50 m (Table 1).

From our preliminary analyses, there appeared to be strong patterning in households of parents and offspring. It was decided to examine these relationships in greater detail, to define more precisely their role in the creation of pattering on the site. Of the parents, the mother is the most likely to be surviving at the time of marriage of her offspring. This is due to her younger age at marriage compared

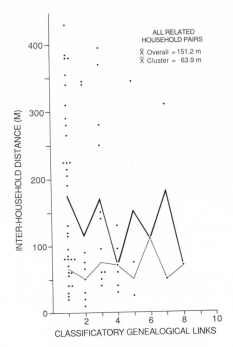

Figure 3. Scatterplot of interhousehold distance and classificatory links using all related household pairs.

Table 1. Summary of Within-Cluster Mean Distances and the Proportion of Households within 50 Meters for Each Category of Relationship

	Mean overall (m)	Mean, cluster (m)	Proportion < 50 m
All household pairs including unrelated	Unavailable	75.5	8%
All pairs related by primary links	147.0	70.1	29%
All pairs related by classificatory links	151.2	63.9	21%
Parent/son	148.0	73.0	18%
Parent/daughter	110.9	52.5	35%
Brothers	123.7	42.7	50%
Sisters	155.3	80.6	13%

to her husband's. Were we to monitor the relationship between children and male parents, or only those in which both parents were living, we would be drawing from a very small sample (e.g., for fathers/daughters, $n = 6$; for fathers/sons, $n = 9$). For this reason, our analyses of parent/child relationships include the mother only. We were still able to observe meaningful patterning; therefore we are confident that there is no loss of robusticity because of our decision.

The observations for parent/child relationships and interhousehold distance are separated by sex and marital status. Figure 4 presents the plot for mothers and male offspring. It demonstrates (1) the tendency for unmarried sons to live in the same cluster as their mother, although still displaying higher than average spacing, and (2) the opposite situation for married males. (As mentioned previously, it is less likely that the married male's parents will be alive, which may explain why there are so few married males in this sample.) High average spacing within clusters, 73.0 m, and only 18% of males living within 50 m of their parents, suggests a weak relationship between parents and sons.

In contrast, Figure 5 illustrates the situation for daughters. The majority live within 60 m (mean distance = 52.5 m) of their mothers, and a relatively high 35% live within 50 m. Seventy-seven percent of females live in the same cluster as their mother, compared with 64% for males. The mother/daughter relationship appears

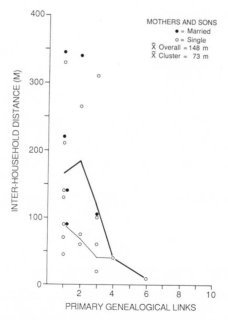

Figure 4. Scatterplot of interhousehold distance and primary genealogical links using mother/son relationship.

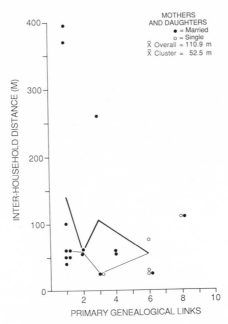

Figure 5. Scatterplot of interhousehold distance and primary genealogical links using mother/daughter relationship.

to be one of the more important in determining the spacing between households, much more important than the parent/son relationship, with an average distance of 73.0 m between them. Indeed, even when we consider the small sample of relationships with fathers present, the observation that a strong relationship exists between mothers and daughters is reinforced: no women live outside of their father's cluster, and on average, they live 58 m from their father's household. The weaker bonding of unmarried adolescent males to their nuclear families and bands of origin is frequently noted in hunter–gatherer literature.

On the other hand, relationships between brothers are known to be close among the aborigines and many other hunter–gatherers. Figures 6 and 7 document an observed disparity in the importance of the brother/brother and sister/sister relationship. Brother pairs have the closest average spacing of any category of relationship analyzed in this study, giving this relationship a high predictive value in terms of interhousehold spacing. Sisters, on the other hand, live further apart than any other relationship: 80.6 m on average. This figure for sisters is higher than the average within-cluster value for interhousehold distance for all household pairs at Papunya, related or not, at 75.5 m. Moreover, the proportion of brothers living within 50 m of each other is 50%, also the highest observed, whereas for sisters this value is 13%, almost as low as the 8% figure for the site as a whole.

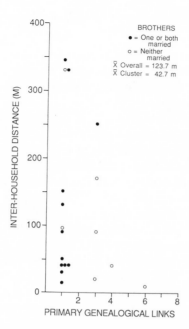

Figure 6. Scatterplot of interhousehold distance and primary genealogical links using brother/brother relationship.

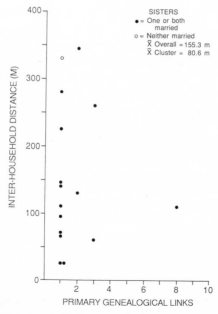

Figure 7. Scatterplot of interhousehold distance and primary genealogical links using sister/sister relationship.

In sum, the most important relationships determining who will reside near whom are brother/brother and parent/daughter. Also, the more primary kinship links there are between households, the closer they are likely to reside to each other.

O'Connell (1987:86) found that 83% of nearest neighbors were related by primary ties or close classificatory equivalents. We find a similar situation at Papunya. A breakdown reveals that 55% of the 29 nearest neighbor pairs are parent/child relationships, natural or classificatory; an additional 14% are natural brother pairs; 7% are classificatory brother pairs; 7% are natural brothers/sisters; the remaining 17% are unknown relationships. All nearest neighbors are within 50 meters of each other (mean = 27.9 m); the closest are 10 m apart. Three-quarters are between 20 and 40 meters of each other. This closely follows O'Connell's finding that Alyawara nearest neighbors are 25 to 40 m apart, suggesting that similar spacing and organizational mechanisms are at work at both sites, as one might expect given their similar conditions and history. These results are important to any discussion of the factors determining site structure. Though they do not in themselves constitute explanations, they nevertheless lend support to the reliability of our data and contribute to our understanding of the creation of site structure.

4. DISCUSSION

4.1. Primary Relationships

For all households related by primary genealogical relationships (Figure 2), the clear trend of the within-cluster mean curve illustrates that, as the number of kin ties between households increases, the likelihood that two households will be close together also increases. The erratic slope of the curve of mean within-cluster spacing in the case of classificatory relationships (Figure 3) suggests that the same mechanisms governing spatial arrangement in primary relationships are not at work between most subsection relatives. Indeed, contrary to the impressions that some anthropologists provide, it is clear from our data that primary kinship ties have more of an impact and a more predictable effect on socio-economic relationships and the structure of sites.

4.2. Parents and Married Offspring

Peterson (1970) discusses the economic value of women in aboriginal society, and particularly their indirect role in determining postnuptial residence as a result of their important productive role. He observes a disconformity between the cultural ideal of a man and his family living on his clan estate, and the apparently anomalous mixed groups, which often occur in fact. He sees residence after marriage as being responsible for the mixed group, determined by both social and economic factors.

Women in aboriginal society procure between 60% and 90% of the bulk of the diet by weight in desert areas, including some animal protein—lizards, for example (Peterson 1970:12). In caloric terms, this probably translates to an equivalent, or possibly lower, contribution than that of males. Nevertheless it is clear that women provide an important fraction of the diet. Women's contribution also contrasts with the hunted game provided by men in that women's returns are more stable and reliable and therefore of critical importance compared to the high-risk, high-return, but fluctuating, contribution of males.

Other factors, such as the failure of eyesight, reducing hunting effectiveness, may also contribute to a shorter productive life for males. The traditional group's dependence on women is demonstrated by its ability to subsist even when the most active males go off for weeks at a time. Women provide for their young and for those relatives too old to provide for themselves. Older males, unable to provide for themselves, but who still want to maintain independence and mobility—not to mention survival viability—have two choices: keep control of young daughters after marriage or take a new, young wife. Gerontocratic polygyny enables a man to live out the latter years of life on his clan estate, which is the cultural ideal. In return for receiving a wife, however, a son-in-law is expected to make significant food contributions to his wife's parents. Thus, habitual sharing is carried on between young married couples and the elderly parents of the wife. The young married man must, for a time, reside near his wife's kin, while assisting in their provisioning, and wait for his time to return to his own estate to build an extended family to look after him in his senescence (Peterson 1970:14).

For these reasons, the most important relationships in the band are between parents and daughters and between a married couple and the wife's parents. This is clearly responsible for close spacing between the households of parents and married women and explains why married males do not live in proximity to their parents: presumably, once a young married male has fulfilled obligations to his wife's parents and retires to his estate, his own parents are deceased. It is curious that a married daughter does not live closer than 40 or so meters to her parents. It could be that the taboo on relations between son-in-law and mother-in-law in aboriginal society keeps the daughter's household at this "safe" distance.

4.3. Parents and Unmarried Offspring

Ethnographically, it is known that unmarried males living apart from their parents move around a great deal, taking advantage of their independence to maintain important relations between bands and, not unimportantly, to be close to marriageable females. Thus we expected them to exhibit more variable, perhaps even random, spacing. As Figure 4 shows, there is a tendency for them to live near their parents, but the average spacing is quite high compared to other relationships in this study. This may reflect either (1) stronger ties existing between parents and unmarried males than indicated by anecdotal ethnographic accounts; (2) relatively brief or episodic wandering and visiting behavior alternating with a more dominant residence pattern focused on parents; or (3) the large permanent aggregation conditions characteristic of living near industrial outposts.

There is a noticeable trend in the mean curve within clusters for spacing between the households of parents and unmarried sons (Figure 4). The more links there are, the closer they live to their parents. By far, this relationship is most visible in the parent/unmarried male data; indeed, it appears to be almost a linear relationship. The situation seems to be largely a function of the number of siblings still residing with the parents. As other siblings leave home, particularly other males, the number of kin ties between the parent's residence and that of the unmarried male must be reduced, and the average distance between all such households must increase. These strong relationships may indicate that unmarried males probably resided close to their parents traditionally when they were affiliated with the parents' band but that they frequently left to visit other groups.

On the other hand, the spatial relationship between unmarried males and their parents is a settlement feature also noted by O'Connell (1987). He attributes their proximity to their parents to the government welfare system that supplies weekly "pensions" to the parents' households but not to the unmarried independent offspring. This would result in the parents provisioning, at least in part, the single male child, and cause high rates of sharing and therefore close spacing between their households.

We also find that, among the Pintupi, unmarried males show a preference for living in the same cluster as their parents. However, as a group, they show high average spacing within the cluster, 73 m, and one of the lowest proportions of households within 50 m—18%. This may be the result of the contradictory social position of the unmarried male in the modern context: one of traditional, culturally prescribed independence and the contemporary imperative of economic dependence on their parents. As a hypothesis for explaining the unexpected regularity in the location of unmarried men's households, the foregoing requires further data for testing. As can be seen in Figure 6, unmarried females are a rarity (women generally are married in adolescence). However, their position is more constrained than that of their male counterparts because, as already explained, they are of great importance in the economy of the group. And they are especially important to their parents. Therefore, it was expected that they should live nearby. (It should be noted, as it was previously, that the data point at 8 links and 110 m is recognized to be anomalous.)

Even though we can perceive possible effects of government rationing on the independence of unmarried males, we cannot detect any great effect on the situation that exists between parents and females. Given the impact of settlement economy and contact (especially the reduced economic contribution of women), we might have expected to see evidence that the previous adaptation of keeping married daughters close to fathers was losing its tenure. Apparently the modern situation has had no visible effect in this regard. Perhaps this relationship was so fundamentally important under traditional conditions that it has persisted over time, even though the conditions to which it was adapted have changed. The foregoing results all support the hypothesis that reliance on food sharing is a major factor affecting site structure.

4.4. Siblings

Unmarried, same-sex siblings generally live together, apart from their parents, or near their married siblings. Ethnographically, sisters may, once married, be widely separated, once their obligation to assist their parents has been fulfilled, unless they are married to the same man, as is often the case. They are expected to follow their husbands, and it is likely that they would live near his kin, at some distance from their own. In the modern settlement at Papunya, sister pairs live in different clusters only 40% of the time. However, they live farther apart on average than any other class of relationship studied there. The within-cluster mean distance between their households is 80.6 m, and only 13% live within 50 m of each other. This does not seem to be a very important relationship ethnographically, nor in the contemporary context, in the structuring of the site.

Brothers, on the other hand, live within 50 m of one another in half of the cases observed. They live closer together, on average, than any other relationship, 42.7 m. Although they may be constrained to live apart for a time, because of marriage arrangements, brothers can be expected to live very close together at other times, married or not. The male's entitlement to eventually live in the same locality as his patrikin, and the strong ethic of cooperation and sharing seen between brothers, probably contributes most to their highly predictable spatial relationship.

4.5. Classificatory Relatives

Classificatory relations generally are not very important as determinants of spacing, as Figure 3 demonstrates. Father's brothers and mother's sisters (classed as "father" and "mother" in the aboriginal kinship system), however, are present in 31% of the nearest-neighbor pairs surveyed at Papunya. It is not clear whether this is due to similar patterns of sharing or to the limited possibilities of the kinship system.

4.6. Determinants of Absolute Spacing

Because one aim of our research ultimately is to explain, rather than simply to describe or monitor these relationships, something must be said about hypotheses concerning variability in spacing among the !Kung, the Alyawara, and the Pintupi. On average, !Kung households are 5 to 7 meters apart; the Alyawara nearest-neighbor residential units are 25 to 40 meters apart. The Pintupi site resembles the Alyawara in this respect, although traditionally they exhibited spacing more characteristic of the !Kung when they foraged in small bands (Howitt 1904:774; Gould 1968:106; Hayden 1979:139ff). This disparity cannot be attributed to physical constraints of the landscape and is thus more apt to be due to cultural or economic factors.

Whitelaw (1983) argues that reliance on food sharing among the group results in closer spacing in the !Kung situation and much greater separation in the case of the inhabitants of the Central and Western Deserts of Australia: the Pitjantjara, the Pintupi, and the Alyawara. At least 60% of the game captured is shared among members of the !Kung camp, and sharing is a vitally important strategy to the survival of the group (Whitelaw 1983:62). In this context, close spacing of households is adaptive; proximity of huts promotes monitoring of activities in other huts, thereby deterring hoarding and ensuring an even distribution of resources. On the other hand, the Alyawara and the Pintupi share much less between households, due to the availability of store-bought foods, and, as Whitelaw argues, this is generally the case in hunter–gatherer aggregation phases. Thus households are an order of magnitude further apart on average.

We feel that the degree to which food is shared is a much more powerful explanation of why distances between households vary than Gould and Yellen (1987) have indicated. Not only do they fail to take into account the pervasive reduction in sharing among the Alyawara (one of their study groups) due to integration into an industrial economy, but they ignore the dramatic variability that is present within the Australian data—variability that cannot be explained on the basis of differential predator dangers as they suggest. Indeed, they ignore the most dangerous and omnipresent predator of all: hostile men from other bands (well documented for Australian and most other hunter–gatherers). They suggest relatively distant spacing of households in Australia (37 to 85 m) due to a lack of predators, in contrast to close spacing (6 to 20 m) of the !Kung where predators are more common.

Gould and Yellen's use of data, however, stands in marked contrast to Gould's earlier (1968:109) observations to the effect that "the camps of a single large extended family tended to be clustered together *within 25 feet of one another* [emphasis added], but the distance between extended family clusters was never less than 50 feet, and generally more than 100." Similar observations were made by Howitt (1904:774) almost a hundred years ago in Southeast Australia.

Gould and Yellen's emphasis on predatory dangers is incapable of dealing with this important kind of variability, and it would appear that they have been rather selective in the manipulation of their raw data to support their hypothesis.

Although the sharing hypothesis explains the reasons for the proximity of the !Kung and other hunter–gatherers to one another, it does not explain why related people live further apart when they are able to, nor does it help to explain the similarity in the interhousehold spacing of the Pintupi and the Alyawara camps evinced by the present study.

There are several possible explanations for this behavior:

1. As Whitelaw (1983) suggests, traditional large aggregation encampments may only occur under conditions of abundant (and reliable?) resources, thus diminishing the need for sharing. Modern settlements, too, provide the same conditions, and therefore it is expected that the distance between households will be greater than in traditional, dispersed-band campsites. Households will want to be far enough away from their neighbors to enable each household to horde small resources but not so far that they will not be able to observe large resources or be subject to unobserved thefts or intruders or to be accused of sorcery or other mischief.

2. The gradual breakdown of the traditional sharing ethic at settlements, coupled with a desire for greater privacy, could contribute to greater physical separation.

3. Each household activity area in the aboriginal settlement is flanked or surrounded by refuse. Including the activity area, the residential unit could span 30 or 40 meters, depending on the length of stay in one spot (O'Connell 1987). Thus the area required for all activities and refuse disposal could put a lower limit on the proximity of two households that do not share resources between them. Neighbors might not want to be in the refuse-toss and long-term accumulation zone of each other.

4. Other factors may operate to prevent maximal isolation of households. It is possible, for instance, that important temporary or long-lasting personal alliances, which are activated when there are disputes or fights in the camp, limit the distance that households are willing to be separated from others.

5. This study could not take into account the important ritual bonds that exist across families. These, too, may affect spatial organization. They may parallel or reinforce those ties already examined.

Thus the kinship system, ritual affiliations, subsistence economy, and refuse disposal all may influence the structure of the site, but given the data at hand, the role of sharing in the economy appears to be the most important factor that determines where people live.

5. CORRELATES OF SOCIAL ORGANIZATION

As we have seen, sharing occurs predominantly along primary kin lines among the Pintupi, and it is precisely along these lines that residence location choices are most often made. Although it may not be possible to determine the precise kinship system of prehistoric societies, the results of this and other studies should make it possible to determine the importance of sharing in communities on the basis of settlement patterns. It is this more basic behavioral adaptation that should be accessible through the archaeological record.

If the subsistence base consists of relatively large-package food, which is sporadically available and which cannot be stored, then sharing among the group should represent an important adaptive strategy (Whitelaw 1983:59). This is a coherent interplay of factors and probably always would tend to create similar site structures: households closely spaced to facilitate sharing. O'Connell mentions the Aché as another example; Whitelaw mentions the Mbuti. Were archaeologists to find such a site, they would feel relatively safe in hypothesizing a similar subsistence pattern for the archaeological cultures, against which to compare other ecological data, including faunal and technological evidence and the presence in nearby habitations of evidence for sharing as indicated by refitted lithics or faunal remains. Moreover, if one household were significantly provisioning the occupants of a nearby household, as demonstrated among the Pintupi, one might expect asymmetrical artifact assemblages in the households, related to the procurement and preparation of food in one of them (for an excavated example, see Hayden 1979:139–149). Similarly, evidence for cooperative resource extraction might be obtained from the pattern of artifacts and faunal remains recovered from two neighboring households.

If archaeologists, however, were to encounter a site whose structure was similar to the Pintupi camp, more care would be required in making inferences, as similar site structures might result from different subsistence activities. High interhousehold spacing should occur under a variety of conditions, all of which contribute to greater economic independence of household units, reduced dependence on sharing, and thus less need to live close together. In general, richer environments should encourage wide spacing. Where the subsistence base allows reliance on small-package food items (especially r-selected species), which are readily and constantly available and do not require storage, the need for sharing is low among the entire group, and thus household spacing should be greater. Food storage, resulting from seasonally available, abundant, reliable, and predictable resources, is another condition that can reduce the need for sharing and lessen the need to live close together.

Other hunter–gatherer strategies might present a different kind of ambiguity. Where procurement follows a seasonal round or where there is periodic or occasional nutritional stress, changing strategies of the group should be mirrored in the site structure. At times closely spaced, at others more distantly, the spatial organization of households would likely indicate the particular strategy employed at any one time. This is suggested by some of the transformations that can be observed in Inuit groups at times during the year (Burch 1975). Observing these differences archaeologically would allow important inferences to be made about the subsistence and seasonal adaptations of groups living in marginal environments. It is worth noting that, at times of severe stress, the group may even break up into nuclear family units, when sharing is discontinued altogether (Woodburn 1972:198; Burch 1975:251; Silberbauer 1981:196). Such variability also seems to typify many Algonkian and Athapaskan prehistoric sites.

6. CONCLUSIONS: RECOGNIZING INTACT HOUSEHOLDS

In order to successfully interpret community patterns, we first need to be able to recognize discrete residential units at a site. The work with hunter–gatherer groups discussed so far suggests several ways that this might be accomplished, even though the scale of recovery or excavation required would be large (on the order of thousands of square meters). The kinds of evidence needed to monitor site structure are the same as those sought for the answers to traditional questions in archaeology; the only difference is one of scale.

1. Hearths and roasting pits are good, lasting evidence of activity. These are usually closely associated with residential units. Even in the absence of evidence for a structure, hearths represent an opportunity to monitor interhousehold spacing. They can be expected to be relatively close to the sleeping/eating area, and thus they should still give relatively accurate observations on household spacing.
2. Refuse concentrations should help to delineate individual subsistence units, especially in the case of groups such as the Pintupi. They should be relatively easy to discern, unless an unusually long occupation occurs and there is a great deal of accumulated refuse, as is the case with the shell middens on the Northwest Coast of North America.
3. Artifact clusters, observable workshop areas (perhaps identified by lithic debitage or microdebitage) may be repeated across a site and be used to distinguish residential units.
4. Posthole or other structural remains are, of course, optimal kinds of evidence for spatial arrangement (e.g., the Gravettian habitations on the loess plains of Central Europe).
5. Refitting analyses might be used to show contemporaneity of residential units, as well as evidence of the kind of social contact concomitant with sharing.

O'Connell (1987) is pessimistic about the usefulness of some of the correlates listed in the recognition of spatial patterning. He finds that, in the kinds of sites the Alyawara now occupy, hearths, refuse areas, and activity areas are quickly blurred by the rearrangement of households through time. Only those at the periphery are clearly discernible. We feel that O'Connell's outlook is too pessimistic. He deals with intensively occupied permanent camps that are the product of contact with the industrial world. Neither these population concentrations nor the intensity of occupation were typical of most prehistoric hunter–gatherer encampments. The kind of spatial analysis in our study, relying as it does on the recognition of intact households, can contribute to an understanding of the prehistoric situation, perhaps even where sites are intermittently occupied over relatively long periods. The employment of rigorous excavation technique, as always, is imperative to the study of site structure, requiring, as it does, the extrication of certain classes of relatable evidence from the often confusing background of penecontemporaneous homologous features scattered across sites.

The problem of recognizing contemporaneous dwellings is one that must be sorted out before proceeding with any analysis of site structure. In single-component sites, such as Vail (Speiss 1982), contemporaneity can be argued for by the formal patterning of refuse, together with refitting data. Refitting and borrowing of materials, as seen at Meer (Cahen, Keeley, and Van Noten 1979) and Pincevent (Leroi-Gourhan and Brézillon 1966, 1972), can provide important insights into habitation contemporaneity. Given these encouraging results, it appears to be archaeologically feasible to recover data needed to make the kinds of inferences we have discussed.

Several interrelated variables contributing to site structure have been discussed in this chapter. Our analysis of a Pintupi encampment lends support to the findings of an earlier study of !Kung site structure by Whitelaw (1983). It has also increased our understanding of the factors governing the choice of where to live in a community, by examining economically important kinship relations. Sharing between individuals and families is a common thread in relationships that display the most predictable spatial patterning. Sharing not only influences how far apart people choose to live, but it also determines whom they live near. Other social and behavioral considerations may only mediate these choices; it is the adaptation of sharing resources that seems to be the fundamental determinant. It is also evident that although kinship can be extended by classificatory means, such extensions do not replace nuclear family bonds. Classificatory relationships appear to be of much less importance even though individuals may be called "brother" or "father."

This model of site structure adds another dimension to inferences drawn from the archaeological record. When recognized in the material remains of a culture, the horizontal organization of residential units can provide insights into the economics of past human groups, especially their relative reliance on sharing as an adaptation to the subsistence base. This will inevitably deepen our understanding of the hunter–gatherer adaptation and cultural dynamics in prehistory. It may not be possible to recover evidence of a specific kinship system, but it certainly seems possible to infer close prehistoric relationships without naming them.

ACKNOWLEDGMENTS

We would like to thank the Australian-American Educational Foundation and the Australian Institute of Aboriginal Studies for providing funding and the research opportunity to collect the data on which this chapter is based. We are very grateful to the entire Pintupi community at Papunya for their cooperation and their indulgence in pursuit of intellectual trivia. Peter White and Bob Edwards were generous with their support and encouragement in this endeavor, for which we are also grateful.

7. REFERENCES

Burch, E. S., 1975, *Eskimo Kinsmen: Changing Family Relationships in Northwest Alaska*, American Ethnological Society, Monograph 59, West Publishing Co., St. Paul.

Cahen, D., Keeley, L., and Van Noten, F., 1979, Stone Tools, Tool Kits, and Human Behavior in Prehistory, *Current Anthropology* 20:661–683.

Gould, R. A., 1968, Living Archaeology: The Ngatatjara of Western Australia, *Southwestern Journal of Anthropology* 24:101–122.

Gould, R. A., and Yellen, J. E., 1987, Man the Hunted: Determinants of Household Spacing in Desert and Tropical Foraging Societies, *Journal of Anthropological Archaeology* 6:77–103.

Hayden, B., 1979, *Palaeolithic Reflections*, Australian Institute of Aboriginal Studies, Canberra.

Honigmann, J. J., 1961, *Foodways in a Muskeg Community: An Anthropological Report on the Attawapiskat Indians*, Department of Northern Affairs and National Resources, Ottawa.

Howitt, A. W., 1904, *The Native Tribes of South-East Australia*, Macmillan, London.

Lee, R. B., 1979, *The !Kung San*, Cambridge University Press, Cambridge.

Leroi-Gourhan, A., and Brézillon, M., 1966, L'habitation Magdalénienne No. 1 de Pincevent près Montereau (Seine-et-Marne), *Gallia Préhistoire* 9:263–385.

Leroi-Gourhan, A., and Brézillon, M., 1972, *Fouilles de Pincevent, Essai d'Analyse Ethnographique d'un Habitat Magdalénien (la section 36)* (*Gallia Préhistoire*, 7th supplement). Monograph published by C.N.R.S., Paris.

O'Connell, J. F., 1987, Alyawara Site Structure and Its Archaeological Implications, *American Antiquity* 52:74–108.

Peterson, N., 1970, The Importance of Women in Determining the Composition of Residential Groups in Aboriginal Australia. In *Woman's Role in Aboriginal Society* (F. Gale, ed.), Australian Aboriginal Studies No. 36/Social Anthropology Series No. 6, Australian Institute of Aboriginal Studies, Canberra, pp. 9–15.

Shapiro, W., 1979, *Social Organization in Aboriginal Australia*, St. Martin's Press, New York.
Silberbauer, G. B., 1981, *Hunter and Habitat in the Central Kalahari Desert*, Cambridge University Press, Cambridge.
Speiss, A., 1982, *Arctic Garbage and New England Paleoindians: The Single Occupation Option*. Paper presented at the annual meetings of the Society for American Archaeology, Minneapolis.
Whitelaw, T., 1983, People and Space in Hunter–Gatherer Camps: A Generalizing Approach in Ethnoarchaeology, *Archaeological Review from Cambridge* 2(2):48–66.
Woodburn, J., 1972, Ecology, Nomadic Movement and the Composition of the Local Group among Hunters and Gatherers: An East African Example and Its Implications. In *Man, Settlement and Urbanism*, (P. J. Ucko, R. Tringham, and G. W. Dimbleby, eds.), Duckworth, London, pp. 193–206.

Chapter 2

The Relationship between Mobility Strategies and Site Structure

SUSAN KENT

1. INTRODUCTION

The spatial organization of hunter–gatherer sites has been the subject of numerous studies over the past 25 years (e.g., Yellen 1977; Binford 1978, 1987; Brooks and Yellen 1987; Hitchcock 1987; Whitelaw 1989 and others). These studies have yielded similar conclusions regarding observed cross-cultural and diachronic variability. The factors are ecological in their orientation. They are that (1) the threat of predators determines camp area in terms of mean hearth-to-hearth distance, or how dispersed a camp is; (2) subsistence strategies and the institutionalization of sharing food (attributed to the size of hunted resources) influence site nucleation; (3) site population is a critical variable for determining camp size; and (4) seasonal and climatic differences create intragroup spatial variation (e.g., Whitelaw 1983; Gould and Yellen 1987; O'Connell 1987). The interrelationship of these four ecological factors is thought to explain the cross-culture variability that exists in the size and structure of modern hunter–gatherer camps, which is considered to be relevant to variability in past sites.

The aforementioned studies arrive at similar conclusions for several reasons. First is the similar theoretical orientation on which they are based, an orientation

SUSAN KENT • Anthropology Program, Old Dominion University, Norfolk, Virginia 23529.

emphasizing human ecology and predicated upon what Whitelaw (1983:63) termed "ecologically dependent density relationships." Another reason is that each author examines groups occupying different environments containing different fauna (i.e., Botswana and Australia; Gould and Yellen 1987; O'Connell 1987). By comparing groups in disparate environments and noting variation, differences in the environment may appear to be responsible for the variation. However, emphasis on related ecological variables alone—such as environment, seasons, and predators—makes it impossible to determine whether the variation would still occur if the groups were in the same setting; that is, that the variation is the result of other factors. This is equally true for variation attributed to ethnicity, economics, and other variables examined without investigating alternative hypotheses. Factors attributed to diversity in spatial patterning must be selectively varied in order to differentiate those that are most influential. Therefore, multivariate analyses are most appropriate to determine the separate effects of independent variables.

In this chapter, I consider spatial patterning and site structure from a perspective different than the more common ecological one. Variation in site structure is examined from the perspective of anticipated mobility. The data are from two ethnic groups inhabiting the identical environment at the same time. Data viewed in light of multiple perspectives often generate more insights than single variable analyses, as has been noted by Binford (1987).

2. AN ALTERNATIVE MODEL OF THE ROLE OF MOBILITY IN SPATIAL ORGANIZATION

2.1. Anticipated Mobility and Site Structure

Causes of mobility among hunter–gatherer groups are complex, involving a number of interrelated factors. Environmental and economic conditions, particularly subsistence procurement, have traditionally been given primacy in explanations of mobility strategies. Thus mobility patterning is often equated with economic and environmental patterning. However, social and political considerations can be crucial factors as well. For example, during the nineteenth century, Batswana chiefs did not permit their Batswana subjects to move from a central village to small multiple- or single-family camps near distant farmland, even if the environment could no longer support the population (Silitshena 1983). This was a concerted effort on the part of the chiefs—who actually punished anyone who disobeyed—to maintain tight political control over the group. As a result, the Batswana were forced to build temporary seasonal residences at agricultural fields located some distance from their village.

There are other nonecological factors that influence mobility, ranging from medical to ceremonial to eduational (Kent 1989). Linking mobility to only one specific variable, however, masks the relationships among site structure and mobility, economics, environment, and other factors. Therefore, it is instructive to look at mobility as an independent variable, as well as other potentially influential factors such as economics, the environment, and ethnicity. This approach will explicate which factors influence particular aspects of site structure and spatial organization.

Following Binford's definition (1983:144), I use the term *site structure* to mean site size, the presence and arrangement of activity areas, and structures and features including huts, hearths, and storage facilities. This discussion of site structure does not include the patterning of artifacts at sites, although future fieldwork will hopefully permit a study encompassing their distribution.

A model of intrasite spatial organization has been dveloped that focuses on *anticipated mobility*—length of time people expect to occupy a site. The study was based on ethnographic data gathered by Helga Vierich and reported and analyzed in Kent and Vierich (1989). As part of a demographic study, Vierich mapped and described 25 Basarwa (San, "Bushmen") camps, 5 Bakgalagadi (Bantu speakers) camps, and one mixed Basarwa–Bakgalagadi camp in Botswana (Table 1). For all but two of the variables we chose to monitor (described later), we found that anticipated mobility was the most influential factor—that is, more important than actual length of site occupation, camp subsistence orientation, season of habitation, number of occupants, or ethnic affiliation. Furthermore, the study indicates that anticipated mobility often accounts for a larger percentage of site structure variability than does subsistence procurement strategies. This finding emphasizes the need to treat mobility, subsistence, and other variables independently.

Anticipated versus actual mobility (i.e., anticipated versus actual length of occupation) was ascertained through informant interviews conducted by Vierich with the head of the household, who initially established the camp, and with other household members. The interviews included why a site was occupied, by whom, what activities occupants planned to conduct, and the like (Vierich 1985:personal communication). Specific questions to determine anticipated mobility, such as why a camp was established, how long the occupants planned to reside at the camp and why, were asked. Anticipated mobility may be analogous to Binford's (1987:498–499) concept of "planning depth." However, there is a range of behavior included within the concept of planning depth that does not necessarily relate to specific mobility patterns, such as planning particular subsistence endeavors. I therefore use the phrase *anticipated mobility* more restrictively to refer to the particular behaviors linked to mobility and length of occupation.

Actual mobility was determined by the length of occupation at the time of abandonment *or*, if still occupied, at the time the site was mapped. Anticipated

Table 1. Bivariate Regression Analysis (from Kent and Vierich, 1989)

Dependent variable	R^2	Prob > F[a]
Square meters per person		
Anticipated mobility	0.5093	0.0001
Number of site occupants	0.3201	0.0014
Subsistence orientation	0.3085	0.0244
Actual mobility	0.2390	0.0287
Ethnic affiliation	N.A.[b]	0.0585
Season of occupation	N.A.	0.3014
Site size		
Anticipated mobility	0.2458	0.0255
Number of site occupants	0.1778	0.0227
Subsistence strategy	N.A.	0.2973
Season of occupation	N.A.	0.4844
Ethnic affiliation	N.A.	0.6956
Actual mobility	N.A.	0.0706
Formal storage facilities		
Anticipated mobility	0.2340	0.0313
Ethnic affiliation	0.2324	0.0081
Susbistence strategy	N.A.	0.1541
Number of site occupants	N.A.	0.1969
Actual mobility	N.A.	0.2300
Season of occupation	N.A.	0.6988
Feature type frequency		
Subsistence orientation	0.3530	0.0112
Ethnic affiliation	0.2705	0.0038
Actual mobility	0.2628	0.0190
Anticipated mobility	0.2109	0.0460
Season of occupation	N.A.	0.7397
Number of occupants	N.A.	0.9419
Hut diameter		
Anticipated mobility	0.3788	0.0020
Actual mobility	0.2773	0.0147
Season of occupation	0.1906	0.0179
Subsistence orientation	N.A.	0.0781
Number of site occupants	N.A.	0.2081
Ethnic affiliation	N.A.	0.6932
Number of huts		
Number of site occupants	0.3844	0.0003
Season of occupation	N.A.	0.4948
Subsistence orientation	N.A.	·0.7923
Actual mobility	N.A.	0.9304
Anticipated mobility	N.A.	0.9909
Ethnic affiliation	N.A.	0.9522

[a] The prob > F value should only be used as a guide to measure the significance of the association because of the nature of the sample.
[b] N.A. = nonapplicable because the association is not significant.

mobility, actual mobility, season of occupation, subsistence strategy, site population, and ethnic affiliation are discussed later. They focus on the variables for which we had data and on the variables most often monitored by archaeologists: square meters per person, site size, formal storage loci, prevalence of activity restricted areas (or monofunctional loci), investment in hut construction, hut diameter, and number of huts per site.

Anticipated length of occupation was divided into three somewhat arbitrary categories. These are *short*, under 3 months duration; *medium*, between 3 and 5.9 months duration; and *long*, duration of 6 months or longer. The categories roughly correspond to the qualitative terms, *nomadic, semisedentary*, and *sedentary*.

Some anthropologists maintain that *sedentism* is a term that should be restricted to groups occupying the same site for many years; however, I feel that this is unrealistic, particularly for the past. Except in urban settings and areas of high population density, the occupation of the same location for many generations was probably a relatively rare phenomenon in the past. For example, few would argue that traditionally the Batswana were not sedentary, yet they moved their camps approximately every 10 to 15 years (Silitshena 1983:191). The same is true for the Zulu, who moved at least every 30 years (Oswald 1987).

To call groups who occupy a site for over 6 months anything but sedentary would, in my opinion, mask the very diversity we seek to examine. Patterns of refuse disposal and morbidity, for instance, are modified in habitations of over 6-month duration (e.g., see Kent 1986). Perhaps a separate category of suprasedentary or hypersedentary for groups that inhabit the same site for generations is required (Kent 1989). Unfortunately, however, not enough long-term sedentary camps were in our sample to separate sedentary from suprasedentary camps, although future research will hopefully rectify this deficiency.

This study revealed that anticipated mobility was a more influential factor than actual mobility at almost every camp. In most situations, anticipated and actual length of occupation coincided. However, the greatest insights were obtained when anticipation did not conform to reality. This did not occur very often because people do not continually anticipate that which never fulfills expectations. But it occurred frequently enough to elucidate patterning that would otherwise have been masked.

2.2. Square Meters per Person

Square meters per person values (m^2/person) was one variable examined to evaluate site investment. It was calculated by dividing camp size (m^2) by the number of site occupants. Visitors present for a brief stay were not included; nor were regular household members not living at the camp (e.g., who were working at the South African mines).

Multiple regression revealed that the m²/person value is directly tied to the anticipated length of stay and not as directly tied to the actual length of stay. Camps with a short, medium, or long anticipated occupation, but with a long actual stay, had variable m²/person values. In contrast, all camps occupied as an anticipated long habitation had the same range of m²/person values regardless of length of occupation.

This was also true for camps occupied with an anticipated short habitation. For example, in three camps, each with the same m²/person range of values, one was occupied for 9 days by 8 people (Site 1), another (Site 23) was occupied by 39 people for 6 weeks, and the third (Site 2) was occupied for 6 months by 31 people. The common variable among these different camps was an anticipated short length of occupation.

A statistical regression analysis was conducted, and anticipated mobility, camp population, subsistence strategy, and actual mobility were all significant variables with an F prob of under .05 (Table 1). The prob > F significance should only be used as a guide, however, because the sample collected was not systematically obtained and was small (n = 31). Even so, we feel confident about the associations because in many cases the statistic is rather robust. Anticipated mobility explains 51% of the variance of m²/person, whereas actual mobility explains only 24%. Thus m²/person, a rough index of site investment, is determined more by how long occupants plan to live at a site than by how long they actually live there.

The anticipated length of stay corresponded to a predictable range of m²/person values. With only one exception, all sites with an anticipated short length of occupation (under 3 months) had a m²/person value of under 32.9. The m²/person value remained constant between 33 and 65.9 for anticipated medium-term occupations (between 3 and 5.9 months), regardless of actual length of occupation. Moreover, these sites differed from anticipated short- or long-term sites with identical actual lengths of habitation. Finally, the same pattern was consistent for the anticipated long-term occupations of over 6 months—all had a value of over 66 m²/person. This situation occurred regardless of the number of site occupants, ranging from 4 to 25 people, type of economic pursuit (including hunting/gathering, farming, and employment), or actual length of habitation, which ranged from only 3 weeks to over 24 months. The data show that there is less correspondence between actual mobility and m²/person than between anticipated length of occupation and m²/person.

The m²/person value was compared to the economic pursuites of the inhabitants for each camp. This included hunting–gathering, farming, paid labor, employment, or a mixture. Although statistically significant, economic orientation explained much less of the variance of m²/person than did mobility. A camp occupied by a hunting–gathering group with an anticipated long-term stay had an m²/person value equivalent to other camps occupied by groups who also anticipated long-term habitations but pursued paid labor or farming activities.

Note that this was not so for similar hunting–gathering camps where occupants had different anticipated lengths of occupation. Anticipated mobility significantly explained more of the variance than economic orientation and was a much stronger predictor of m²/person (see Table 2).

The number of site occupants also had a significant correlation with m²/person, but not as strong an association as anticipated mobility, actual mobility, or subsistence orientation (Tables 1 and 2). Finally, m²/person values were assessed from the perspective of season and the different ethnic groups in the study. Neither was a significant variable. Therefore, the analysis shows that anticipated mobility explains more variance and is a better predictor of m²/person values than any other single variable.

2.3. Site Size

Particularly important for archaeologists, who attempt to estimate population from site area measurements, is the finding that anticipated mobility determines site size (Tables 1 and 2). Not only did this analysis find anticipated mobility a much stronger predictor of site size than number of occupants, but also, that anticipated mobility accounted for more variance than did site population (25% versus 18%). The regression analysis indicated that actual mobility, ethnic affiliation, subsistence strategies, and season of occupation were not significantly associated with site size.

2.4. Formal Storage Areas

Another component of site structure, the presence of formal storage areas or loci containing facilities used specifically for storage, was analyzed. Formal storage areas and storage huts were located only at sites with either an anticipated medium or long occupation. No formal storage areas occurred at any sites with an anticipated short occupation, regardless of actual length of occupation. This was the case even at one Mokgalagadi (singular of Bakgalagadi) camp that was specifically inhabited for farming endeavors. Interestingly, this was in contradiction to the frequently assumed correlation between horticultural activities and storage facilities. That is, neither economic orientation nor season of occupation were significantly correlated with the presence of storage areas, whereas anticipated mobility was (Table 1). For reasons yet to be determined, ethnic affiliation was the only other variable with a significant association.

2.5. Feature-Type Frequency

Areas where only a range of specific activities are performed are defined here as activity-restricted or monofunctional areas. These include storage huts, thresh-

Table 2.   Multivariate Regression Analysis

Dependent variable	Spread[a]
Square meters per person	
Anticipated mobility	43.907
Actual mobility	26.276
Subsistance orientation	21.678
Number of site occupants	1.638
Ethnic affiliation	N.A.[b]
Season of occupation	N.A.
Site size	
Anticipated mobility	1125.203
Number of site occupants	42.595
Subsistence strategy	N.A.
Season of occupation	N.A.
Ethnic affiliation	N.A.
Actual mobility	N.A.
Formal storage facilities	
Anticipated mobility	1.405
Ethnic affiliation	1.311
Subsistence strategy	N.A.
Number of site occupants	N.A.
Actual mobility	N.A.
Season of occupation	N.A.
Feature-type frequency	
Ethnic affiliation	1.965
Actual mobility	1.406
Anticipated mobility	1.051
Subsistence orientation	0.825
Season of occupation	N.A.
Number of occupants	N.A.
Hut diameter	
Anticipated mobility	0.719
Actual mobility	0.417
Season of occupation	0.360
Subsistence orientation	N.A.
Number of site occupants	N.A.
Ethnic affiliation	N.A.

[a] This is a measurement of the strength of the predictor variable. The spread was calculated by taking the predicted values for each dependent variable and subtracting the low predicted value from the high predicted value for each set of dummy variables. Nonsignificant bivariate relationships were not included because there were only 29 cases which, in order to increase the power of the test, necessitated a minimum number of predictor variables.
[b] N.A. = nonapplicable since the bivariate association is not significant.

ing floors, and grain cribs. This is perhaps the most problematic category because function was inferred primarily through an area's artifact content (as an archaeologist excavating a site would) without actually observing the activities performed at the locus over a period of time. Hence, there may be fewer or more activity-restricted loci at any one site than were recorded. As a result, caution should be exercised when using this category. Even so, regression analysis suggested that subsistence orientation explains more variance than do, in descending order, ethnic affiliation, actual mobility, or anticipated mobility (Table 1). However, also in descending order or magnitude, ethnic affiliation, actual mobility, and anticipated mobility are stronger predictors of feature-type frequency than is subsistence strategy (Table 2). Season of occupation and site population are not significantly correlated with feature-type frequency. A similar relationship between mobility and the rigidity of the use of space, reflected in the presence of monofunctional activity areas and corresponding facilities, also occurs among Tarahumara Indians of northern Mexico who inhabit camps for varying periods of time (Grahm 1990). More research is needed to isolate and understand the variables influencing the number and different types of features located at various sites.

2.6. Hut Diameter

Somewhat unexpectedly, the size of huts was not correspondingly associated with the number of occupants (this is also true for Efe Pygmies, see Fisher 1986, and highland Maya, see Hayden and Cannon 1984). Hut diameter was instead associated with—in order of the predictor variable strength and amount of variance explained—anticipated mobility, actual mobility, and season of occupation. Hut diameter was the only variable for which season of occupation had a significant association. This may relate to the climatic differences characteristic of the two main seasons in the Kalahari—wet and dry. Even so, anticipated mobility explains more variance and is a stronger predictor of hut diameter than is season of occupation (Tables 1 and 2).

2.7. Number of Huts

As illustrated in Table 1, the number of huts at a camp was correlated *only* with the number of site occupants and not with any other variable monitored. Site population explained 38% of the variance of the number of huts at a camp. Although the data did not support the standard assumption that population can be estimated from site size or hut diameter, they did indicate that population can be inferred from the number of huts at a camp. In some ways, this may prove to be a more reliable indicator of population for archaeological sites because it is often easier to count the number of huts at a site than to determine either absolute hut diameter or site size.

2.8. Hut Construction and Investment

Construction investment was reflected in the three different types of huts located at the camps. These included grass huts, requiring the least amount of time for construction; grass-and-woven-branches huts, requiring more time; and mudbrick huts requiring the most time. Both Basarwa and Bakgalagadi build all three types of huts. All three types were built at sites, regardless of the subsistence orientation of the occupants. Thus differential investment in hut construction was associated with neither the occupants' ethnicity nor with their subsistence strategies. It was, however, correlated with the anticipated (but not actual) mobility. With the one exception of an anticipated medium occupation, only those camps where inhabitants anticipated a stay of over 6 months contained huts constructed of either mudbrick or grass and woven branches. This included mudbrick huts located at Site 31, where the inhabitants had anticipated a stay of 6 months or longer but moved after only 3 weeks. It also accounts for the grass huts located at Site 2, where the inhabitants had anticipated a short occupation of fewer than 3 months, but actually stayed for 6 months. This resulted from the inhabitants' continual anticipation of a short occupation and consequent choice to build grass huts rather than mudbrick huts. When asked why more substantial huts were not constructed, the occupants said they did not plan to stay much longer (Vierich 1986:personal communication).

3. ALTERNATIVE VIEWS AND PERSPECTIVES OF SITE STRUCTURE

3.1. The Role of Anticipated Mobility and Ecology in Influencing Site Structure

Anticipated mobility needs to be considered as an alternative factor affecting site structure. The preceding analysis differs from the spatial studies conducted by other authors who use either data from similar geographical areas and ethnic groups (e.g., Yellen 1977; Binford 1978), data from dissimilar areas and groups (O'Connell 1987; Gould and Yellen 1987), or data from a range of areas and groups (Whitelaw 1983, 1989). The analysis differs in that it examines groups inhabiting the same environment, thereby factoring the environment out as an influential variable while varying mobility, mode of subsistence, ethnicity and other variables.

As mentioned earlier, the ecological explanation can be lumped together into a number of related factors: that (1) environment (including the local fauna and particularly predators), (2) subsistence strategy (including procurement strategies), and (3) population directly influence site size and structure (Gould and Yellen 1987; O'Connell 1987; Whitelaw 1983). Contrasting anticipated mobility with these ecological factors will indicate which are stronger predictors of site size and structure.

Despite the attraction of elegance and parsimony for explanations and understanding (Lave and March 1975:62–64), simplicity of an explanation has frequently proven to be invalid for explicating human behavior. It should not be a sufficient criterion for the acceptance of an explanation. The opposite is also true; explanations with multiple independent variables do not necessarily explain more data any more than do explanations with one variable. Because the ecological explanation presented above is more complex, with more independent variables, does not *pro forma* mean that it has more explanatory power.

Each explanation needs to be tested with data. Vierich's data are used because, unlike what has been used in other cross-cultural studies, her data set allows some factors to be held constant while selectively varying others. This permits us to determine which factors are most influential and delineate patterns that might otherwise be masked. Because previous work has addressed variability in the site structure of groups inhabiting very different environments (Whitelaw 1983; Gould and Yellen 1987), I examine site structure within and between different environments.

The aforementioned authors noted variability in site structure among groups occupying different ecological settings, and they attributed this variability to the different ecologies. However, the data from Kent and Vierich (1989) show that variability in site structure also occurs at camps located in the same environment, with the same seasons and predators. Whereas, on a larger scale, environment may account for some variability, it cannot explain the variability at sites located in the same environment, sometimes at the same settlement. Anticipated mobility, however, does explain the variability present within a single environment.

For example, proponents of an ecological explanation of site structure note differences among !Kung, Alyawara Aborigine, and Nunamiut site structure, which they attribute to the vastly different seasons characterizing the environment each group inhabits (i.e., attributed to different ecologies: O'Connell 1987:103). Instead, the differences in site structure are suggested to actually be the result of dissimilar mobility patterns. This can be seen by contrasting the mobility patterns among the nomadic !Kung, as described by Yellen (1977), the seasonally semisedentary Nunamiut, as described by Binford (1978, 1980, and elsewhere), and the now-sedentary Alyawara, as described by O'Connell (1987). These groups not only occupy different environments, they also have very different mobility patterns.

The presence of dangerous predators in the Kalahari and their absence in Australia was one reason proposed by Gould and Yellen (1987) to explain the difference in site size between the two environments. However, nomadic African Pygmy camps, where there are no dangerous predators in the inhabited areas, resemble the anticipated short-term camps of the nomadic Basarwa, where lions are a common threat, more than they do the Aborigine camps with a longer planned occupation, but where there are no dangerous predators (e.g., see Fisher 1986). Predators, then, cannot account for the variation between Basarwa and Aborigine site size or people per square meter.

Environmental factors must be treated as constants and selectively varied so as not to attribute unwarranted influence to them and in order to detect other significant factors. For example, despite inhabiting the same environment and often the same dispersed settlement during the same season, site spatial organization varies substantially between and within each ethnic group examined. Bivariate analysis shows that differences in subsistence strategies and ethnic affiliation are usually not significant nor as strong a predictor variable as anticipated mobility. Discrepancies in Aché, Alyawara, and !Kung camp hearth-to-hearth distances used as an index of site size, are, within the ecological explanation, attributed to different subsistence activities that result from different degrees of resource sharing (O'Connell 1987:101–102). It would be interesting, however, to view these in terms of anticipated mobility because both the Aché and !Kung camps are short-term habitations, in contrast to the more sedentary Alyawara.

What about other factors often subsumed within the ecological explanation? Holding the environment constant by using data collected by Vierich, we can examine the variables of site population, seasonality, ethnic affiliation, and subsistence procurement strategies (e.g., hunting) in relationship to site size (see Tables 3, 4, 5, and 6). As mentioned earlier, both population and anticipated mobility are significantly correlated with site size. Anticipated mobility, however, is a substantially stronger predictor of site size than population. The other variables of the ecological explanation are not significantly associated (see Table 3). Sites ranging in area from 401 to 600 m² are occupied by groups ranging from 2 to 4 and from 29 to 31 individuals (Table 7). The largest site in the sample is occupied by fewer people than the site with the largest number of occupants. Employment-oriented households tend to inhabit larger sites than households characterized by other economic orientations (Table 5), although this is not a statistically significant trend (Table 1). I think this may be partially related to the tendency of people whose subsistence orientation is employment to have anticipated long occupations.

Examining households engaged in different subsistence strategies reveals similar variations within the same ecological setting as between different settings. Groups that are primarily hunter–gatherers, but occupy different environments, do not exhibit the same amount of variation. For example, Whitelaw's (1983) innovative discussion of the relationship between food sharing, game size, and

Table 3. Site Population by Site Size

Number of occupants	Site size (square meters)											
	188–400	401–600	601–800	801–1000	1001–1200	1201–1400	1401–1600	1601–1800	1801–2000	2001–2200	2201–2400	2401–2600
2–4	2	1										
5–7	2	1		2		1						
8–10	1											
11–13					1							
14–16		1	1	1	2							
17–19						1				1		
20–22			1	2				1		1		
23–25									1			
26–28				1								1
29–31		1										
32–34												
35–37												
38–40					2							

Table 4. Ethnic Affiliation by Site Size

Ethnic affiliation	Site size (square meters)											
	188–400	401–600	601–800	801–1000	1001–1200	1201–1400	1401–1600	1601–1800	1801–2000	2001–2200	2201–2400	2401–2600
Basarwa	4	4	1	4	4	4		1	1	2		
Bakgalagadi	1			2	1							1
Mixed Basarwa–Bakgalagadi			1									

Table 5. Economic Orientation by Site Size

Economic orientation[a]	Site size (square meters)											
	188–400	401–600	601–800	801–1000	1001–1200	1201–1400	1401–1600	1601–1800	1801–2000	2001–2200	2201–2400	2401–2600
h/g	1	2			1	1						
f	2		2									1
e	2	1	1	2		3		1	1	2		
h/g;e	1		2	3								
f;g	1											
f;e		1			1							
h/g;e;f					1							

[a] Hunter/gathering = h/g; farming = f; employment (including herding, odd jobs, domestic work, mine wage work, etc.) = e; gathering = g.

Table 6. Season by Site Size

Season of occupation	Site size (square meters)											
	188–400	401–600	601–800	801–1000	1001–1200	1201–1400	1401–1600	1601–1800	1801–2000	2001–2200	2201–2400	2401–2600
Dry season	1	1		1	1	1						
Wet season	3		3		1							
Dry+[a] season (6 months or longer occupation)				2	1							1
Wet[a] season (6 months or longer occupation)	1	2		2	2	3		1	1	2		

[a] + refers to season of site mapping because sites were actually occupied at least 6 months. Site 21 is not included because its actual length of occupation is unknown, and therefore it cannot be assigned with confidence to the wet or wet+ categories.

camp size was based on data drawn from a number of different groups. All were hunter–gatherers, many of whom exploited very different types of fauna that had different behaviors. Because the hunter–gatherers practiced noticeably different patterns of sharing, which were attributed to the different species procured, variations in the size seemed to be explained by these two factors. Nonetheless, by examining hunter–gatherers who exploit the same prey species and who practice other subsistence strategies, such as farming or employment, the variability in site size noted by Whitelaw was *still* present. Therefore, other variables have to be explored. Anticipated mobility is the single most consistent variable found responsible for variation between areas with different prey and may be equally responsible for variation in groups with different modes of sharing, although the latter needs to be further systematically tested.

Some researchers have used hearth-to-hearth distances to measure site size and dispersal (e.g., Gould and Yellen 1987). Their view of average hearth-to-hearth distances indicates it does not vary according to mobility strategy. Instead, it seems to be sensitive to the factors emphasized in the ecological explanation (see Gould and Yellen 1987). This variation is perhaps due to the presence of dangerous predators in Botswana and their absence in Australia, as has been suggested. However, because camp size as measured by the number of square meters is primarily the result of anticipated mobility (Table 8), it may mean that hearth-to-hearth distance is equated with absolute site size or site square meters. Hearth-to-hearth distance may alternatively result from patterns of sharing and kinship (see Gargett and Hayden, Chapter 1 in this volume), or there might be an as yet undetermined factor influencing their distribution at sites.

Table 8 shows that anticipated length of occupation—short, medium, and long—is a good indicator of site size, whereas actual length of occupation is not. Sites inhabited with an anticipated occupation of medium duration average 700 m^2, whereas sites inhabited with an anticipated long occupation are almost twice as large, averaging 1,266 m^2. As with the m^2/person value, and no doubt related to it, mobility affects the size of sites. However, the variability within each category of anticipated mobility may be influenced by the extremes of site population, even though site population *per se* does not affect site size (see Table 3). That is, the two largest sites in the anticipated short occupation category in Table 9 (1001 to 1200 m^2) also had extremely large populations (39 and 40 people). The five smallest camps (1000 m^2 or less), which were inhabited by people with an anticipated long occupation, all also had the least number of inhabitants for sites in the anticipated long occupation category. The smallest site at which people anticipated a long habitation was occupied by only 3 people. The next smallest camps occupied by people anticipating a long stay were inhabited by only 4 and 5 people each. The two camps in the next size category with groups anticipating a long occupation were both occupied by 7 individuals. At the opposite extreme in size was the largest site, occupied by people in the same anticipated long-mobility category, that was inhabited by the most people, 25 individuals.

Table 7. **Number of Site Occupants by Number of Huts at a Site**

Number of site occupants	\[Number of huts\]										
	1	2	3	4	5	6	7	8	9	10	11
2–4	2	1									
5–7	2	3	1	1							
8–10				1							
11–13			1								
14–16			1	2	1	1					
17–19				1	1						
20–22				3	1		1				
23–25								1			1
26–28									1		
29–31						1					
32–34											
35–37											
38–40				1	1						

This appears to be consistent with the other size categories, as well; the smallest camps at which inhabitants anticipated as a medium occupation were populated by only 2 and 7 people each. Other larger camps, where occupants also anticipated a medium occupation, were inhabited by more people, between 16 and 28.

From these data, population appears to be a straightforward explanation of *intracategory* variability and anticipated mobility an explanation of *intercategory* variability. However, the effects of site population actually become ambiguous when we examine the midrange 1000 to 1200-m^2-size category. Here, individual camps occupied by groups anticipating a long stay were inhabited by 5, 13, and 16 people. The population varied from 6 to 17 individuals at sites occupied with the anticipation of a long habitation and within the 1201-1400-m^2-size category. One would not expect to see such a range in camp population sizes if population were the primary explanatory variable. This reveals why anticipated mobility is a

Table 8. Mobility Patterns by Site Size

	Site size (square meters)											
	188–400	401–600	601–800	801–1000	1001–1200	1201–1400	1401–1600	1601–1800	1801–2000	2001–2200	2201–2400	2401–2600
Anticipated length of occupation[a]												
Short	2	2			2							
Medium	2		2									
Long	1	2		2		3	4	1		2		1
Actual length of occupation												
Short	3	1		2		1	2					
Medium[b]		1	1			1						
Long	1	2		4		3	2	1	1	2		1

[a] Short = less than 3 months; medium = between 3 and 5.9 months; long = over 6 months.
[b] Site 21 has an unknown actual occupation length and hence cannot be included here.

Table 9. Anticipated Mobility and Actual Mobility at Time of Mapping Compared to
Number of Huts Located at Site

				Number of huts (includes storage huts)							
Mobility, site number	1	2	3	4	5	6	7	8	9	10	11
Anticipated short[a]											
Actual short											
#1				X							
#7	X										
#20			X								
#23					X						
Anticipated short											
Actual medium											
#10				X							
Anticipated short											
Actual long											
#2						X					
Anticipated medium											
Actual short											
#5				X							
#15	X										
#16									X		
Anticipated medium											
Actual medium											
#6	X										
#22							X				
Anticipated medium											
Actual long											
#4			X								
#19			X								
Anticipated long											
Actual short											
#8		X									
#31					X						
Anticipated long											
Actual medium											
#3		X									

(*Continued*)

Table 9 (*Continued*)

	Number of huts (includes storage huts)										
Mobility, site number	1	2	3	4	5	6	7	8	9	10	11
Anticipated long											
Actual long											
#9		X									
#11			X								
#12											X
#13		X									
#14				X							
#17		X									
#18				X							
#24			X								
#25								X			
#26				X							
#27			X								
#28			X								
#29	X										
#30				X		X					

[a]Short = less than 3.0 months; medium = between 3 and 5.9 months; long = over 6 months.

stronger predictor of site size than is camp population (Table 2). Extremely large or small populations may affect the variation in camp size *within* a category of anticipated length of occupation, but variation in camp size between the two extremes seems to be the result *not* of population differences but of anticipated mobility.

Even though still somewhat preliminary, I would like to suggest that the reason Gould and Yellen (1987) found no correlation, and O'Connell (1987) found only a slight correlation between mobility and site area and/or m²/person, may be that planned reoccupation was not a variable they examined. According to Gould (1987:personal communication), conclusive data on reoccupation was not possible to obtain from the Aborigines he studied. This may be due in part to their extremely nomadic and opportunistic mobility patterns, unlike the people in Vierich's sample. Although perhaps not easy to obtain, my fieldwork among the Basarwa and Bakgalagadi indicates that such information can be collected through a variety of questions that cross-check informant replies concerning anticipated length of occupation. This method may not be possible with all groups, and certainly may be more difficult with some groups.

In the data collected by Vierich, the Bakgalagadi inhabitants at Site 7 had both an anticipated and actual short length of occupation whereas the camp had a medium range of m²/person value and site area size. The site, however, was reoccupied each season. I think the planned reoccupation resulted in an increase in both site investment (measured by the m²/person value) and site area. How does this most tentative hypothesis fare when compared to Gould and Yellen's (1987) data? Because reoccupation was not a variable specifically discussed, I can only provisionally suggest that reoccupation accounts for the m²/person values for !Kung DBC base camps described in their Table 2 (Gould and Yellen 1987:85). I speculate that had the !Kung planned neither a long stay nor a reoccupation at the Dobe base camps, their m²/person values would be much lower, excluding the artificial 1969 example, which was influenced by the presence of an anthropologist (see Yellen 1984:58–64). On a cross-cultural level, anticipated reoccupation tends to mimic the next category of anticipated mobility in groups with transhumant and other mobility strategies (e.g., Grahm 1990; Tomka 1989). This illustrates the importance of obtaining information concerning inhabitants' future plans through intensive interviews.

There are, however, variables that cannot be accommodated by the anticipated mobility explanation. As mentioned earlier, the number of huts at a camp is not mobility dependent, although their diameter is. For example, and as is illustrated in Table 9, sites occupied for a short stay have an average of 3.8 huts per site, whereas sites inhabited for a medium stay have an average of 3.4 huts per site. Camps occupied for a long stay have an average of 4.4 huts per site. This is not statistically significant (Table 1). Table 10 illustrates that season is not an important factor in the number of huts. The number of huts located at a site appears to be directly correlated with the number of site occupants.

4. DISCUSSION

The principle of anticipated mobility, as noted, is related to Binford's (1977) concept of planning depth. At some point in human evolution, hominids developed the capacity for planning depth in general and anticipated mobility in particular. When in prehistory this capacity evolved now becomes an important issue. If the principle of anticipated mobility is, in fact, responsible for specific site structures and sizes, then those pre-*sapiens* hominids who did not have the ability for such anticipation would not—could not—produce spatial patterns directly correlated with anticipated mobility. If, on the other hand, the patterns are correlated with actual length of site occupation, or environment, season, site population, predators, or subsistence strategies, then pre-*sapiens* hominids could have produced the patterns much earlier in their evolution. At what point pre-*sapiens* acquired the potential for anticipation and planning depth is currently

Table 10.   Season of Site Occupation by Number of Huts Present at a Camp

	Number of huts (includes storage huts)										
Season[a]	1	2	3	4	5	6	7	8	9	10	11
Dry	1		2	1	1						
Dry+ (6 months or longer)		2	1								1
Wet	2	1	2	1	1		1		1		
Wet+ (6 months or longer)		1	1	5	3		2		1		

[a] +refers to season of site mapping because these sites were actually occupied at least 6 months and span the wet or dry season. Site 21 is not included because its actual length of occupation is unknown.

being debated in the literature (Binford 1987 and elsewhere). Other authors may not attempt to grapple with the issue because they do not see it as an influential factor. However, it becomes a crucial issue in light of the anticipated mobility explanation of site structure variability, not with the ecological explanation because it is not a major component of the latter. This is a critical point because many anthropologists attempt to determine population and related factors from Olduvai and other Early Paleolithic sites based on analogs from modern Basarwa (who use anticipated mobility) to extrapolate behavior concerning hominids who may or may not have used anticipated mobility to structure or lay out their sites (e.g., Jewett and Clark 1987). I submit that all anatomically modern humans utilize the principle of anticipated mobility. If so, it makes anticipated mobility valid as a beginning point from which to embark on studies of the spatial patterning of *Homo sapiens sapiens* in Upper Paleolithic and later sites. Further study is necessary to determine whether or not pre-*sapiens*, much less pre-*Homo*, hominids also used anticipated mobility (e.g., see Septh 1990).

The whole issue of archaeological visibility is crucial to our understanding of the past. Brooks and Yellen (1987) have shown that reoccupied hunting stand sites among the !Kung Basarwa are much more visible in the archaeological record than are more ephemeral single-component anticipated short-term habitation camps. This information, coupled with the tendency for people with anticipated long occupations to construct more archaeologically visible facilities such as formal storage loci, can lead to questions concerning the perceived population increase at the beginning of the Neolithic (also see Testart 1988). Are we seeing more sites in the Neolithic when there was a shift to horticulture because there was a shift to anticipated longer site occupations? In other words, is the increase in sites the result of changed mobility strategies that emphasized longer habitations rather than the result of a population increase?

As noted by a number of authors, "The patterns of early hominid behavior may well have been profoundly different from those of any living system we can observe. If we are to explore the record and detect its originality, we need to avoid adopting interpretations and hypotheses that project ethnographic or primate patterns into the remote past. . . . [We] need to engage in restless thinking about processes and patterns, and to develop a heirarchy of testable hypotheses" (Kroll and Isaac 1984:28). This can only be achieved by replacing studies based on ethnographic analogs with studies based on cross-culturally valid relationships and patterning of site structure. They are, as a result, not tied to a specific time and therefore are applicable to archaeological data (Kent 1987). Though both explanations examined here, that is, ecological and mobility, attempt to accomplish the latter, clearly more research is called for. We have come a long way from the early simplistic views of site structure and spatial patterning. However, we still have a long way to go before we can confidently predict when and when not to expect specific patterns.

5. CONCLUSIONS

Among the multiple explanations concerning spatial patterning examined, cross-cultural data in most cases best fit the anticipated mobility explanation. Generally, when the ecological variables were tested independently (held constant, and then selectively varied), anticipated mobility accounted for the largest amount of variation. However, it was not exclusively the case, as in the number of huts per site. The number of huts at a site seems to be better explained by the variables emphasized by the ecological explanation and specifically by site population.

When mobility is the influential variable, anticipated length of occupation appears to be more influential than actual length. Anticipated length of occupation is vital for understanding the principle behind mobility and spatial patterning but is not immediately germane for understanding site structure in the archaeological record because anticipated and actual length of occupation usually coincide. Moreover, and with only a few exceptions of unusual obvious departures, it is probably not possible to distinguish between the two archaeologically. This fact does *not* in any way diminish the need to delineate the role of anticipated versus actual mobility. Only through understanding the principles behind patterns, rather than just describing their presence or absence, is it possible to develop realistic and predictive models of the past. Future work will hopefully be directed toward developing research strategies that will allow us to obtain some measure of anticipated behavior (planning depth in the larger sense) from the archaeological record. Certainly the presence of specific features, such as formal storage areas and the relative amount of time invested in particular facilities, may ultimately be productive measures.

Understanding the presence or absence of certain patterns is equally important to determine. This is the only way we can begin to understand the rich variability present in the spatial patterning of diverse modern groups and their evolution. Furthermore, it is the only way we can really begin to understand the archaeological record, be it concerned with the Paleolithic, Mesolithic, Neolithic, or beyond. If nothing else, I hope this chapter will stimulate more debate and research in the directions outlined here.

ACKNOWLEDGMENTS

I would like to thank Jay Teachman and Garland White for help with the statistical analyses. Their invaluable aid made the quantitative portion of the chapter possible. I am indebted to Doug Price and Ellen Kroll for the invaluable editorial comments. I also am grateful to them for inviting me to participate in their Society for American Archaeology symposium (1987) and their resulting book. In addition, I sincerely thank Dick Gould, Jim O'Connell, Denise Lawrence, Debra Pellow, Mike Schiffer, and Libby Monk-Turner for valuable comments on rough drafts and Jean Johnson for typing Tables 3–10. Any inadequacies, however, are my sole responsibility.

6. REFERENCES

Binford, L., 1977, Forth-Seven Trips: A Case Study in the Character of Archaeological Formation Processes. In *Stone Tools as Cultural Markers: Change, Evolution and Complexity* (R. V. Wright, ed.), Canberra, Australian Institute of Aboriginal Studies, pp. 24–36.
Binford, L., 1978, Dimensional Analysis of Behavior and Site Structure: Learning from an Eskimo Hunting Stand, *American Antiquity* 43(3):330–361.
Binford, L., 1980, Willow Smoke and Dogs' Tails: Hunter–Gatherer Settlement Systems and Archaeological Site Formation, *American Antiquity* 45:4–20.
Binford, L., 1983, *In Pursuit of the Past: Decoding the Archaeological Record*, London, Thames and Hudson.
Binford, L., 1987, Research Ambiguity: Frames of Reference and Site Structure. In *Method and Theory for Activity Area Research: An Ethnoarchaeological Approach* (S. Kent, ed.), New York, Columbia University Press, pp. 449–512.
Brooks, A., and Yellen, J., 1987, The Preservation of Activity Areas in the Archaeological Record: Ethnoarchaelogical and Archaeological Work in Northwest Ngamiland, Botswana. In *Method and*

Theory for Activity Area Research: An Ethnoarchaeological Approach (S. Kent, ed.), New York, Columbia University Press, pp. 63–106.

Fisher, J., 1986, *Shadows in the Forest: Ethnoarchaeology among the Efe Pygmies,* Unpublished Ph.D. dissertation, Department of Anthropology, University of California, Berkeley.

Gould, R., and Watson, P. J., 1982, A Dialogue on the Meaning and Use of Analogy in Ethnoarchaeological Reasoning, *Journal of Anthropoligical Archaeology* 1:335–381.

Gould, R., and Yellen, J., 1987, Man the Hunted: Determinants of Household Spacing in Desert and Tropical Foraging Societies, *Journal of Anthropological Archaeogology 6(1):77–103.*

Grahm, M., 1990, *Periodically Abandoned Residences among the Tarahumara: Settlement Organization and Assemblage Variability.* Paper presented at the 55th annual meeting for the Society of American Archaeology, Las Vegas, Nevada.

Hayden, B., and Cannon, A., *The structure of Material Systems: Ethnoarchaeology in the Maya Highlands.* Society for American Archaeology Papers No. 3. Washington, DC: Society for American Aracheology.

Hitchcock, R., 1987, Sedentism and Site Structure: Organizational Changes in Kalahari Bosarwa Residential Locations. In *Method and Theory for Activity Area Research* (S. Kent, ed.) Columbia University Press, New York, pp. 374–423.

Isaac, G., Ll., 1983, Bones in Contention: Competing Explanations for the Juxtaposition of Early Pleistocene Artifacts and Faunal Remains. In *Animals and Archaeology* (J. Clutton-Brock and C. Grigson, eds.), *British Archaeological Reports* No. 163, pp. 3–19.

Jewett, R., and Clark, J., 1987, Observations on Estimating Local Group Size at Olduvai Gorge, Tanzania. In *Coasts, Plains and Deserts: Essays in Honor of Reynold J. Ruppé* (Sylvia Gaines, ed.). Arizona State University Anthropological Research Papers No. 38, pp. 117–127.

Kent, S., 1984, *Analyzing Activity Areas: An Ethnoarchaeological Study of the Use of Space,* Alburquerque, University of New Mexico.

Kent, S., 1986, the Influence of Sedentism and Aggregation on Porotic Hyperostosis and Anemia in the Southwest: A Nondiet Approach, *Man* 21(4):605–636.

Kent, S., 1987, Understanding the Use of Space: An Ethnoarchaeological Approach. In *Method and Theory for Activity Area Research: An Ethnoarchaeological Approach* (S. Kent, ed.), New York, Columbia University Press, pp. 1–62.

Kent. S., 1989, Cross-Cultural Perceptions of Farmers as Hunters and the Value of Meat. In *Farmers as Hunters: The Implications of Sedentism* (S. Kent, ed.), Cambridge, Cambridge University Press, pp. 1–17.

Kent, S., and Vierich, H., 1989, The Myth of Ecological Determinism: Anticipated Mobility and Site Organization of Space. In *Farmers as Hunters: The Implications of Sedentism* (S. Kent, ed.), Cambridge, Cambridge University Press, pp. 97–130

Kroll, E., and Isaac, G. L., 1984, Configurations of Artifacts and Bones at Early Pleistocene Sites in East Africa. In *Intrasite Spatial Analysis in Archaeology* (H. Hietala, ed.), Cambridge, Cambridge University Press, pp. 4–31.

Lave, C., and March, J., 1975, *An Introduction to Models in the Social Sciences,* New York, Harper and Row.

O'Connell, J., 1987, Alyawara Site Structure and Its Archaeological Implications. *American Antiquity* 52(1):74–108.

Oswald, D., 1987, The Organization of Space in Residential Buildings: A Cross-Cultural Perspective. In *Method and Theory for Activity Area Research: An Ethnoarchaeological Approach* (S. Kent, ed.), New York, Columbia University Press, pp. 295–344.

Septh, J., 1990, *Champanzee Studies and Their Implications for Understanding Early Hominid Ranging Behavior.* Paper presented at the Society of Africanist Archaeologists, Gainesville, Florida.

Silitshena, R. M., 1983, Intra-Rural, Migration and Settlement Changes in Botswana, *African Studies Centre Research Reports* No. 20.

Testart, A., 1988, The Social Anthropology of Hunter–Gatherers, *Current Anthropology* 29(1):1–31.

Tomka, S., 1989, *The Ethnoarchaeology of Site Abandonment in an Agro-Pastoral Context.* Paper presented at the 54th annual meeting of the Society for American Archaeology, Atlanta, Georgia.

Whitelaw, T., 1983, People and Space in Hunter–Gatherer Camps: A Generalizing Approach in Ethnoarchaeology, *Archaeological Review of Cambridge* 2(2):48–66.

Whitelaw, T., 1989, *The Social Organization of Space in Hunter–Gatherer Communities*, Unpublished Ph.D. dissertation, Cambridge University, Cambridge.

Yellen, J., 1977, *Archaeological Approaches to the Present*, New York, Academic Press.

Yellen, J., 1984, The Integration of Herding into Prehistoric Hunting and Gathering Economies. In Frontiers: Southern African Archaeology Today (M. Hall *et al.*, eds.), *British Archaeological Reports International* Series 207, pp. 53–64.

Yellen, J., 1987, *The Effect of Non-Human Predators on Intra-Site Spatial Organization*, Paper presented at the 52nd Annual Meeting of the Society for American Archaeology, Toronto, Ontario.

Chapter 3

Distribution of Refuse-Producing Activities at Hadza Residential Base Camps

Implications for Analyses of Archaeological Site Structure

JAMES F. O'CONNELL, KRISTEN HAWKES, AND
NICHOLAS BLURTON JONES

1. INTRODUCTION

Recent research on prehistoric hunter–gatherer site structure continues to be concerned primarily with the identification of discrete, activity-specific areas within sites (e.g., Carr 1984; Hietala 1984; Flannery 1986). However, an increasingly large body of ethnoarchaeological data suggests that such areas may be rare in the archaeological record, especially among middle- and low-latitude foragers (Yellen 1977; O'Connell 1987). Here we present additional data pertinent

JAMES F. O'CONNELL and KRISTEN HAWKES • Department of Anthropology, University of Utah, Salt Lake City, Utah 84112.   NICHOLAS BLURTON JONES • Graduate School of Education and Departments of Anthropology and Psychiatry, University of California at Los Angeles, Los Angeles, California 90024.

to this topic, derived from recent fieldwork among the Hadza of northern Tanzania. Preliminary analysis indicates that although activity areas can be identified within Hadza base camps, the range of activities associated with each are broad and broadly similar from area to area. Assumptions commonly made by archaeologists about the differential distribution of activities are only weakly supported by our data.

Comparison of the Hadza data with those on other hunter–gatherers shows certain general cross-cultural similarities in site structure but also reveals significant differences in the distribution of refuse-producing activities within sites. These differences further challenge common archaeological assumptions and underline the need for a better, more comprehensive understanding of the relationship between human behavior and site structure. Recent ethnoarchaeological research suggests that site structure may reflect, among other things, variation in food procurement, sharing, and storage practices. This surprising prospect deserves attention. Further ethnoarchaeological research may be especially informative.

2. THE HADZA

The Eastern Hadza are a group of 600 to 800 people who currently occupy a 2500 km^2 area south and east of Lake Eyasi in northern Tanzania. Much of this region is rough and hilly and covered with mixed savannah woodland. Medium and large herbivores, notably elephant, buffalo, zebra, and several species of antelope, are locally common (Smith 1980). The climate is warm and dry; annual average rainfall is in the 300 to 600 mm range, most of it falling in the 6-month wet season from November to April (Schultz 1971).

At the time of first European contact around the beginning of this century, only the Hadza occupied this country (Woodburn 1964 and references therein). They apparently lived entirely by hunting and gathering. Since then, the Hadza have suffered gradual encroachment by pastoral and agricultural groups and have also been subjected to a series of government-sponsored settlement schemes (McDowell 1981). Most Hadza now support themselves by a combination of hunting and gathering, farming, and farm labor. The precise mix of strategies pursued varies locally. Some 200 Hadza are essentially full-time subsistence foragers. During 1985–1986, we spent 188 days over 14 months living among the latter, collecting quantitative data on time allocation, foraging returns, and other topics (Blurton Jones et al. 1989; Hawkes et al. 1989; O'Connell et al. 1988). Data reported here are derived from this fieldwork. Earlier ethnographic reports concerning the Hadza have been provided by Kohl-Larson (1958), Woodburn (e.g., 1964, 1968a, 1970, 1972), and Vincent (1985a), among others.

Table 1. Site Population, Site Area, and Nearest Neighbor Distance at Six Hadza Base Camps

Site	Date Mapped	Sleeping areas				Number of Residents	Area (m^2)	Mean distance between nearest neighbors (m)
		Family	Women	Adolescents	Total			
Tsipitibe B	12 September 85	5	2	1	8	36	1000	4.2+1.1
Tsipitibe C	24 September 85	7	4	1	12	49	700	5.8+5.1
Mugendeda	24 November 85	6	5	2	13	46	1250	7.3+3.6
Umbea A	12 December 85	6	4	2	12	43	600	6.5+3.0
Umbea B	13 April 86	7	3	2	12	39	650	5.6+1.9
Dubunghela	21 May 86	6	3	2	11	34	575	6.0+1.9

The Hadza we observed pursued a seasonally variable, central-based foraging strategy (see Woodburn 1968a for additional description). During the dry season, when medium to large game animals were concentrated near water sources, adult men practiced both encounter and intercept hunting (*sensu* Binford 1978), the latter from blinds near water sources or along heavily used game trails. Both were typically solitary activities, although tracking wounded prey usually involved parties of men and boys. Weapons were limited to the bow and arrow (often poisoned); traps and snares were not employed, except rarely for small birds. Small game were not often taken by men, though they frequently shot at ground nesting birds. Groups of women foraged daily for roots and baobab fruit. In the wet season, when game animals were dispersed, intercept hunting was abandoned. Men continued encounter hunting, again mainly for medium to large mammals, often in the context of honey collecting trips with their wives. Parties of women also foraged separately for berries and roots. Many of these resources were consumed away from camp, but substantial quantities were also brought back for redistribution, processing, and consumption.

3. HADZA RESIDENTIAL BASE CAMPS

Six Hadza base camps at which we lived had populations of 35 to 50 individuals, and covered areas of about 550 to 1250 m^2 at the time they were first mapped (Table 1). (Woodburn [1972] reported camp populations of up to 100 individuals.) All were located within walking distance (usually within 15 minutes, sometimes up to 60 minutes) of a seasonally reliable source of water. All were associated with rocky outcrops that, according to the Hadza, provide potential refuge from elephants.

Base camp populations were divided into sleeping groups whose members usually shared the same shelter or sleeping area each night they were in camp. Three types of sleeping groups could be identified on the basis of age and sex composition:

1. *Nuclear families.* These consisted of a man, his wife, and their pre-adolescent children. They ranged in size from two to eight individuals, averaged about four to five, and were relatively stable in composition.
2. *Older women.* These groups consisted of older unmarried or widowed women, their unmarried adolescent daughters or granddaughters, and their preadolescent children or grandchildren. They included as many as five members, but usually numbered two to three. Senior women in such groups were often sisters or first-generation cousins. Their composition changed frequently as individuals moved between camps.
3. *Adolescents.* Theses groups included teenagers and young adults of the same sex, usually males. They included two to five members but averaged

about three. Members were sometimes (but not always) closely related; group composition changed frequently.

4. ACTIVITY AREAS

All activities in residential base camps took place in one of three kinds of areas: household, communal, and special activity areas (Figure 1). *Household*

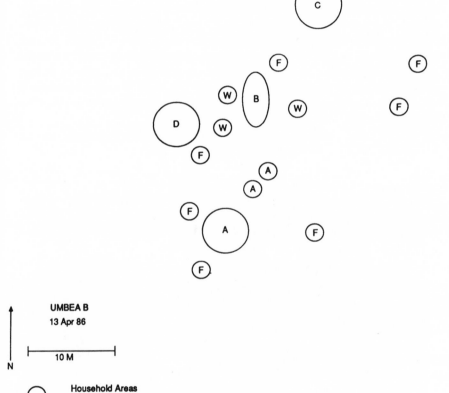

Figure 1. Distribution of household and communal activity areas at Umbea B, 13 April 1986. See text for details.

areas were occupied and used by one of the sleeping group types mentioned (Figure 2). They were the settings for a wide range of domestic activities, including the preparation and consumption of food, and the manufacture and maintenance of tools, clothing, and other equipment. Each was marked by a circle of cleared ground 2 to 6 m in diameter. Each contained a simple shelter and one or more hearths and was flanked by one or more secondary refuse areas. Shelters varied in form depending on the season of the year. During the wet season, they were usually simple, dome-shaped huts, 2 to 3 m in diameter and about 1.6 m in height, with a woven brush frame and grass cover. Similar huts were also built in the dry season, although unroofed or partly roofed brush windscreens of about the same size were also common then. Shelters were often positioned to one side of their respective activity areas but sometimes covered or enclosed them completely.

Household shelters usually contained hearths. These were small features, about 30 cm in diameter, located at the center of the hut floor or just inside the entrance. Outside hearths were also common and were generally positioned within 1 to 3 m of the hut entrance. Like interior hearths, they were relatively small but were often flanked by two to three large stones that served as stands for cooking vessels.

Activity areas were kept clear of refuse, mainly by frequent sweeping with

Figure 2. Household activity area at a residential base camp, April 1986. Secondary disposal areas at margins of cleared space.

leafy boughs or grass brooms. Hearths were also periodically cleared of ash. Much of the cleared material was deposited in secondary refuse areas along the edge of the activity area. There it appeared as a diffuse scatter, in dense circular or subcircular concentrations up to 2 m in diameter, or in well-defined windrows along the edge of the swept zone. Some size sorting occurred in disposal, depending on the hardness or penetrability of the ground surface in the activity area. Large items were always likely to be removed, but where sediments were soft or loose, some fraction of the smaller items were trampled into the ground rather than swept into secondary disposal areas (cf., Gifford-Gonzalez *et al.* 1985). Refuse was also occasionally deposited in small piles, up to 30 cm in diameter, located just to one side of the hut entrance. These "door middens" usually consisted of small items of food waste (e.g., small bone fragments or fruit pits), which accumulated during meals taken inside the hut.

Communal areas (Figure 3) were used for essentially the same range of activities as household areas but were not associated with any particular household or sleeping group. Members of different households were routinely seen in these areas, often in single-sex groups. Some areas were used by one sex to the complete or near complete exclusion of the other; others were used by members of both sexes, but not often simultaneously. Communal areas were always marked by the presence of one or more hearths and were periodically swept clear of refuse.

Figure 3. Communal area at a residential base camp, May 1986. Man at left shapes a metal arrowhead on rock anvil with a metal hammer; man at top right shapes a wooden arrow shaft; man at right sews a leather bag; others recline, watching.

Most varied in size from 4 to 6 m across. Structures of any kind were seldom found within these areas, nor did people often sleep in them at night.

Special activity areas (Figure 4) included bedrock grinding facilities, and defecation areas. The former were large, relatively flat-topped outcrops of granite or schist, whose surfaces were marked by small pecked and polished patches, 30 to 50 cm diameter, where baobab and other hard seeds were ground. Small handstones were frequently found in association with such features. All residential base camps had these facilities, which suggests their presence was a determinant of camp location. Defecation areas were located at the margins of camp, often forming a discontinuous ring around it.

5. DISTRIBUTION OF ACTIVITY AREAS WITHIN CAMPS

Household areas were often arrayed in a roughly circular pattern, with nearest neighbors 4 to 7 m apart (center of area to center of area; see Figure 1). In some camps, household areas were grouped in loosely defined clusters; in others, they were not. The position of individual household areas probably reflected kin relationships among household members, primary kin camped close together, less closely related individuals further apart (see also Woodburn 1972). Comprehensive analysis of this aspect of camp organization has not yet been

Figure 4. Woman processing baobab on a rock outcrop at a residential base camp, August 1986. Child watches, occasionally eats pulverized fruit.

undertaken. Communal areas were usually found both within and at the margins of camps. Their precise location was determined primarily by the distribution of morning sunlight and midday shade. Special activity areas were almost always peripheral to the camp.

6. DISTRIBUTION OF ACTIVITIES WITHIN CAMPS

One of the principle objectives of our fieldwork was to obtain information on time allocation among the Hadza. Toward this end, we pursued a program of systematic behavioral scan sampling, or "spot checks" of the activities of all individuals present in camp at selected intervals during the course of each day (Altmann 1974; Borgerhoff Mulder and Caro 1985; Hawkes *et al.* 1987). Data recorded included each individual's identity, location in camp, activity, and equipment and facilities involved, if any. More than 25,000 individual observations were recorded at seven different camps during the 14-month study period. A subset of the data has been subjected to preliminary analysis with attention to implications for site structure. We report some results of the preliminary study here.

Data analyzed were from scans perfomed on nine days over a 21-day period, from 26 March–16 April 1986, at a camp called Umbea B (Figure 1). The scans yielded about 1,000 individual behavioral observations. The camp retained essentially the same configuration of household and special activity areas throughout this period. It consisted of 12 household activity areas, 6 used by nuclear families, 1 by an adult man temporarily separated from his wife, 3 by older women, and 2 by adolescents. Four communal activity areas were used frequently, 2 (A and B) located at the center of the camp, 2 (C and D) at its northern and western edges.

Our particular concern here is with the distribution of refuse-producing activities within the camp. Four broad categories of activities were defined: (1) weapons maintenance, (2) clothing maintenance, (3) tool maintenance, and (4) food processing. Weapons maintenance includes all activities related to the manufacture and repair of men's hunting gear. The most common single activity in this category was arrow making. Clothing maintenance includes the manufacture and repair of garments. Tool maintenance refers to the manufacture and repair of all implements other than weapons, mainly women's digging sticks. Food processing includes all steps in the processing of foods for consumption. During the period under consideration, only about 16% of all food-processing activities involved meat, the rest plant foods. Food processing and the maintenance of women's digging sticks also often took place away from camp; other refuse-producing activities did not.

Table 2 shows how often these activities were observed at the site in daylight hours during the sample period. The sample is fairly large, about 200 individual

Table 2.   Refuse-Producing Activities Observed at Umbea B, 26 March–16 April
1986

	Actors		
	Men	Women	Total
Activity			
Weapons maintenance	129	0	129
Clothing maintenance	4	10	14
Tool maintenance	1	10	11
Food processing	2	42	44
Total	136	62	198

observations. This should be sufficient to provide a rough indication of the relative frequency of daytime activities performed at the site as a whole and at various locations within the site. The most common activity by far was weapons maintenance, which accounted for 65% of the total number of observations. Food processing accounted for 22% of the total, clothing repair 7%, and tool maintenance 6%. Table 2 also shows the distribution of these activities by sex. The distinctions are very clear: Weapons-related activities were associated exclusively with men, all other activities (especially food processing) primarily with women.

Table 3 shows the distribution of activities by location. Two patterns are immediately apparent. First, activity areas can be distinguished by the frequency of activities of all types recorded at each. The great majority of activities, 86% of the total observed, took place in the four communal areas. The remaining 14% were distributed among the 12 household areas. Second, communal activity areas located on the periphery of the site (Areas C and D; Figure 1) differ sharply from both centrally located communal areas (Areas A and B) and household areas in the relative proportions of associated activities. Peripheral areas were exclusively associated with male activities (more than 95% of the total observed), mainly weapons maintenance. Centrally located communal areas and household areas witnessed a broader range of activities associated with both men and women. Men's activities accounted for about 49% of the total observed in both central communal areas and about 52% of those in household areas. Weapons maintenance represented about 47% of the activities observed in central communal areas, 41% in household areas. Chi-square tests indicate that differences in the relative frequency of activities associated with household and centrally located

Table 3. Spatial Distribution of Refuse-Producing Activities at Umbea B, 26 March–16 April 1986

Activity	Communal areas								Household areas (n = 12)	
	A		B		C		D			
	n	%	n	%	n	%	n	%	n	%
Weapons maintenance	18	46	27	47	57	97	16	100	11	41
Clothing maintenance	5	13	4	7	2	3	—	—	3	11
Tool maintenance	4	10	5	9	—	—	—	—	2	07
Food processing	12	31	21	37	—	—	—	—	11	41
Total	39	100	57	100	59	100	16	100	27	100

communal areas, respectively, are not significant, given the sample sizes under consideration.

7. DISCUSSION

These data are sufficient to support several preliminary observations. First, the structure of Hadza residential base camps is a variant of a general pattern defined on the basis of recent ethnoarchaeological work among the Alyawara, !Kung, and (less certainly) the Nunamiut (Yellen 1977; Binford 1983; O'Connell 1987). Among each of these groups, residential base camps contain household, communal, and special activity areas. Household areas witness a wide range of domestic activities and are the most common activity areas in the camp. Communal areas (called shaded areas among the Alyawara and !Kung) are settings for essentially the same range of activities. They contain some of the same facilities but are less frequently reported. Special areas see a much narrower range of activities, usually only one per area. They are generally peripheral to household areas and often peripheral to the site as a whole. They are comparatively uncommon among the Hadza, !Kung, and Alyawara but are apparently encountered quite frequently among the Nunamiut.

The spacing of these areas differs significantly from group to group. Among the Hadza and !Kung, household areas are located on average about 4 to 8 m apart, whereas among the Alyawara and other central Australian groups (Gould and Yellen 1987; Gargett and Hayden 1987, Chapter 1 this volume), the distances are in the 25 to 45 m range. For the Aché of eastern Paraguay, who also display a variant of this same pattern of residential site organization, the mean inter-household distance is no more than 3 to 3.5 m (Jones 1984). A survey by Whitelaw (1983) shows substantial variation in this aspect of site structure among ethnographically known hunter–gatherers worldwide.

Hadza camps also differ from those of the !Kung and Alyawara with respect to the quantitative distribution of daytime refuse producing activities. Data presented here show that among the Hadza, more than 85% of these activities occur in communal activity areas, less than 15% in household areas. Similar data on the Alyawara (Denham 1978; Moslak and Tucker 1987) show just the opposite: More than 90% of all activities are confined to household areas, less than 10% in communal areas. Yellen (personal communication) reports the latter pattern for the !Kung. The Aché abandon foraging camps during the day, but in the late afternoon and early morning hours, when the camps are in use, the distribution of activities is like that described for the !Kung and Alyawara, unlike that for the Hadza (Lupo 1987).

Data presented here indicate that Hadza camps display little significant variation in the relative proportions of different refuse-producing activities pursued in communal and household areas. The exceptions to this generalization are peripherally located communal areas, which are dominated by men's activities, particularly weapons maintenance. Household and centrally located communal areas all witness essentially the same range of activities in about the same proportions. Analysis of a larger sample of behavioral scan data should enable us to distinguish older women's household areas from nuclear family and central communal areas by the absence of men's activities. Proportions of other activities in these areas should be fairly constant. Similar or perhaps somewhat more pronounced patterns of interhousehold variation in the relative importance of male versus female activities should be present among the Alyawara, although this has not yet been demonstrated quantitatively (but see O'Connell 1987). Preliminary analysis of scan sample data from the Aché shows no evidence of such a pattern (Lupo 1987). All household activity areas witness the same range of activities in about the same proportions.

8. ARCHAEOLOGICAL IMPLICATIONS

A common objective of site structural analysis is the identification of activity areas and tool kits used in the past (Carr 1984; Hietala 1984; Flannery 1986). Recent approaches to this goal are based on some common assumptions, among them that activities will be differentially distributed within sites and that there will be a consistent quantitative relationship between the performance of particular activities and the deposition of certain categories of refuse. Note that the first of these assumptions does not necessarily require that different activities be completely segregated, only that they be performed in some areas more often than in others. If these conditions prevailed during the formation of a site, then quantitative analysis of the spatial distribution of various categories of refuse should reveal covariant sets associated with particular activities.

The Hadza data provide only limited support for the first assumption. Men and women pursue distinctive sets of refuse-producing activities, which are differentially distributed over the site as a whole. Given a consistent quantitative relationship between the performance of those activities and the deposition of certain kinds of refuse (it remains to be seen whether such a relationship actually exists; cf. Ammerman and Feldman 1974), it might be possible to distinguish men's from women's activities and to determine their distribution and relative frequency in different parts of the site. Such an exercise would require analysis of a large sample of activity areas, including peripheral communal or older women's household areas. Men's and women's activities would *not* be distinguishable in an analysis of central communal and/or nuclear family household areas alone. Moreover, spatial analysis at any scale would be unable to separate the three refuse-

producing activities most often pursued by women because their relative frequency is apparently correlated in the areas in which they take place.

Comparison of the Hadza with other modern hunter–gatherers further limits
the confidence we can place in assumptions commonly made about the segregation of activities. Segregation by sex and sex-related activity may be common
between household areas among the Alyawara, and among the Nunamiut, both
within household areas and between such areas and special activity areas. It is not
common among the Aché and apparently of only limited significance among the
!Kung.

These results should not be surprising; Yellen (1977) made essentially the
same point 10 years ago. Nevertheless, its importance often remains unapprec-
iated. For example, in an analysis of site structure at Guila Naquitz, Flannery
(1986) and his colleagues make the initial operating assumption that men's
activities will be spatially separated from women's. No ethnographic support
pertinent to matters of site structure is cited. Patterns observed in the distribution
of debris within the site are interpreted primarily in terms of the initial operating
assumption. Alternate explanations grounded in the recent ethnoarchaeological
literature on site structure are never considered.

Ethnoarchaeological data reviewed here underline the inappropriateness of
this approach. Analyses of site structure must be based on a theoretically and
empirically justified set of expectations about behavior and its archaeological
reflection.

The research reported here contributes to this goal. Our description of the
Hadza and comparison with other groups reveals both a general pattern and some
marked differences in the use of space among hunter–gatherers. The fact that
three groups compared, the Hadza, !Kung, and Alyawara, live in superficially
similar environments makes the differences especially intriguing. Some of these
differences have received attention and may be at least partly explained. For
example, Whitelaw (1983), Gould and Yellen (1987), Gargett and Hayden (1987),
and O'Connell (1987) have all speculated on the relationship between interhousehold spacing and the relative importance of food sharing and predator pressure.
O'Connell (1987) and Binford (1987) have attributed certain differences in the
form and relative frequency of special activity areas among foragers and collectors
to the relative importance of food storage. The reasons behind other differences,
especially the completely unanticipated contrast in the distribution of activities
between communal and household areas between the Hadza, Alyawara, and
!Kung, remain unclear. Like other aspects of site structure, they may reflect basic
differences in local ecological circumstances, particularly related to food procurement and redistribution.

Though still only tentatively suggested, these relationships have great potential interest: Questions concerning food procurement, sharing, and storage
have long been of general concern to students of human evolution. The research
needed to explore this potential is also clearly indicated. Instead of continuing to

look for activity areas and tool kits, we must begin to ask how and why behavior is organized as it is within sites, how that organization is reflected in the distribution of refuse, and whether our knowledge of the relationship can be applied in archaeological context. These questions can only be answered where both behavior and its archaeological reflection can be observed directly, that is, in ethnoarchaeological situations.

ACKNOWLEDGMENTS

This work was supported financially by the National Science Foundation, the Swan Fund, Ms. B. Bancroft, the University of Utah, and the University of California (Los Angeles). We thank Utafiti (Tanzanian National Research Council) for permission to pursue fieldwork, L. C. Smith for introducing us to the Hadza and for access to unpublished data, D. Bygott and J. Hanby for vital assistance in the field, and K. Heath, C. Inoway, and D. Zeanah for help in analysis. D. Metcalfe, D. Grayson, and J. Yellen offered useful comments; D. Gillett and A. Lichty provided technical support.

9. REFERENCES

Altmann, J., 1974, Observational Study of Behavior: Sampling Methods, *Behavior* 48:1–41.
Ammerman, A., and Feldman, M., 1974, On the "Making" of an Assemblage of Stone Tools, *American Antiquity* 39:610–616.
Binford, L., 1978, *Nunamiut Ethnoarchaeology*, Academic Press, New York.
Binford, L., 1983, *In Pursuit of the Past*, Thames and Hudson, London.
Binford, L., 1987, Researching Ambiguity: Frames of Reference and Site Structure. In *Method and Theory for Activity Area Research: An Ethnoarchaeological Approach* (S. Kent, ed.), Columbia University Press, New York, pp. 449–512.
Blurton Jones, N., Hawkes, K., and O'Connell, J., 1989, Modeling and measuring the costs of children in two foraging societies. In *Comparative Socioecology: The Behavioral Ecology of Humans and Other Mammals* (V. Standen and R. Foley, eds.), Blackwell Scientific, London, pp. 367–390.
Borgerhoff Mulder, M., and Caro, T., 1985, The Use of Quantitative Observational Techniques in Anthropology, *Current Anthropology* 26:322–335.
Carr, C., 1984, The Nature of Organization of Intrasite Archaeological Records and Spatial Analytic Approaches to Their Investigation, *Advances in Archaeological Method and Theory* 7:103–222.
Denham, W., 1978, *Alyawara Ethnographic Data Base*, HRAFlex Books 015-001, Human Relations Area Files Press, New Haven.
Flannery, K., 1986, *Guila Naquitz: Archaic Foraging and Early Agriculture in Oaxaca, Mexico*, Academic Press, Orlando.
Gargett, R., and Hayden, B., 1987, *Site Structure, Kinship, and Sharing in Aboriginal Australia: Implications for Archaeology.* Paper presented at the 52nd Annual Meeting of the Society for American Archaeology, Toronto.

Gifford-Gonzalez, D., Damrosch, D., Damrosch, D., Pryor, J., and Thunen, R., 1985, The Third Dimension in Site Structure: An Experiment in Trampling and Vertical Dispersal, *American Antiquity* 50:803–818.

Gould, R., and Yellen, J., 1987, Man the Hunted: Determinants of Household Spacing in Desert and Tropical Foraging Societies, *Journal of Anthropological Archaeology* 6:77–103.

Hawkes, K., Hill, K., Kaplan, H., and Hurtado, M., 1987, A Problem of Bias in the Ethnographic Use of Scan Sampling, *Journal of Anthropological Research,* 43:239–245.

Hawkes, K., O'Connell, J., and Blurton Jones, N., 1989, Hardworking Hadza Grandmothers. In *Comparative Socioecology: The Behavioral Ecology of Humans and Other Mammals.* (V. Standen, and R. Foley, eds), Blackwell Scientific, London, pp. 341–366.

Hietala, H., 1984, *Intrasite Spatial Analysis in Archaeology,* Cambridge University Press, Cambridge.

Jones, K., 1984, *Hunting and Scavenging by Early Homonids: A Study in Archaeological Method and Theory.* Ph.D. Dissertation, University of Utah, Salt Lake City.

Kohl-Larson, L., 1958, *Wildbeuter in Ost-Afrika: die Tindiga, ein Jager-und Sammlervolk,* Dietrich Reimer, Berlin.

Lupo, K., 1987, *Preliminary Analysis of the Spatial Distribution of Activities at Aché Camps.* Unpublished manuscript, Department of Anthropology, University of Utah, Salt Lake City.

McDowell, W., 1981, *A Brief History of the Mangola Hadza.* Unpublished manuscript prepared for the Rift Valley Project, Ministry of Information and Culture, Division of Research, Dar es Salaam, Tanzania.

Moslak, K., and Tucker, T., 1987, *Preliminary Analysis of the Spatial Distribution of Activities at an Alyawara Residential Base Camp.* Unpublished manuscript, Department of Anthropology, University of Utah, Salt Lake City.

O'Connell, J., 1987, Alyawara Site Structure and Its Archaeological Implications, *American Antiquity* 52:74–108.

O'Connell, J., Hawkes, K., and Blurton Jones, N., 1988, Hadza Scavenging: Implications for Plio-Pleistocene Hominid Subsistence, *Current Anthropology* 29:356–363.

Schultz, J., 1971, *Agrarlandschaftliche Veranderungen in Tanzania (Mbulu/Hanang Districts),* Weltform Verlag, Munich.

Smith, L., 1980, *Resource Survey of Hadza Hunter–Gatherers.* Unpublished manuscript, Department of Anthropology, University of Utah, Salt Lake City.

Vincent, A., 1985a, *Wild Tubers as a Harvestable Resource in the East African Savannas: Ecological and Ethnographic Studies.* Ph.D. Dissertation, University of California, Berkeley.

Vincent, A., 1985b, Plant Foods in Savanna Environments: A Preliminary Report of Tubers Eaten by the Hadza of Northern Tanzania, *World Archaeology* 17:131–148.

Whitelaw, T., 1983, People and Space in Hunter–Gatherer Camps: A Generalizing Approach in Ethnoarchaeology, *Archaeological Review from Cambridge* 2(2):48–66.

Woodburn, J., 1964, *The Social Organization of the Hadza of North Tanganyika.* Ph.D. Dissertation, Cambridge University, Cambridge.

Woodburn, J., 1968a, An Introduction to Hadza Ecology. In *Man the Hunter* (R. Lee and I. DeVore, eds.), Aldine, Chicago, pp. 49–55.

Woodburn, J., 1968b, Stability and Flexibility in Hadza Residential Groupings. In *Man the Hunter* (R. Lee and I. DeVore, eds.), Aldine, Chicago, pp. 103–110.

Woodburn, J., 1970, *Hunters and Gatherers: Material Culture of the Nomadic Hadza,* The British Museum, London.

Woodburn, J., 1972, Ecology, Nomadic Movement and the Composition of the Local Group among Hunters and Gatherers: An East African Example and Its Implications. In *Man, Settlement, and Urbanism* (P. Ucko, R. Tringham, and G. Dimpleby, eds.), Duckworth, London, pp. 193–206.

Yellen, J., 1977, *Archaeological Approaches to the Present: Models for Reconstructing the Past,* Academic Press, New York.

Chapter 4

Variability in Camp Structure and Bone Food Refuse Patterning at Kua San Hunter–Gatherer Camps

LAURENCE E. BARTRAM, ELLEN M. KROLL,
AND HENRY T. BUNN

1. INTRODUCTION

As part of a widening interest in site formation processes, archaeologists have turned to ethnoarchaeology for insight into the factors that contribute to variability in the spatial makeup of prehistoric hunter–gatherer sites (e.g., Binford 1978a, 1983; Gould 1980; O'Connell 1987; Schiffer 1983; Spurling and Hayden 1984; Yellen 1977a). The structure of this volume reflects the fact that ethnoarchaeology complements archaeology in the development of methods for the discovery, description, and interpretation of intrasite spatial patterns. Together these approaches constitute an effective method for investigating prehistoric hunter–gatherer sites.

In this chapter we present a preliminary report on recent ethnoarchaeological research into the factors that affect the intrasite distributions of bone food

LAURENCE E. BARTRAM, ELLEN M. KROLL, and HENRY T. BUNN • Department of Anthropology, University of Wisconsin–Madison, Madison, Wisconsin 53706.

refuse. Understanding the variability among processes of bone assemblage accretion and modification in ethnoarchaeological contexts is of vital importance if we hope to identify and interpret the traces of similar processes in the archaeological record. This kind of research is especially helpful to archaeological spatial analysts because many of the intrasite patterns they attempt to interpret are also composed of the plotted positions of bones. The data generated by ethnoarchaeological research are also a source of useful test cases for evaluating the effectiveness of new analytical methods in detecting meaningful spatial patterns from which formation processes may be inferred (see Gregg et al., Chapter 5 this volume; Yellen 1977a).

In the tradition of "middle-range" or "actualistic" research, many recent efforts to understand site formation processes have systematically considered the various agents that accumulate and modify bones. Motivated both by the desire to better understand how stone artifacts and animal bones came to be juxtaposed in African Plio–Pleistocene sedimentary contexts and by an interest in the peopling of the New World, among other topics, archaeologists and paleontologists have been engaged in lively and enlightening research into the taphonomic history of bone assemblages. As a result of this research, the effects of many physical and biological processes on modern bone assemblages have been closely evaluated and are providing archaeologists with the methodological tools to recognize and discriminate between the effects of these natural agents and of ancient hominids (e.g., Bartram n. d.; Behrensmeyer 1978; Behrensmeyer et al. 1986; Binford 1978b, 1981; Binford and Bertram 1977; Blumenschine 1987; Bonnichsen 1973; Bonnichsen and Sorg 1990; Boaz and Behrensmeyer 1976; Brain 1967, 1969, 1980, 1981; Bunn et al. 1980; Bunn 1982, 1983a; Bunn and Kroll 1986; Crader 1974; Gifford 1978; Gifford 1981; Gifford and Behrensmeyer 1977; Hanson 1980; Haynes 1983; Hill 1979; Isaac 1967; Johnson 1985; Morlan 1980; Richardson 1980; Sutcliffe 1970; Vrba 1980).

Although the contributions of such research continue to catalyze debate, and in some cases, to supplant long-accepted notions of ancient hominid behavior, the overall research endeavor can still be usefully expanded. Much taphonomic research by archaeologists has spotlighted noncultural agents of bone accumulation and modification, although there are notable exceptions to this trend (e.g., Binford 1978b; Bunn 1983b; Bunn et al. 1988; Crader 1983; Noe-Nygaard 1977; Yellen 1977b). The emphasis on noncultural agents of bone assemblage formation and modification may in part derive from an intuitive (but debatable) notion that they are relatively "well-behaved" by comparison with cultural processes and are therefore more easily and comprehensively recognized and explicated. It also derives in part from the need for distinguishing "noise" from the human behavioral "signals" in the archaeological record. Cultural processes and the patterning that they create in bone assemblages have been examined to some degree (e.g., intrasite spatial distributions of bones, carcass-processing behavior), but more taphonomic research is required in this area before even central tendencies can be documented.

Although it is critical for the effects of nonhominid taphonomic agents to be recognized and evaluated before interpretations are made about the nature of a bone assemblage, it could be argued convincingly that even if provided with a bone assemblage formed exclusively by the actions of hominids, free from the effects of any taphonomic masking or distortion, archaeologists would still have great difficulty in making defensible inferences about the behavior of hominids that created it, especially from the spatial characteristics of the assemblage. It is precisely here that ethnoarchaeology can help to refine our methodology, and it is incumbent upon ethnoarchaeologists to provide the tools to link spatial patterns with behavioral processes. The fact that most of today's archaeologists painstakingly plot the locations of the bone specimens they excavate means numerous useful data sets now exist where ethnoarchaeologically derived principles can guide inferences about the meaning of archaeological bone distributions revealed by spatial analysis.

Despite significant work conducted in other parts of the world (e.g., Binford 1978b), quantitative ethnoarchaeological data on African faunal assemblages and their spatial attributes remain regrettably scant. Among modern sub-Saharan African subsistence hunters, who are arguably the most ecologically relevant contemporary subjects vis-à-vis the range of habitats and species represented at ancient hominid sites, available information has been limited to six societies, including the !Kung San (Yellen 1974, 1977a) and the Kua San (Bunn 1982, 1983b; Kroll n. d.) of the Kalahari Desert, the Bisa of Zambia (Crader 1974, 1983; Marks 1976), the Efe of the Ituri Forest in Zäire (Fisher 1987), the Dassanetch *gal dies* near Lake Turkana, Kenya (Gifford 1977, 1980; Gifford and Behrensmeyer 1977), and the Hadza of Tanzania (Bunn *et al.* 1988). Our continuing ethnoarchaeological fieldwork among two of these groups, the Kua San and the Hadza, is part of an effort designed to help improve this situation (also see O'Connell *et al.*, Chapter 3 this volume).

The work reported here is based upon 170 days of observation among the Kua San (hereafter called Kua) in the east-central Kalahari of Botswana between late September 1985 and early August 1986. We concentrated on documenting formation processes and camp structure, especially as they were reflected in potentially durable bone food refuse. Through notes, photographs, videos, maps, and bone collections, which included detailed skeletal part and bone modification data, we documented the range of activities associated with the procurement, processing, and discard of animal carcasses during an annual subsistence cycle of the Kua. In addition, by accompanying men and women on their foraging trips into the bush, we were able to document the nature and frequency of activity performance away from camps, including hunting, primary butchery, and transport of carcasses, and, to a lesser degree, the gathering and processing of plant foods. The Kalahari data consist of maps, observational records, and the entire complement of bones from over 30 camps. The bones represent more than 100 larger mammals obtained and processed by the Kua. Our analyses of the Kua bone and spatial data are underway at the University of Wisconsin–Madison.

In this chapter, we offer some initial observations about the spatial structure of Kua camps and how this structure is reflected in the bone refuse. Future publications will provide more detailed, quantitative assessments of the Kua camp data. We first provide some background information on the study area and the Kua. Next, we characterize the five types of Kua camps we observed and the processes that formed the material refuse recovered from them, and we present examples to illustrate the structure of each type. Finally, we offer some preliminary conclusions about the nature of the spatial structure of these camps, especially the patterning in the bone food refuse, and we summarize some of the implications these may have for archaeological spatial analysis.

2. BACKGROUND

2.1. The Field Area

The study area is located near the eastern border of the Central Kalahari Game Reserve in the Western Sandveld region of Botswana's Central District, about 75 km south-southwest of the diamond-mining town of Orapa (Figure 1). There is little topographic relief in the unconsolidated aeolian sands that mantle the Western Sandveld, except for occasional dunes and pans. In 1978, traveling with Robert Hitchcock, Kroll and Bunn first observed our informants living near one of these pans (Bunn 1983b; Hitchcock 1982, 1987; Kroll n. d.).

The climate of the region is subtropical and semiarid. Rainfall is strongly seasonal and falls generally in the form of convectional thunderstorms occurring between November and April (Pike 1971; Cooke 1982). The Kua recognize three main seasons in a year. A hot dry season lasts from late August through late October, a time aptly described by George Silberbauer as one of "crushing heat" (1981). This is a stressful time in the Kalahari, during which sources of food and fluid become scarce. Beginning in late October or early November a short period of isolated storms follows; however, these storms are sporadic and localized, and in most respects this period is much like the preceding hot dry season. With the rising humidity, many of the Kalahari trees develop leaves in anticipation of the longer summer rainly season. The rain normally arrives in mid-December and lasts until the end of March, with a peak in precipitation during January and February. Next ensues a cool dry season (with below-freezing nights by June and July) that lasts into August when the heat returns again.

The vegetation in this part of the Kalahari is dominated by grasses and low shrubs, punctuated with "islands" of trees dominated by *Acacia* species. The

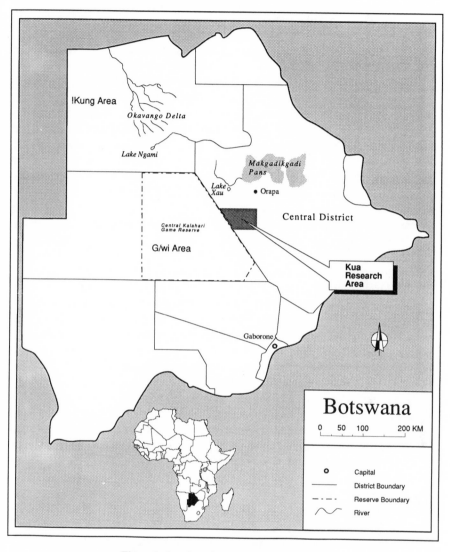

Figure 1. Location of research area in Botswana.

overall impression is that of a vast and generally treeless grassland. In this way the area differs markedly from the more densely vegetated area of northwestern Botswana that is home to the !Kung. Notably, and unlike the habitat of the !Kung, there are no monogongo groves to provide a dietary staple or choice of shade trees (Yellen 1977a; Lee 1979). In numerous features, the Western Sandveld region is similar to the area inhabited by the G/wi (Silberbauer 1981). The presence of significant sources of fluids in the tubers and fruits of several plant species enables animals and people to live in a land characterized by an almost total lack of surface water. Most plant food species are present only seasonally, with a rain-related peak in availability between February and June (Vierich and Hitchcock 1978).

More than 50 mammalian species, plus abundant birds and reptiles, inhabit this part of the Kalahari. Among them, at least a dozen are hunted regularly by the Kua, including eland, greater kudu, gemsbok, wildebeest, hartebeest, duiker, bat-eared fox, porcupine, and steenbok (Table 1). At least a dozen more are (or were, e.g., giraffe) taken less frequently. Several of the commonly hunted species are gregarious bovids who migrate vast distances in search of water and fresh grass. Some species, notably gemsbok and eland, are able to meet all of their moisture requirements from the consumption of the same fruits and tubers that permit human foragers to live in the region.

Veterinary fences erected in the Kalahari since the 1950s, combined with an ever increasing number of cattle, are taking a heavy toll on Botswana's mammalian fauna, especially the migratory antelope that depend on much of the same browse and grass. The grass that grows so luxuriantly in this part of the Western Sandveld had drawn a burgeoning population of people and their cattle from other locations lacking adequate grazing. People and their herds are sustained by water raised through drilled boreholes from deep beneath the Kalahari (often from hundreds of meters down) by diesel-driven pumps that provide a semireliable source of water. These boreholes are central features of cattle posts, a settlement type by no means new to this part of the Kalahari (Yellen 1985; Denbow and Wilmsen 1986), but certainly more abundant now than in the past. The ecology of pastoralism in the east-central Kalahari is complex and dynamic, but generally speaking, as the cattle population increases, the yields of economically vital plant and animal species for human foragers decrease (Hitchcock 1987:391–393). It should be noted that many of the wild species are also important subsistence items for sedentary cattle post residents (Hitchcock 1982:298).

2.2. The Kua

The Kua speak a language (Traill 1978:252–260) belonging to the Tshu-Khwe group of the Khoe family of southern African languages (Westphal 1979). Bleek's "Central Group" of Bushmen languages (Bleek 1956) is a roughly equivalent name for this language family, which also includes the languages of the G/wi, G//ana, and Naron, with whom the Kua share numerous economic and social characteristics. The constellation of linguistic, economic, and physical attributes shared by the Kua place them into the much debated and vaguely defined categories of Bushman, San, or Basarwa (e.g., Elphick 1985:xxi–xxii, 4–7, 23–42; Lee 1979:29–35; Silberbauer 1981:3–6; Tobias 1978:1–3). Based on 1978 census data, some 2,709 Basarwa, most of whom are Kua, comprised about 77% of the

Table 1.   Some Mammals Hunted by the Kua

Taxon	Common name	Weight range (kg)[a]
Giraffa camelopardalis	Giraffe	703.0 to 1395.0
Taurotragus oryx	Eland	400.0 to 700.0
Oryx gazella	Gemsbok	210.0 to 240.0
Connochaetes taurinus	Blue wildebeest	180.0 to 250.0
Tragelaphus strepsiceros	Greater kudu	119.6 to 258.2
Alcelaphus buselaphus	Red hartebeest	105.0 to 156.0
Orycteropus afer	Antbear	40.4 to 64.5
Antidorcas marsupialis	Springbok	30.4 to 47.6
Hyaena brunnea	Brown hyena	28.0 to 47.5
Sylvicapra grimmia	Duiker	15.3 to 25.4
Hystrix africaeaustralis	Porcupine	13.6 to 24.1
Raphicerus campestris	Steenbok	8.9 to 13.2
Proteles cristatus	Aardwolf	7.7 to 10.0
Manis temminicki	Pangolin	4.5 to 14.5
Otocyon megalotis	Bat-eared fox	3.2 to 5.4
Pedetes capensis	Springhare	2.9 to 3.9

[a]Weights for each taxon are from Smithers (1971).

population living in the Western Sandveld of the Central District (Hitchcock 1978a:219).

We lived among Kua who were full or part-time foragers. An economic spectrum is evident among the inhabitants of the Western Sandveld, ranging from sedentary cattle post living to mobile foraging (Hitchcock 1978a), and Kua may be found from one end of this economic spectrum to the other. In fact, at different times of the year, the same Kua individuals may shift from complete dependence on the cattle post economy to full-time foraging. Flexibility and mobility, the keys to adaptive success in the frequently hostile habitat of the Kalahari, are conspicuous features of both the subsistence pursuits and residences of the region's inhabitants.

Because of habitat deterioration, the foraging Kua we observed are now restricted to an area along the western frontier of a "borehole front," which is advancing rapidly into the region from the east. As the progressive degradation of the fragile Kalahari savanna continues under the hooves of cattle, any purely foraging mode of subsistence among the Kua will likely be supplanted by a sedentary, livestock-based economy during the next decade. The ongoing process of sedentism among the Kua attendant with this incursion has been the subject of much work by Robert Hitchcock and his colleagues (Hitchcock 1978a, 1980, 1982, 1985, 1987). Against this background, we shall now present information about the camps themselves.

3. KUA CAMPS: OVERVIEW

3.1. Camp Variability

Seasonal differences in Kua mobility strategies result in different types of camps and play an important part in determining their size and structure. Most of the Kua living in the Western Sandveld occupy large camps during the hot dry season, but they disperse into smaller camps in the rainy season and cool dry season, when they are sustained by water-bearing melons and tubers. This residence pattern is broadly similar to that reported for the !Kung of Ngamiland (Marshall 1976; Lee and DeVore 1976; Yellen 1977a), although it has appeared only recently among the Kua in this part of the Western Sandveld. During the period from 1975 and 1979, Hitchcock observed the same Kua practicing a different residential mobility pattern than what we recorded in 1985–1986. The difference led Hitchcock (1982:339) to contrast the Kua residence pattern with the dry season residence pattern of the !Kung.[1] The change coincided with the drilling of many new boreholes in the Kua territory of the Western Sandveld. To the Kua, these boreholes present an irresistible and previously unavailable alternative for dry season residence.

The pattern of Kua residential mobility produced four distinct types of occupations during our period of observation: (1) base camps (*sensu* Binford and Binford 1966; Binford 1978b:488, 491) of hot dry, cool dry, and rainy season

---

[1]The residence types observed among the Kua in the late 1970s were similar to those reported for the G/wi (Silberbauer 1972) and illustrated by Binford as typical of a "foraging" subsistence-settlement system [Binford 1980:Figure 1] with one influential exception: Because pans are relatively less numerous in the Western Sandveld than they are in the G/wi area to the west, rainy season occupations were less focused upon them. We did not observe any human occupation at pans during the 1985–1986 rainy season, although such an occupation was observed in 1978 (Hitchcock 1982, 1987; Kroll and Bunn personal observations). We were, however, told by some of our Kua informants that they would have camped near the 1978 location had enough rain fallen there to fill the pan.

varieties; (2) transient camps; (3) special-purpose camps; and (4) special-purpose locations, which are places where the activities performed were similar to those performed at special-purpose camps but did not involve an overnight stay[2] (Binford 1980:9). Kua camps can be placed into one of these categories based on season of occupation, length of occupation, population size, camp area, and the kinds of activities performed. Data for each of the camps we observed are summarized acording to these variables in Table 2. Table 3 presents these data grouped by each camp type.

Base Camps. As mentioned before, during the hot dry season, most of our Kua informants in the Western Sandveld occupied relatively large settlements of up to about 75 people. These took the form of "borehole base camps," a distinctive settlement type located near cattle posts operated by Tswana and Herero herdsmen for nonresident owners. The Kua camps were peripheral to the main cattle post settlement and borehole but within easy walking distance to the borehole itself, usually within a kilometer or so.

Despite their appearance as welcome oases, cattle posts had several shortcomings for the Kua. Many more Kua than the herdsmen would have liked stayed near the cattle posts during the tremendous heat of this season, and occasional conflicts flared up between the herdsmen and Kua over rights to water or payment for labor. Nonetheless, Kua priority in these places was recognized (Kua place names were in common use among all residents), and their presence was grudgingly tolerated by the cattlemen.

A particularly unyielding problem posed by cattle post residence was the local deficiency of economically important fauna and flora. The dilemma was that although wild food resource densities increased as a function of distance from the cattle posts, the availability of water decreased. Observations of foraging distances and wild food harvests from both cattle post and noncattle post residences during the dry season illustrate this (Hitchcock 1982:188–189; Bartram, n. d.). The limitations posed by the virtual absence of water sources in the bush during the hot dry season thwarted plans for lengthy foraging excursions. For example, on rare ocasions when a large animal had been shot on a hunting trip in this season, tracking was undertaken with clear knowledge of the potential hazards of remaining in the bush overnight without water. In several instances we received reports of large, fatally wounded animals being abandoned because of the danger of dehydration posed by further tracking. This meant that although routine hunting trips originated from hot dry season base camps, they rarely resulted in the formation of overnight special-purpose camps.

---

[2]Functionally equivalent terms used by Binford to describe these same kinds of places are "work camps" (Binford and Binford 1966), "special-purpose sites" (Binford 1986:256; 1982; 1983a:133–138), "special-purpose locations" (Binford 1978b:490; 1984), and "special-use locations" (Binford 1978b:483–495).

Table 2. Kua Camp Data

Camp name	Type	Season	Arrival date	Abandon date	Nights occupied	Population Minimum	Maximum	ALS area	Total structures
Doatara	S(K)	HR	≈12/84	≈12/84	1	1	1	≈20	1
Taela	S(K)	HR	≈12/84	≈12/84	≈2	1	1	79	1
Kani//am/odi HHG-2	B	HD-HR	≈7/27/85	2/22/86	≈210	1	15	309	3
Kani//am/odi HHG-4A	B	HD-HR	≈7/27/85	≤12/27/85	≈153	14	16	451	7
Kani//am/odi HHG-5	B	HD	≈7/27/85	≈10/20/1985	≈85	6	6	204	3
Kani//am/odi HHG-7	B	HD	≈7/27/85	≈10/15/1985	≈80	10	10	714	7
Kani//am/odi HHG-3	B	HD	9/30/85	≤12/27/85	>88	5	5	421	2
Kani//am/odi HHG-4B	B	HR	<12/27/85	1/16/86	>20	26	33	345	5
Kani//am/odi HHG-4C	B	HR	1/16/86	2/19/86	34	33	33	761	6
//oabe I	B	HR	1/29/86	2/5/86	7	9	17	399	1
Four/amguu	S(R)	HR	2/10/86	2/14/86	4	4	4	≈100	1
Kani//am/odi HHG-8 (East)	B	HR-CD	2/19/86	4/13/86	53	10	18	474	8
Kani//am/odi HHG-8 (West)	B	HR-CD	2/19/86	6/6/86	107	2	17	504	11
Senyabe	L(K)	HR	3/2/86	3/2/86	0	4	4	66	0
Koka//a/u I	S(K)	HR	3/4/86	3/6/86	2	3	3	72	1*

Koka//a/u I death site	S(K)	HR	3/4/86	3/5/86	1	3	3	20	0
KunahajinaA	B	HR	3/14/86	3/22/86	8	18	26	—	4
//oabe II	B	HR	3/22/86	3/29/86	7	5	7	147	1
Ke am	L(K)	HR	3/25/86	3/25/86	0	2	2	≈25	0
Hitso/nu	L(K)	HR	3/26/86	3/26/86	0	7	7	≈100	0
Minipara death site	L(K)	HR	3/29/86	3/29/86	0	5	5	14	0
Minipara	S(K)	HR	3/29/86	3/30/86	1	5	5	62	1
//eba	T	HR	3/30/86	3/31/86	1	5	5	70	1
Basuni	T	CD	4/10/86	4/11/86	1	17	17	≈45	1
//udiku	T	CD	4/11/86	4/12/86	1	18	18	≈45	1
Tsautsaba	B	CD	4/12/86	4/15/86	3	9	16	—	1
Kunahajina B	B	CD	4/13/86	7/20/86	98	6	16	601	6
Gonatsa	B	CD	4/14/86	4/18/86	4	4	12	34	1
Zaitekaiwa	T	CD	4/14/86	4/15/86	1	5	5	—	1
≠oo/o	S(K)	CD	4/17/86	4/18/86	1	5	5	≈30	1*
Bohomau A	B	CD	4/19/86	≈4/27/86	≈8	12	12	—	1
Koka//a/u II	S(K)	CD	4/27/86	4/28/86	1	3	3	14	1
Tu'kai death site camp	S(K)	CD	≈4/27/86	≈4/28/86	1	12	12	18	1*
Tu'kai	S(K)	CD	≈4/28/86	≈4/30/86	2	12	12	86	1*

(Continued)

Table 2 (*Continued*)

Name	Type	Season	Arrival	Abandon	Nights	Minimum	Maximum	ALS area	Structures
Bohomau B	B	CD	≈4/30/86	≈5/7/86	≈7	12	12	—	1
≠oozoro	S(K)	CD	≈5/7 /86	≈5/10/86	3	12	12	274	1*
≠oo/watsia	L(K)	CD	5/13/86	5/13/86	0	2	4	≈50	0
Bohomau C	B	CD	≈5/10/86	≈5/16/86	≈6	12	12	—	1
N//ameguu	T	CD	≈5/16/86	≈5/18/86	2	12	12	≈100	1
N//ame/waguu	T	CD	≈5/18/86	≈5/20/86	2	12	12	≈15	1
Bohomau D	B	CD	≈5/20/86	≈6/2/86	≈13	12	12	259	2
Uwekiachere A	B	CD	≈6/2/86	≈6/4/86	≈2	11	12	—	1
≠oo/wakoa	B	CD	≈6/4/86	≈6/9/86	5	11	12	49	1*
Uwekiachere B	B	CD	≈6/9/86	≈6/18/86	≈9	5	12	—	1
Tarataguu	L(K)	CD	≈6/17/86	≈6/17/86	0	5	5	—	0
N//ameoo	T	CD	≈6/18/86	≈6/20/86	2	6	6	≈20	1
Dutara	S(K)	CD	≈6/20/86	≈6/23/86	3	5	5	118	1
Bohomau E	T	CD	≈6/23/86	≈6/24/86	1	12	12	—	1
'Gaenkiapaho death site	L(K)	CD	7/27/86	7/27/86	0	5	5	14	0
'Gaenkiapaho	S(K)	CD	7/27/86	7/30/86	3	5	7	93	1

Note: Name: Roman numerals denote different camps in the same named area. Arabic numerals indicate household groups at the same large basecamp. Letters indicate subsequent occupations at the same camp. Type: B = Basecamp; L = Special-purpose location; S = Special-purpose camp; T = Transient camp; (R) = Reconnaissance; (K) = Kill. Season: CD = Cool dry; HD = Hot dry; HR = Hot rainy. Arrival/abandon dates < = before; ≤ = on or before; "≈" = approximate date. Nights: Number of nights spent at the camp. "≈" = approximately; ≥ = more than. Population: Minimum = Minimum number of residents observed at camp (exclusive of temporary visitors). Maximum = Maximum number of residents observed at camp (exclusive of temporary visitors). ALS area: Area in square meters contained within the absolute limit of scatter (Yellen 1977). Structures: Total number of residential structures built during the occupation. * = Minimally modified bush windbreak.

Table 3. Kua Camp Summary Statistics

Occupation type	Season	Total observed	Nights			ALS area (m²)			Population minimum			Population maximum			Number of structures		
			n	Mean	S. D.	n	Mean	S. D.	n	Mean	S. D.	n	Mean	S. D.	n	Mean	S. D.
Basecamp	Hot dry	5	4	132.0	61.7	5	419.8	191.3	5	7.2	5.0	5	10.4	5.0	5	4.4	2.4
	Hot rainy	7	7	31.4	38.0	5	457.0	220.4	7	14.7	11.4	7	21.6	9.6	7	5.1	3.6
	Cool dry	10	10	15.4	29.2	4	264.3	191.3	10	9.4	3.2	10	11.6	4.2	10	1.6	1.6
	Total	22	21	43.0	58.3	14	380.5	227.2	22	10.6	7.7	22	15.1	7.3	22	3.4	3.0
Special purpose reconnaissance	Hot dry	0	0	—	—	0	—	—	0	—	—	0	—	—	0	—	—
	Hot rainy	1	1	1.0	0.0	1	≈100	0.0	1	4.0	0.0	1	4.0	0.0	1	1.0	0.0
	Cool dry	0	0	—	—	0	—	—	0	—	—	0	—	—	0	—	—
	Total	1	1	1.0	0.0	1	100.0	0.0	1	4.0	0.0	1	4.0	0.0	1	1.0	0.0
Special purpose kill	Hot dry	0	0	—	—	0	—	—	0	—	—	0	—	—	0	—	—
	Hot rainy	5	5	1.4	0.5	5	50.6	28.6	5	2.6	1.7	5	2.6	1.7	5	0.8	0.4
	Cool dry	7	7	2.0	1.0	7	90.4	90.6	7	7.7	4.1	7	8.0	3.9	7	1.0	0.0
	Total	12	12	1.8	0.9	12	73.8	72.1	12	5.6	4.1	12	5.8	4.1	12	0.9	0.3
Kill location	Hot dry	0	0	—	—	0	—	—	0	—	—	0	—	—	0	—	—
	Hot rainy	4	4	0.0	0.0	4	51.3	39.5	4	4.5	2.1	4	4.5	2.1	4	0.0	0.0
	Cool dry	3	3	0.0	0.0	2	32.0	25.5	3	4.0	1.7	3	4.7	0.6	3	0.0	0.0
	Total	7	7	0.0	0.0	6	44.8	34.1	7	4.3	1.8	7	4.6	1.5	7	0.0	0.0
Transient	Hot dry	0	0	—	—	0	—	—	0	—	—	0	—	—	0	—	—
	Hot rainy	1	1	1.0	0.0	1	70.0	0.0	1	5.0	0.0	1	5.0	0.0	1	1.0	0.0
	Cool dry	7	7	1.4	0.5	5	45.0	33.7	7	11.7	4.9	7	11.7	4.9	7	1.0	0.0
	Total	8	8	1.4	0.5	6	49.2	31.8	8	10.9	5.1	8	10.9	5.1	8	1.0	0.0

Thus, despite the trouble, their desire for access to reliable water prompted the Kua to practice the common Kalahari risk management strategy of minimizing distance to water (Silberbauer 1981; Brooks and Yellen 1987:67). In the Western Sandveld, this manifested itself in dry season settlements focused on the large borehole base camps. Extreme seasonal fluctuations in population were characteristic of these large camps because of the temporary presence of otherwise mobile foragers. Later, during the rainy season, the cattle post population diminished to only the herdsmen and some sedentary Kua, although there were also occasional visits from individuals and small groups in transit. There were few special purpose camps associated with these base camps.

With the coming of the rains in January, most Kua moved away from cattle post camps to smaller, rainy season base camps located at distances of 5 to 40 kilometers from the cattle posts. On the eve of one such residential move, a Kua informant told us that it was now time to "sleep near the melons." He was referring to the renewed availability of several vital, water-bearing plants (principally the gemsbok cucumber [*Citrullus naudinianus*] and later, the tsamma melon [*Citrullus lanatus*]). During this season, the populations of the camps averaged about 10 to 20 individuals, within two to four households. As was so at dry season camps, households were primarily based around nuclear families. Daily foraging trips were made by all camp members to exploit the range of fresh resources. Even the youngest individuals rode along on their mother's backs, and the oldest individuals foraged in areas near to camp. As was also the case at dry season camps, food was consumed in the bush while foraging, but now large quantities were returned to camp for consumption by the group.

Rainy season and cool dry season base camps formed the hub of a network of special purpose camps. Subgroups left the base camp to go to special-purpose camps for stays of up to several days in order to hunt and butcher game or to collect locally abundant plant foods. The large number of special-purpose camps affiliated with rainy season and cool dry season base camps contrasts conspicuously with the smaller number of special-purpose camps associated with hot dry season base camps.

Transient Camps. Transient camps were places where people spent the night while traveling (Binford, 1978b). Similar to special purpose camps, the examples we observed were attributable almost exclusively to rainy season and cool dry season periods. By virtue of their immediacy and short-term occupation, these camps were represented only by low-density debris scatters (Kent, Chapter 2 this volume).

Special-Purpose Camps and Locations. Special-purpose camps (and special-purpose "locations" [*sensu* Binford 1980]) were extractive in nature. The special-purpose camps were distinguished from special-purpose locations by an overnight stay and the construction of some sort of shelter. Activities performed at these camps tended to be restricted in number, and the duration of the occupation generally was a function of the amount of time required to complete the tasks at hand. During our period of observation, these tasks most commonly centered around the butchery of a large bovid carcass.

Before we examine the spatial characteristics of each of these types of camps, we shall first consider some common structural components of Kua camps, and second, some common aspects of the accumulation of bone refuse. Despite variations in occupation length, number of residents, activities conducted, and season of occupation, most Kua camps that we observed combined a relatively small assortment of structural components and facilities to produce the diversity in Kua camp types as variations on a basic structural theme.

3.2. Camp Structure

We begin our discussion of Kua camp structure at the scale of the *household cluster* (*sensu* Winter 1976), an elemental unit of virtually all camps that is composed of the associated sets of facilities and structures belonging to an individual household (Figure 2). Kua camps variably comprised a household

Figure 2. A cool dry season household cluster. The roasting pit in the foreground contains *ka* melons (*Citrullus naudinianus*).

cluster or one or more *household groups* that were formed by an aggregation of two to as many as seven or more household clusters. At the larger dry season camps, household groups often consisted of multiple household clusters, whereas at the dispersed rainy season and cool dry season camps, they sometimes consisted of a single household cluster.

For the following discussion, Figure 3 is a schematic rendering of a Kua household group comprising two household clusters. The Kua household cluster always included a windbreak or hut (sometimes both), a primary and normally secondary hearth(s), and sometimes other associated facilities or structures as

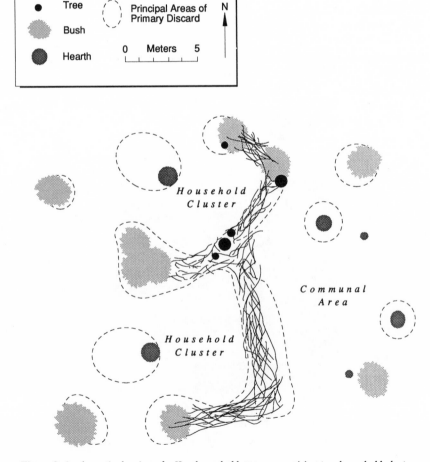

Figure 3. A schematic drawing of a Kua household group comprising two household clusters.

well. The individual household cluster conforms closely to the "nuclear activity area" of Yellen (1977a:95) and was most frequently occupied by a nuclear family unit, although other household configurations were observed (e.g., unmarried adolescents of the same sex, widowed adults, etc.). Visitors were accommodated just outside the hut or just inside the windbreak near the primary hearth.

Areas of shaded ground most often governed the positioning and layout of household clusters and groups, but this was much more apparent at hot dry season and hot rainy season camps than at cool dry season camps. One of the shaded areas in a camp invariably formed the focus for the principal "structural" component of the household group, a "communal activity area" (Yellen 1977a:95). Although not necessarily circumscribed by structures or centrally located in a ring of huts as they were with the !Kung (Yellen 1977a), communal areas were normally so closely adjacent to individual household clusters that they could be defined "in negative" (Yellen 1977a:95), that is, by a lack of architecture. This was because the tree(s) into which windbreaks were built were typically the only nearby source of shade (Figure 4). If other trees were present in the vicinity, the shaded ground beneath them would sometimes be swept and cleared of low branches to provide additional communal areas (or play areas for children).

Aside from the structural elements furnished by specific natural features of the place, the most prominent architectural element in many Kua household clusters and groups was a windbreak or hut. Windbreaks were simply constructed,

Figure 4. A household group's communal activity area.

arcuate arrangements of cut branches and grass roughly 1 to 1.5 meters in height, woven into or simply laid against an existing "skeleton" of brush and small trees. The quality of construction often reflected how long the residents had lived there; that is, at short-term occupations, windbreaks were never elaborate affairs but merely minimally modified bushes (see Kent, Chapter 2 this volume). The concave side invariably opened to the west. As discussed later, the opposite (eastern) side of the windbreak was also used, resulting in a functionally bilateral structure. The primary functions of these roofless structures (in addition to their nominal role as shelters from the wind) were to provide storage for personal belongings, private space, and a modicum of protection from carnivores. The floor near (or even inside of) the back wall of the concave side of the windbreak and the branches forming its back and side wall were both places used for the storage of household items.

Windbreaks were built one per household and were commonly arranged end to end in a linear plan (Figure 5). When closely related households built adjacent windbreaks, the intersection between them was routinely attenuated to the point of producing a single, long windbreak. In these instances, two or more hearths appeared in a row in the opening, most often one per nuclear family. Such an

Figure 5. Windbreaks at Kani//am/odi Household Group 7, viewed from the southwest (see Figure 9 for locations).

arrangement of windbreaks was common at all dry season camps. In fact, a similar linear arrangement of functionally bilateral windbreaks and huts was also observed in 1978 (Hitchcock 1982:341, 1987:397–398; Kroll n. d.; Kroll and Bunn, personal observation 1978) among the same Kua. Where shade was restricted but kin links were close, windbreaks would sometimes "bend" around a tree to provide each household unit with maximum shade and thereby modify the otherwise linear pattern.

Huts were shelters constructed primarily during the rainy season and cool dry season (Figure 6). They were assembled by digging up to about a dozen principal postholes in a circular (or among more sedentary Kua at dry season cattle post settlements, rectangular) arrangement, into which cut poles or branches were placed. These were bent and lashed together at various points along the frame to form the principal supporting members of the hut. Onto this framework more brush was placed, and their smaller branches were woven into the structure. Finally, bundles of grass were carefully arranged to cover the structure, woven into and laid onto the hut. The entire construction could be completed in a few hours by several people; the most time-consuming tasks were the chopping of poles and gathering of grass. Huts were used for sleeping and

Figure 6. Huts at Kani//am/odi Household Group 7 viewed from the northwest (see Figure 9 for location; huts 2, 3, and 4 are visible). Additional posts and thatching were added later in anticipation of rain.

storage during the rainy season and the cool dry season, but almost no daytime activities were conducted within them. Hut arrangements did not conform as frequently to a linear plan as did windbreaks, although this arrangement was observed.

Once built, structures strongly conditioned both the location of activity performance and the distribution of refuse, mainly by restricting the flow of traffic through the camp and providing a protected space where individual activities could be conducted near hearths. The central area enclosed by the windbreak or hut was kept relatively free of debris, and it was occasionally swept with a broom of bundled grass. The floor inside the structures was always swept during construction to clear the area of unseen thorns, scorpions, and other possible hazards.

Another type of structure was a pole-supported platform used for storage and shade (Figure 7). The platforms were built almost exclusively at dry season camps. They were constructed of a varying number of trimmed poles set vertically into the sand and roofed with a lattice of smaller poles, which were lashed to the forked uprights. The structure was sometimes finished with a layer of grass. Platforms provided a surface on which food, cooking utensils, bedding, and sundry household items were stored, but they also provided gratifying shade in the heat of the day. In the latter role, they were often a focus of midday activity. They were frequently located near the windbreaks or huts to facilitate easy retrieval of the personal belongings stored there.

Figure 7. A pole-supported storage platform at a Kua hot dry season camp.

Hearths were located in both household and communal activity areas. The hearths in the two areas were not functionally distinct, although there were typically pronounced differences in the duration and intensity of their use. At all Kua camps, fires were simply kindled on the ground with no special containment basins or structures (although live coals and hot sand would occasionally be swept into pits adjacent to hearths to roast *ka* [*Citrullus naudinianus*—see Figure 2] or small game). Each household had a primary hearth positioned in front of the concave windbreak, roughly centered between the two ends of it. The hearths in the windbreak openings were typically the largest in camp. These were the hearths used for cooking morning and evening meals, and they were usually the only ones used to provide night-time illumination and heat. For these reasons, they grew in size at a much faster rate than did the hearths in other areas (such as those in areas of afternoon shade), and they were cleaned out more frequently.

Most small fires in or near communal activity areas were used at times when the primary hearths were not in use, and they were kindled primarily for lighting tobacco pipes while people rested during the heat of the day. Others were built as needed around the camp for special uses including the straightening of bows, arrows, or digging sticks, the production of hot coals for adjacent roasting pits, or the manufacture of quivers (obtained by steaming the woody sheaths off the lateral roots of *Acacia nilotica*). The latter activity and others like it (e.g., head roasting and skin pegging) that created a big mess were generally conducted on the periphery of the camp (Hitchcock 1982:356) or in "special activity areas" (Yellen 1977a:92–93).

The distinction between hearths and roasting pits was often a blurry one. Frequently, a hollow was simply dug in an existing hearth to accommodate the material to be roasted. These pits quickly disappeared as the hearth was used again. Special single-purpose pits were excavated only when larger animals or large amounts of *ka* melons were to be roasted.

In order to avoid the buildup of a large and potentially dangerous mound of ash and hot coals immediately adjacent to sleeping areas, frequently used hearths were emptied of their contents in two ways. First, hearths were cleaned out by pushing or sweeping the contents away from the opening of the adjacent hut or windbreak. This activity regularly produced a large ash scatter adjacent to most primary hearths on the side opposite the opening of the hut or windbreak. A second, less frequent, and more effective method of solving the problem was through the periodic shoveling of hearth contents, an activity that produced ashdumps elsewhere at the camp. Ashdumps were often located near the periphery of the camp. These dense midden deposits typically contained waste generated by activities conducted near the hearths as well as sweepings from inside the windbreaks.

Overall, it is helpful to think of the framework of a Kua camp (i.e., the distribution of the structures and facilities described) as the product of a hierarchy of sequentially operating structural controls that fashioned the perception of camp space and therefore the distribution of refuse. Certain individual controls were powerful and ubiquitous among Kua camp types, whereas other controls were variable in the magnitude of their effects or were operable only at certain kinds of camps. At all camps, primary control over the site framework was exerted by natural microgeographic features, such as the distribution of shrubs and trees that cast shade for the communal area and for individual household clusters and provided convenient sources of building materials. Once potential building areas had been identified, the individual household clusters were arranged to accommodate factors of secondary importance, such as kinship links with other households, with their component parts (e.g., windbreaks) sized according to the space required by the co-resident population. In this way, the individual household clusters were formed, and they became the building blocks of the household group. The framework of all camps was characterized by varying numbers of structurally and functionally redundant household clusters. Finally, after individual household clusters were arranged, activity areas (e.g., butchery areas) were positioned in an around the household group with a new perception of the architecturally modified space.

The structure outlined here was similar among all camps, regardless of the season of occupation. Variations in camp population and occupation length account for differences in the number and spacing of household clusters/nuclear areas among camps. The camp framework was not immutable, but once formed it strongly conditioned the subsequent perception and use of space, including the places that refuse generated in the household group should and should not be discarded. Garbage tolerance thresholds were occasionally crossed, especially at longer term occupations, and secondary refuse areas would appear—but not just anywhere. Middens were usually located near the camp's periphery. At long-term occupations, even secondary disposal eventually proved ineffective, and the whole household cluster might be moved to another area of the camp, often into an area not initially regarded as optimum ("If we do not move, we will be sleeping in the fire," one Kua woman laughed as she moved her hut a short distance away from her family's overflowing hearth). If a household cluster *was* moved during an occupation, the effect could be to overprint and/or obscure an earlier living surface and the refuse thereon. Although the household cluster shifted in an absolute sense, activities were still conducted in the same "kinds" of places relative to the new placement of the household framework, and this could necessitate preparation of the area (by sweeping, etc.). Acceptable and unacceptable refuse discard areas were also reconsidered accordingly.

The faunal assemblages were deposited within this general framework. Before discussing examples of their variability and spatial characteristics, we shall first consider the processes that formed the bone assemblages, including the hunting and butchery techniques that generated them, and the taphonomic factors that modified them. These processes and factors are considered here because they determine the composition and distribution of the bone refuse at the camps.

3.3. Formation of Bone Assemblages

Kua behavior was varied in the procurement, processing, consumption, and discard of carcasses, all of which can leave diagnostic traces in a bone assemblage. Although modes of procurement, processing, consumption, and discard activities were not mutually exclusive by camp type, differences in their intensity and specific combination varied with season, duration, and size of occupation. Thus overall similarities in content, modification patterns, and spatial patterning are evident among the bone assemblages collected from camps of the same type. Later we summarize the dominant cultural formation processes observed for bone assemblages at each type of Kua camp (details of the specific techniques employed and their effects on the bone assemblages will be more fully discussed in future articles).

During the hot dry season, the frequency of kills was relatively high, but the size of the animals obtained was generally small. This is partly explained by the fact that several migratory species (e.g., wildebeest and hartebeest) were absent from this part of the Western Sandveld during this season. At hot dry season camps, the principal animals obtained included the steenbok (*Raphicerus campestris*), the common duiker (*Sylvicapra grimmia*), and the springhare (*Pedetes campestris*).

Hunters at hot dry season camps, frequently working together, obtained animals by three methods: snaring, using springhare poles, and walking animals to death, with or without dogs. Spring-loaded noose snares made of twined *Sanseveria scabrifolia* cord (in combination with low brush drive lines) were sometimes placed along frequently used game trails to catch the highly territorial steemboks and duikers that lived in the vicinity of the cattle post. They were also set near the terrestrial nests of gallinaceous birds. Springhare poles are limber wooden poles with a hook made from a steenbok horn lashed to the end (Silberbauer 1981:215; Hitchcock 1982:232–233). These were used to impale springhares and porcupines in their burrows, from which they were subsequently excavated by the hunter. Some hunters occasionally employed dogs for flushing and chasing small animals, including steemboks, duikers, bat-eared foxes, porcupines, and aardwolves. The dogs ran down small prey that was then killed with spear or club (Lee 1979:142–144; Hitchcock 1982:233). Dogs were not always used for this purpose, however. Another physically more demanding method of pursuit hunting was sometimes employed by Kua hunters in the hot dry season. Occasionally a hunter or group of hunters working together left camp in search of a fresh spoor, carrying nothing more than clubs or digging sticks. Through the use of tracking skills at which we could only marvel, the hunters relentlessly pursued their quarry. The animal was not always in sight, but the hunters were always on its trail, keeping it moving. Such tenacious pursuit eventually forced the animal to collapse from pain induced by the intense heat of the sand, as well as from its inability to lie down in the shade and ruminate. When the hunters caught up with the incapacitated animal, it was clubbed with a digging stick. It should be noted, however that this technique worked only during the hottest part of the year, and it was a method generally employed by younger hunters in their physical prime. Finally, although men were observed departing from camp during this season carrying their bow-hunting equipment, we recorded no instance of a kill made with bow and arrow (see Silberbauer 1981:214).

At rainy season and cool dry season camps, men were primarily occupied with the bow hunting of larger game (principally gemsbok [*Oryx gazella*], eland [*Taurotragus oryx*], and greater kudu [*Tragelaphus strepsiceros*]). Additionally, some snaring was also practiced at cool dry season camps. Hunting was predictably better at these more remote camps as game densities increased substantially with distance from cattle posts (Hitchcock 1982). Another important reason that larger game was more easily taken was that primary source of Kua arrow poison, the *Diamphidia sp.* larva (Wollard 1986), became available during the first part of the rainy season and could be collected for several months thereafter. This meant the arrows could be repainted with fresh poison and restored to a strength lethal to the largest game. Bowhunters left camp alone early in the morning in search of a fresh spoor. If a promising track was located, it would be followed until the animal was sighted or until the spoor indicated stalking was in order. While stalking, the hunter would arm his bow and slink in as close as possible (usually within 10 to 40 meters) and shoot.

If the hunter missed, there was rarely a chance for a second shot, and the alerted animal was abandoned. The hunter started home by a different route, often continuing the circular path he had started out on, with hopes of encountering another spoor, which would be pursued upon discovery or during the next day. On the way home, it was common for a hunter to make frequent stops to gather plant foods and firewood. Occasionally snares were also set, especially during the cool dry season, to be checked the next day.

If the arrow found its mark, the hunter noted his location and then usually returned to camp. This break served several purposes: First, the delay gave the poison time to take effect. Second, the animal was more likely to settle down and rest rather than to run even further and extend the distance the trackers would need to cover. Third, it provided the hunter the opportunity to communicate the results of his effort to the other members of the camp and arrange for a party to track, butcher, and transport the animal. Finally, it gave the hunter a chance to rest after what was often a long, hard day. For smaller game, the hunter only rested near the shooting spot a few hours before tracking his prey because the poison more quickly overpowered a smaller animal.

If the tracking was successful, primary butchery and transport decisions were based on a number of variables. These included distance to the base camp, time of day, number of potential carriers, and size of the carcass obtained. Analysis of each situation resulted in the choice of one of five transport strategies: (1) carrying the entire intact carcass (not practiced for larger animals); (2) carrying the entire carcass in partially disarticulated units; (3) carrying selected carcass parts; (4) caching meat; and (5) moving camp to the kill.

If the hunt originated from a hot dry season camp, the prey was usually small enough (e.g., duiker and steenbok) to be simply field-dressed and carried home, or even returned to camp intact. Water was a special concern during this season, and all efforts were made to get home quickly. If more time was available, as was often so at rainy season and cool dry season kills, further processing of these small carcasses was typicaly conducted at the kill site. If it was to be field-dressed, the prey was eviscerated (but left unskinned), and the liver was roasted in a small hearth at or near the death site. The heart, lungs, kidneys, and intestines were given to the dogs (if present) or discarded. Next, the metapodials of the smaller antelope were removed from their encasing skin. Sometimes they were cracked (with the periosteum intact) on a long anvil with either a metal knife or small axe, and the marrow was eaten on the spot; sometimes the metapodials were left uncracked for processing back at the base camp. This method of skinning the metapodials allowed the skin to be tied to the opposite leg, forming a parcel with a sling that could be slipped over the hunter's shoulder in transport. To give still greater flexibility to the package, the fully fleshed upper limb bones were sometimes broken by blows delivered with a digging stick.

Larger carcasses obtained during the rainy and cool dry seasons (e.g., gemsbok and eland) were treated differently. The handling of these animals varied, but processing decisions depended primarily on the kill-to-camp distance. If the animal was recovered near the base camp, the carcass was generally skinned and quartered at or near the death site, and the primary butchery units were carried back to camp for further processing. However, if a large carcass was recovered at a relatively distant location, the Kua chose one of the last three alternative transport strategies listed. A short-term, special-purpose camp was sometimes made at or near the death site where the carcass was most often processed for immediate transport to the base camp. Sometimes, because of the overwhelming quantity of meat obtained (especially from an eland), only a fraction could be carried home. Then, the remainder was bundled and stored in a brush-covered tree platform. The platform was heavily constructed and placed out of reach of all but the most persistent scavengers. As a final alternative, the base camp might be abandoned when the occupants moved their residence to the kill. Large game processing involved the skinning, eviscerating, filleting of meat off of the bones at the kill site, and the production of biltong (sun-dried strips of "jerky"), which was tied into bundles (average individual weight of a bundle after one day of drying was 4.65 kg [*n* = 31]). Marrow-containing bones were broken, their marrow consumed, and the fragments were discarded during the filleting process. Unless adhering to transported meat, marrow bone fragments were discarded at the filleting location.

When transported carcasses arrived at the base camp, the butchery and distribution of parts to other camp members were conducted, commonly by a close male relative of the hunter. Smaller carcasses were skinned and eviscerated if necessary, and the internal organs were roasted and/or cut up and fed to the dogs. Metapodials were removed for marrow processing (if this had not already been done), sometimes after roasting them. The carcass was then cut or chopped into primary butchery units, which were then distributed to individual households. Once in the hands of the recipient, the larger muscle masses (such as the meat on the femora, humeri, and pelves) were filleted off of the bone, and the marrow-containing elements were cracked. However, if parts were not to be eaten immediately (e.g., when a share was apportioned to an absent hunter), the small primary butchery units were laid on the absentee's hut where they dried quickly in the sun.

When larger carcasses arrived in camp, emphasis was on the production of biltong; the meat was cut into strips and dried immediately to prevent it from becoming fly-blown. This was especially important at rainy season camps. This job usually involved all camp members old enough to wield a knife, who worked on the parts of the carcass that had been given to them by the hunter or by his designated butcher. Parcels carried from the kill site were customarily kept by the carrier and his/her household. Unlike the smaller carcasses that tended to be brought to camp skeletally complete or virtually so, for larger animals the inventory of skeletal material introduced into base camp assemblages was far more variable. If the animal was recovered at some distance from the base camp, much of the skeleton was often abandoned at the kill site. On the other hand, if the kill site was relatively close to the base camp, most of the skeleton was brought into camp for filleting and marrow cracking.

At the hot dry season camps, carcasses of all sizes were consumed almost immediately. Some of the Kua preferentially boiled meat in small, three-legged iron pots, the size of which determined the maximum size of the cuts cooked therein. Axial elements and sometimes long bones were chopped to size with small metal axes while encased in meat, and this way, much of their grease and marrow was released during boiling to be consumed as gravy (Binford 1984:161). Alternatively, the Kua roasted carcasses in shallow pits filled with live coals, for which the carcass was eviscerated and skinned, and all bones distal to the femora and humeri were removed. Juvenile animals were roasted with the hide on, after the hair was plucked or removed by singeing and then scraping it from the skin. The skinned radio-ulnae and tibiae were sometimes put in the cleaned rumen without being filleted, and this parcel was placed back inside the body cavity for roasting.

Cooking methods at rainy season and cool dry season camps differed from hot dry season camps only to the extent to which meat was boiled. At the former camps, roasting was a more frequent method of cooking, although meat was also boiled. Liquid for boiling was provided by melon slices placed in the pot along with the meat. Sometimes the boiled meat was mixed with animal fat that had been melted separately, and both were mixed by pounding with a *hiko* (mortar) and pestle (*hiko !ua*). The hiko was made of wood but was sometimes improvised by digging a hole in the sand and lining it with the hide of the animal. However prepared, during consumption, small metal knives were used to cut meat away from any bones cooked along with it. The knives were also used as probes and scrapers to remove adhering bits of meat.

At all types of camps, primary bone discard occurred in or adjacent to both butchery and consumption areas. Limb bones, especially metapodials, were frequently cracked for marrow during primary butchery and were often represented by a pile of "pure" epiphyseal and limb shaft fragments discarded on or adjacent to the log anvil on which they were cracked. In group consumption areas, bones tended to be discarded as primary refuse in one of three specific locations in and around the windbreaks:

1. Within several meters of the windbreak or hut opening, where they were placed in the hearth or tossed into a zone just beyond the hearth (similar to Binford 1980:355).
2. In and adjacent to bushes, which acted as "bone magnets" because of their use as targets for tossed and dropped bones.
3. Within structures themselves, especially near the ends of the windbreaks or in the back and side walls of the windbreaks. The latter location resulted mainly from nighttime consumption; bones were simply piled near the walls of the windbreak to keep them out of sleeping areas.

Once discarded, other processes operated to modify and/or move bones. Bones discarded in frequently used hearths were burned to varying degrees and sometimes completely destroyed. Kua dogs were perpetually hungry and were regarded as hunting tools rather than as pets. At the camps where dogs were present, they were barely tolerated in nuclear household areas and regularly scavenged for bones whenever they could find them, but bones discarded in the windbreaks were relatively "safe" from the camp dogs, who, if not chased away, were frequently discouraged by the thorns. Dogs were most likely, therefore, to obtain bones from discard areas adjacent to hearths and near butchery areas, where processing activities generated primary bone debris. The dogs then took their prizes to the camp perimeter to enjoy them in peace. Bushes were also used by dogs as favored shady locations to which they took bones they managed to acquire. Human traffic across the camp floor was another important factor in the modification of primary bone distributions. Bones discarded in both communal and nuclear areas tended to be kicked aside or, if they were small enough, were trampled and buried as later activities were conducted in the same space. Larger bones tended to be kicked out of the way if discarded in frequently used paths. Finally, the cleaning of hearths and windbreaks at longer term occupations generated concentrations of varied materials (including many bones) that were discarded in secondary refuse middens or ashdumps. After abandonment of camps by the Kua, brown hyenas and other scavengers typically visited the sites and further modified the bone assemblages.

We now consider in more detail the spatial characteristics of the different types of Kua camps, illustrating each type with a specific camp that we observed and mapped. We examine how the camp structure and activity performance described above are reflected in the spatial distribution of bone food refuse. Finally, we turn to a comparative discussion of the archaeological significance of these patterns.

4. KUA CAMPS: EXAMPLES

4.1. Hot Dry Season Base Camps

The largest of the hot dry season base camps we observed was called *Kani//am/odi*. It was located about one kilometer from a borehole-equipped cattle post. The borehole provided barely potable water for approximately 800 head of cattle and other small stock, as well as for the resident herdsmen, their families, and a hot dry season population of some 25 to 50 Kua. Except for one period of borehole failure that lasted several weeks, Kani//am/odi was occupied more or less continuously during the entire period of our fieldwork; for much of the year, however, the resident population was low, consisting only of the herdsmen and a few relatively sedentary Kua and their families who were empolyed at the cattle post.

The hot dry season occupation at Kani//am/odi comprised varying numbers (up to seven) of simultaneously occupied and spatially discrete household groups. These were unevenly distributed in an roughly linear fashion over a distance of approximately 800 meters (Figure 8) and were linked by a network of well-used paths. A powerful influence on the location and spacing of household groups was the local distribution of isolated groups of *Acacia* trees that furnished much-needed shade. The spacing of the household groups at Kani//am/odi varied between about 40 and 200 meters. Though we have yet to conduct a thorough analysis of the relationship between household spacing and kin relations, we think it is accurate to generalize that most Kua resided within or immediately adjacent to the household groups of their closest kin (see Gargett and Hayden, Chapter 1 this volume). What is important is that the occupants of the individual household

7

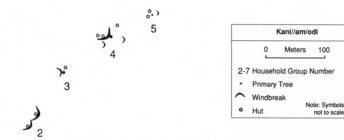

Figure 8. Hot dry season distribution of household groups at Kani//am/odi. The huts were added near the end of the occupation in anticipation of rain.

groups at dry season camps commonly formed the membership nuclei of the smaller, dispersed rainy season and cool dry season camps, as well.

Thus the combined influences of the availability of suitable shade trees, a large number of dry season residents, the kinship links between household units, the position of the borehole itself, the employment obligations of some individuals and their families to the cattle post, and possibly other considerations (e.g., security from carnivores [Gould and Yellen 1987], which may have contributed to the tight packing of huts within each household group), account for the specific configuration of household groups evident at the Kani//am/odi camp.

To illustrate the following discussion, Figure 9a presents a typical hot dry season household group at Kani//am/odi, which we have named Household Group 7 (HHG-7). The site was occupied for nearly 3 months during the hot dry season of 1985 (Table 2). When we first observed it, the household group consisted of unroofed, connected, brush windbreaks built into the group of trees and bushes seen at the center of Figure 9a. Several storage platforms were located to the east and south of the windbreaks (indicated by connected posts in the figure). Three individual but closely related nuclear family households, each with its own hearth, resided in the connected windbreaks. During the last few weeks of the occupation, in anticipation of the coming rains, four huts were constructed to the

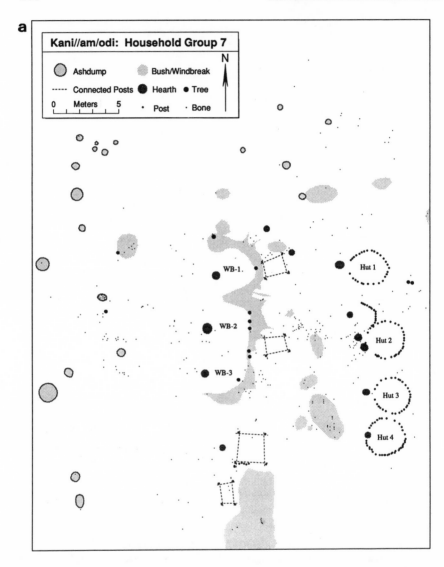

Figure 9. Kani//am/odi Household Group 7 (HHG-7), hot dry season 1985: Distribution of bones, hearths, and ashdumps with (9a) and without (9b) structures and vegetation. See text for the temporal relationship of the windbreaks and huts.

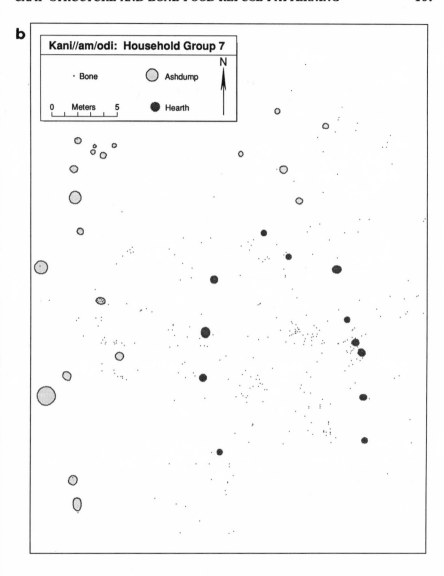

b

Kani//am/odi: Household Group 7

· Bone   ◯ Ashdump

0   Meters   5   ● Hearth

N

east of the connected windbreaks into which all of the inhabitants of HHG-7 moved their belongings. At this time, the western side of the windbreaks was virtually abandoned.

A distinct daily routine was observed in the use of space at HHG-7. Activity positioning was distinctly bilateral with respect to the camp framework, both before and after the construction of the huts. Before the huts, most morning and evening activities occurred near the concave opening on the western side of the windbreak, but most midday activities were performed on the opposite (i.e., eastern) side of the windbreak. People slept in the concave western side of the windbreak, which during the early morning hours was the focus of activity as the night's fire was rekindled and a meal was prepared. As the sun and the temperature climbed, people either left camp to forage or to visit others, or they gradually moved to the eastern side of the windbreak to rest in the shade of the storage platforms or under shrubs fitted with shade-enhancing additions of grass or brush. For those who remained in camp, most of the day was spent in these shady locations resting, talking, or performing maintenance chores. People returned to the western, "morning" side of the windbreak around dusk and remained there for the night. This flip-flop in the daily use of camp space was observed at virtually all camps, as people followed the shade through the day.

Although there was a clear daily rhythm to the use of morning and afternoon activity areas, there was little functional differentiation between them (Yellen 1977a:65–96; O'Connell 1987). Both midday and morning/evening areas were, at various times, the locations of the full range of activities typically conducted in household areas. These activities included sleeping, food preparation and consumption, the manufacture and maintenance of tools and other goods, and divining (a pastime practiced exclusively by men, but witnessed and discussed by all present [Campbell 1968]). Although the areas were not functionally different from each other in most respects, clear differences were evident between them in the intensity and/or frequency of activities performed on each side of the windbreak. For example, the hearths on the western side of the windbreak were the sites of the preparation of the largest meals (morning and evening), whereas the smaller hearths served intermittently during the midday as a source of convenient fire for tasks conducted in the afternoon shade. Some food was consumed by these hearths as well, and primary refuse from these meals was discarded nearby.

After construction of the huts shown in Figure 9a, the pattern of morning and evening activities shifted, reflecting the new occupation of the huts as nighttime sleeping structures and storage facilities. Morning activities previously conducted in the opening of the windbreak near primary hearths were now performed in comparable locations west of the structures, immediately in front of or adjacent to the huts. The midday pattern of moving with the shade was not disrupted, but as the sun climbed in the sky, rather than use the area behind the huts (as might be expected if the huts functioned in the same manner as the earlier windbreaks), people continued to occupy the eastern side of the windbreaks in the same way as they had previously. The implications of this shift for spatial patterning are considered later.

There are several notable spatial features of the HHG-7 bone assemblage that reflect this use of space. In Figure 9a there is a nonrandom distribution to the bones; they are found mostly in four kinds of locations: (1) in and immediately adjacent to hearths, as at the central hearths just to the west of the row of huts; (2) in scatters from 1 to 3 meters of hearths, usually on one side only; (3) in isolated clusters associated with ashdumps between about 4 and 8 meters west of primary cooking hearths; and (4) in and adjacent to bushes.

In the first kind of location, the cluster of bones next to the hearth associated with Hut 2 in Figure 9a was formed by primary discard of bones consumed in this nuclear area. By contrast, the three westernmost hearths associated with the connected windbreaks exhibited only a small amount of spatially associated bone refuse, despite the fact that they were the most heavily used of all camp hearths. Why the discrepancy, if both areas were used for similar purposes in similar locations?

The answer rests with the second and third kinds of locations, those located on the perimeter of, or just beyond, the nuclear areas. The second kind of location contained a combination of primary and secondary bone refuse; some of the bones in these more diffuse scatters on the western side of hearths got there by being tossed beyond the hearths during meals, whereas some of the bones were swept out of nuclear areas at later times. The bones in the third kind of location were exclusively redeposited. These ashdump deposits were created when the contents of heavily used hearths and their associated nuclear areas were scooped up and dumped near the site perimeter. Hearths and adjacent nuclear areas were swept only when primary refuse densities reached unpleasant levels and because this threshold was not reached by the time of abandonment of the nuclear area associated with the huts to the east, the primary bone refuse at these huts remained *in situ*. Bones in the ashdumps were not always burned, for sweeping of the nuclear areas around the hearths collected many unburned bones as well.

The fourth type of bone cluster, associated with bushes, also contained both primary and secondary discard elements. Because larger bushes (smaller ones were often pulled out or trampled flat) prevented the space from being used for other activities, they were a convenient place to discard refuse. Many bones were tossed into nearby bushes as primary refuse during meals, and ashdumps were occasionally located in or next to them for the same reason. Primary bone refuse in bushes was often concentrated on the side closest to the hearths around which the diners sat.

Two important processes complicated the interpretation of the skeletal part data of the HHG-7 bone assemblage. The first process operated at the scale of the entire Kani//am/odi camp, but it affected the bone assemblages of individual household groups. As noted earlier, the size of the animals brought into hot dry season camps was typically small, and HHG-7 was no exception. Because of their small size, whole carcasses were brought to a household group with virtually all of the skeleton intact. Despite the potentially complete representation of skeletal parts from a given carcass in the household group's bone assemblage, the probability of such representation was low. This was because even the small animals obtained by residents of HHG-7 were commonly shared among residents living at other houseshold groups. In one instance, a duiker butchered at HHG-4 was shared with residents of *all* the other household groups throughout the entire *ca.* 800-meter length of the camp. Carcass parts were transported to these remote household groups and discarded as refuse. This sharing was common at dry season camps and tended to distribute bones of nearly all carcasses across the entire camp.

Second, the destructive processes operating on bones from the small carcasses obtained during this season of hunger were potent. Camp dogs were particularly hungry in this season, and they searched for any greasy or tissue-covered bones with a sense of purpose. The small size of the dogs, however, limited the amount of damage they could do; gnawing and secondary abandonment of bones may have occurred more frequently than complete destruction of bones, at least for the fully formed bones of adult carcasses. Because of the relatively long duration of these occupations and their large human population, scavengers other than camp dogs (e.g., hyenas or jackals) were never present, and by the time these camps were abandoned, the majority of the bone refuse had lost its appeal to them.

Further, bone fragmentation from human processing was also high at these camps. This was probably from an extra effort on the part of the Kua to extract the maximum nutritional benefit from the carcasses they obtained during this season. Even the phalanges of small antelopes were cracked for marrow, producing many additional tiny bone fragments. Also, the small size of the iron pots used for boiling meat (rim diameters of less than 25 cm) necessarily led to the reduction of carcass portions, including the bones contained in them, to fit the dimensions of available cooking pots.

Figure 9b shows HHG-7 at the same scale as Figure 9a, but as a visitor to the site after 25 years or more might see the household group; here only bones hearths, and ashdumps are displayed. It is clear that the kinds of bone distributions illustrated in Figure 9a are still visible, but with their structural context removed, the reconstructive challenge to archaeologists is daunting. Further spatial and zooarchaeological work is being conducted on this camp and should reveal additional spatial patterning in skeletal part distributions, the locations of the refitted fragments of individual elements, bone surface modifications, and size sorting of fragments, all of which can be assessed for their utility in reconstructing site formation processes in the absence of structures.

4.2. Rainy Season Base Camps

Acting on reconnaissance information about the abundance of melons and game at specific locations, Kua groups abandoned the cattle post camps after the first rains and established camps close to the newly available food resources. In many respects, the rainy season base camps they constructed at these locations were analogous to the individual household groups of the dry season occupations. Again, positions of the primary components of the camp framework were selected largely with respect to shaded locations under trees and shrubs, with a concern for minimizing the amount of work required to obtain and assemble the constituent parts of a windbreak or hut.

Unlike dry season camps, however, large *Acacia* trees were intentionally avoided in the bush in favor of smaller trees, despite the fact that these smaller ones often required some additional trimming and ground clearing before they provided satisfactory shelter. The large and enticing pools of shade under the expansive canopies of large trees were likely to harbor great numbers of ticks who had waited patiently for any large mammal (including people) to stop and take refuge there. The selection of smaller trees and shrubs gave these camps a more "closed-in" feeling than was so at the hot dry season camps. Ordinarily, construction was minimal at rainy season camps, and no storage platforms were observed, although branches of trees adjacent to windbreaks or huts were occasionally enhanced with additional brush in order to provide more shade.

The rainy season camp illustrated in Figure 10a was called //oabe I. It was occupied over 7 nights (29 January to 5 February 1986) by a group who, for most of the occupation, numbered 14 people. The structures at the camp consisted of a single windbreak (surprisingly, no huts were constructed), which was built into a clump of trees and bushes, and associated hearths and roasting pits.

As was also observed at hot dry season camps, a pronounced daily shift in the use of space was apparent. The northwest side of the windbreak in Figure 10a was functionally analogous to the western side of the windbreaks at the dry season camp (see previous discussion), for it was in these nuclear areas that most morning and evening consumption, cooking, and maintenance activities took place. During the heat of the late morning and afternoon, camp residents shifted their activities to the southeast side of the windbreak or to the area near Hearth 7 in Figure 10a. Both of these areas were enveloped in deep shade for much of the afternoon, and there camp members sought refuge from the heat. Women returning from gathering in the early afternoon typically unloaded and sorted out their hefty burdens of plant foods on the east side of the windbreak, as well. Melons were deseeded and eaten there, whereas the abundant *Grewia flava* berries were dried in the open sun on the concave side of the windbreak. The shaded area near Hearth 7 in Figure 10a was also used for midday relaxation, and

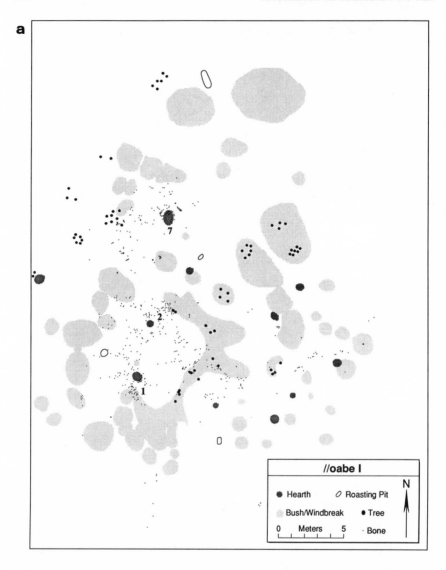

Figure 10. //oabe I, hot rainy season 1986: Distribution of bones, hearths, and roasting pits with (10a) and without (10b) structures and vegetation. Hearth numbers reflect field designations; Hearths 3–6 not numbered.

b

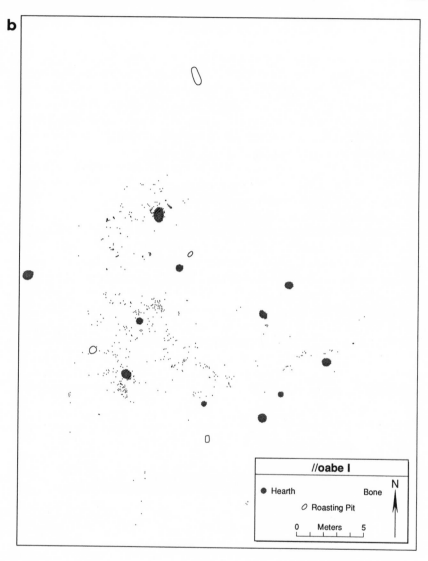

//oabe I

● Hearth   Bone   N

O Roasting Pit

0   Meters   5

it had the additional distinction of being the place where five bovid carcasses were butchered.

Sixteen animals were obtained during the occupation of //oabe I (Table 4), and a rib slab from a cow was brought with the Kua from their previous camp at Kani//am/odi. The nine bovids listed in Table 4 were juvenile or neonatal, and all were obtained by pursuit hunting, with or without the aid of dogs. Because the young of gemsbok, duiker, and steenbok remain hidden in cover during the day while the mother leaves to forage (Smithers 1983; Bartram, personal observation), they were easy prey to dispatch once their hiding places were located. All nine bovid carcasses were returned whole to //oabe I, where they were butchered and eaten. Of the 773 bone specimens recovered from this camp, 704 could be precisely mapped and are plotted in Figure 10a.

The bone distribution displayed in Figure 10a reflects the use of space described earlier in this chapter. Three clusters of bones are visible. The southern (Hearth 1) and central (Hearth 2) clusters each represent areas of primary disposal adjacent to morning and evening cooking and consumption areas, and they are centered on the two primary nuclear area hearths at the camp. The northern cluster is located adjacent to Hearth 7, and it was used during the afternoons while a variety of activities were conducted in the shade of this area. Other areas of bone distribution are evident on the southeastern side of the windbreak, and these extend out to the isolated hearths on the eastern perimeter of the camp.

The clusters of bones in the nuclear areas to the south (Hearths 1 and 2) were concentrated at the ends of the windbreak itself, as well as in and immediately adjacent to the two primary hearths. Most of the remaining bone refuse in this

Table 4. //oabe I Faunal Species List

Taxon	Common name	Total
Bovidae		
Tragelaphus strepsiceros	Greater kudu	1
Raphicerus campestris	Steenbok	1
Sylvicapra grimmia	Duiker	5
Oryx gazella	Gemsbok	2
Aves		
Eupodotis ruficrista	Red-crested korhaan	7

area extended from the nuclear area of the windbreak to about 3 meters out from the nuclear hearths. The majority of these bones are on the "outside" of the nuclear area, that is, northwest of the hearths. Virtually all of this refuse represents bones discarded during the meals eaten in and just outside of the nuclear areas. Many of the bones recovered in the ends of the windbreak represent the remains of late-night snacks placed there while the consumer lay prone in the windbreak. The northern cluster (Hearth 7) was comprised of the bones of juvenile bovids butchered and processed for marrow in that area, and it contains a number of fragments from this activity. Several of those carcasses were also cooked at the nearby hearth; there is refuse from consumption activities located in this cluster as well. The bones to the east of the windbreak lay in another shaded afternoon rest area, and many of those bones are from birds (*Eupodotis ruficrista*) that were plucked and roasted in the small hearths in this shady area soon after being brought to camp. The primary use of the hearths in this area was for lighting tobacco pipes, not for cooking; hence the relative lack of bone refuse in and adjacent to them.

The most striking fact about the overall distribution of bone at this camp is its concentration in nuclear areas as primary refuse near hearths. There is a virtual absence of secondary refuse. Figure 10b emphasizes this patterning when the bushes, windbreak, and trees are removed from view. When the bone distribution is combined with the distribution of activities, it is clear that a close correspondence exists. Thus at this camp, bones are clustered in the areas in which they were generated and do not occupy peripheral areas except as primary refuse.

Because the bones from this camp have been fully analyzed, it is useful to examine the spatial patterns when viewed according to taxon, skeletal part, or bone size (measured by maximum length). Based on field and laboratory identifications, 767 of 773 bones (99%) could be identified to a specific skeletal part, 630 of the 704 plotted bones (89%) were identifiable to species, and 446 (63%) of the same specimens could be identified to a specific carcass.

An interesting pattern emerges when the distributions of bovid axial and appendicular parts are compared. Figure 11a shows the distribution of appendicular parts (including, humeri, radio-ulnae, and metacarpals, femora, tibiae, and metatarsals) and scapulae, whereas Figure 11b shows the distribution of axial elements (including cranial bones, mandibles, vertebrae, and ribs) and pelves. The scapula is grouped with the appendicular elements and the pelves with axial elements for analytical purposes because these two girdle elements are typically butchered and transported as parts of the appendicular and axial units, respectively. Inspection of these figures shows that the axial parts tend to be found in tight clusters within nuclear areas, whereas the appendicular elements are more evenly distributed in primary refuse areas across the camp. The northernmost cluster (Hearth 7), which was the main butchery area of the site, is better represented by limb bones than by axial parts. This pattern reflects the fact that many limb elements were cracked for marrow and discarded during consumption

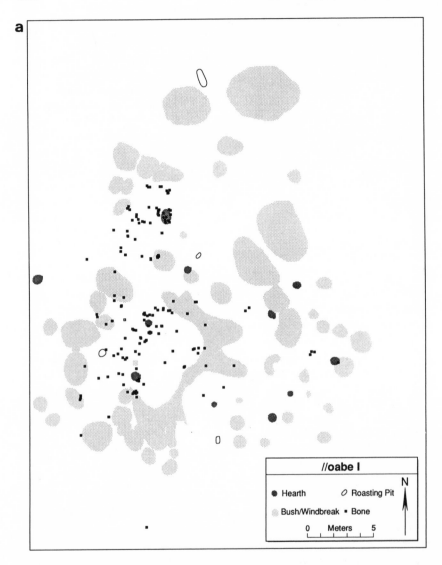

Figure 11. //oabe I, hot rainy season 1986: Distribution of (11a) appendicular bones (humeri, radioulnae, metacarpals, femora, tibiae, metatarsals) and scapulae; and (11b) axial bones (cranial elements, vertebrae) and mandibles and pelves.

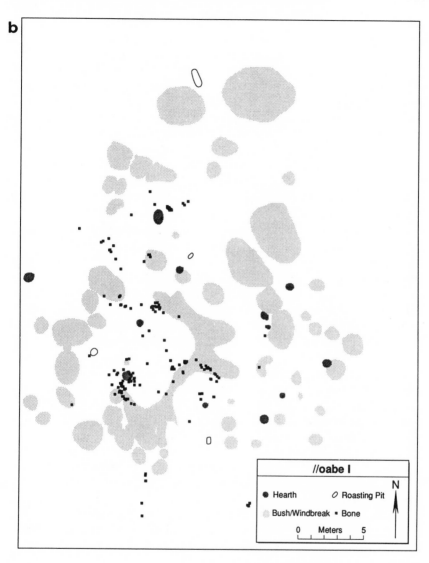

b

//oabe I

● Hearth   𝒪 Roasting Pit

Bush/Windbreak   ▪ Bone

0   Meters   5

N

near the main butchery area. Axial parts, on the other hand, generally were not consumed first, nor were they consumed quickly because of difficulty in removing the adhering meat. This was also true of the tissues surrounding the distal appendicular elements (e.g., phalanges in hooves). The processing of skulls involved fragmenting the bones to extract the brains and cranial pulps. Thus more deliberate attempts to remove less accessible tissues resulted in a more clustered spatial distribution near consumption locations in nuclear and shaded afternoon areas.

Additional patterning is evident among the various individual carcasses recovered from //oabe I. Of the five duikers brought to camp, the distributions of the bones of two are illustrated in Figures 12a and 12b, respectively. The duiker in Figure 12a was skinned and had its metapodials removed in the shady area represented by the northern cluster (Hearth 7). The skinned carcass was then roasted in the pit at the north edge of the camp. No bone refuse remained in this location, however. The carcass was then returned to the area where it had been initially skinned for secondary butchery and distribution. Some parts were carried into the windbreak for consumption and discard, whereas others were eaten near the butchery area. Figure 12b illustrates the patterning associated with another duiker whose butchery and consumption areas were more coincident. In this instance, few bones were discarded outside the processing and consumption areas because this duiker was butchered, cooked, and consumed after dark by the light of the primary hearths.

Figures 13a and 13b illustrate the relative lack of disturbance to the primary refuse at the camp. The first bones that were discarded at the camp (as mapped at the end of the occupation) are displayed in these figures; the cow-rib shafts that were brought from the previous camp are shown in Figure 13a, and the bones of a juvenile greater kudu killed on the day of arrival at //oabe I are plotted in Figure 13b. Both the kudu and the cow-rib slab were roasted in the southernmost nuclear area (Hearth 1) and were eaten in the windbreak during the first evening by all camp members. The bone refuse from these carcasses lies within the "toss zone" in front of the windbreak and stops at the row of bushes to the northwest. As can be seen from Figure 10a this was also so with the majority of the other bone refuse discarded by tossing from within the opening of the windbreak and from the shady afternoon area near Hearth 7. Had the bushes not acted as a barrier to tossing, the distribution would likely have extended a meter or so further. Finally, Figures 14a and 14b show the distributions of bone fragments that are smaller and larger than the median maximum length of 48 mm. Because most of the bones refuse remained in primary discard locations, there is not a marked difference in the overall distributions of smaller and larger pieces other than the occurrence of more large pieces in the toss zone beyond Hearths 1 and 2.

Overall, rainy season camps are characterized by high frequencies of bone refuse remaining in primary discard locations. This is reflected spatially by clusters of bone located close to frequently used hearths and structures and gradually diminishing densities of bone as one moves away from the cluster centers. Ashdumps are also lacking. Both conditions can be attributed to the brief occupation spans of these camps. The gradual reduction in refuse density serves to distinguish these camps from hot dry season camps where the aberrantly high local densities of bones are associated with secondary ashdump locations.

4.3. Cool Dry Season Base Camps

Next we consider camps occupied during the Kalahari's easiest season, the late rainy season/cool dry season. This was a time when many plant foods, such as the water-bearing melons, peaked in abundance and quality, and when many animals could be stalked from the cover of luxuriant vegetation. An example of a base camp from this season is Kunahajina, illustrated in Figure 15. The camp was occupied for 8 nights (Kunahajina A), abandoned, and then reoccupied (Kunahajina B) 3 weeks later for just over 3 months (see Table 2). Kunahajina was located at the same spot that had been used about 2 years earlier as a transient camp during a hunting trip by one of the current occupants. His earlier windbreak was barely visible on the northern side of the tres as a pile of grass (which was incorporated into one of the new huts soon after the occupation began).

During the first occupation, the huts were arranged in a row to the west side of the trees and placed so their openings faced the west and southwest. These huts are labeled with an *A* in Figure 15. During the second, longer occupation, the structures labeled with a *B* were used (although not all simultaneously). Activities were performed in the same types of locations as those described for the hot dry season and rainy season camps. These included nuclear areas near the openings of the huts and windbreaks and in the camp's communal area, which was located just to the south and east of the trees. What is important is that this communal area was the only large naturally shaded area at the camp.

Activities performed at the camp differed little from those discussed at the rainy season camp of //oabe I, except that at Kunahajina different plant species were processed more intensively. In particular, in this season, melons were used for more than just fluids; their seeds were collected in large numbers and roasted in hearths. The roasted seeds were separated from the sand with grass sieves, then pounded in the hiko. The resulting meal was a major food source during the occupation of Kunahajina.

Only three mammal carcasses were obtained during the first occupation of Kanahajina, an immature gemsbok and two bat-eared foxes. Thus little of the bone refuse shown in Figure 15 is attributable to the first occupation, with the exception of the bone scatters in front of the huts in use at that time. There were

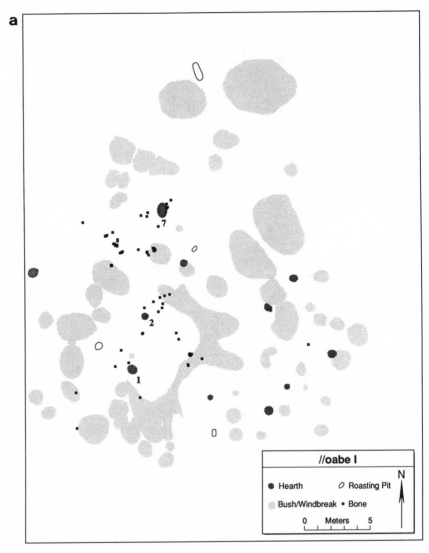

Figure 12. //oabe I: Distribution of bones of duiker carcasses #1 (12a) and #5 (12b).

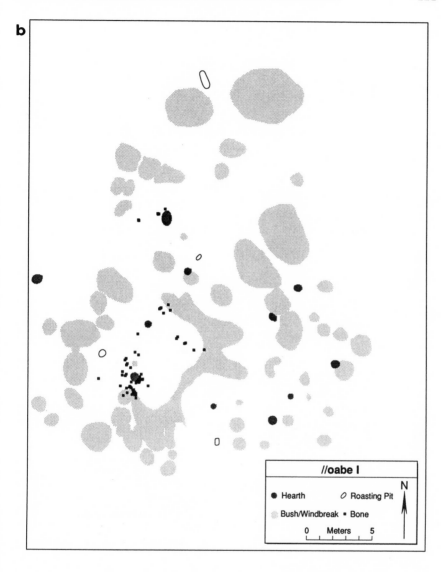

b

//oabe I

● Hearth   O Roasting Pit

Bush/Windbreak   ▪ Bone

0   Meters   5

N

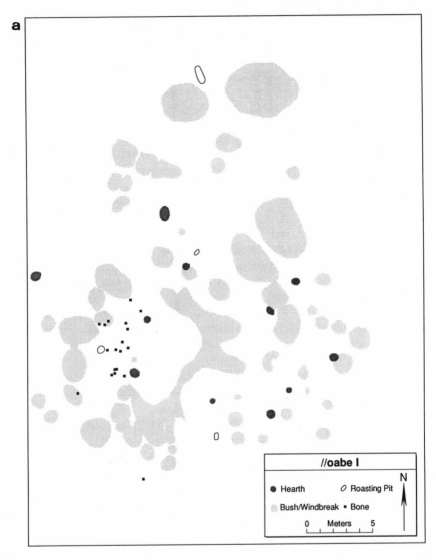

Figure 13. //oabe I: Distribution of cow rib shafts (13a) and juvenile greater kudu #1 (13b).

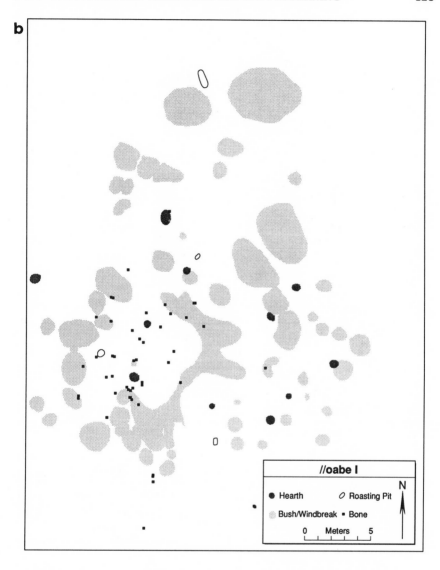

b

//oabe I

● Hearth   ⃝ Roasting Pit

Bush/Windbreak ▪ Bone

0   Meters   5

N

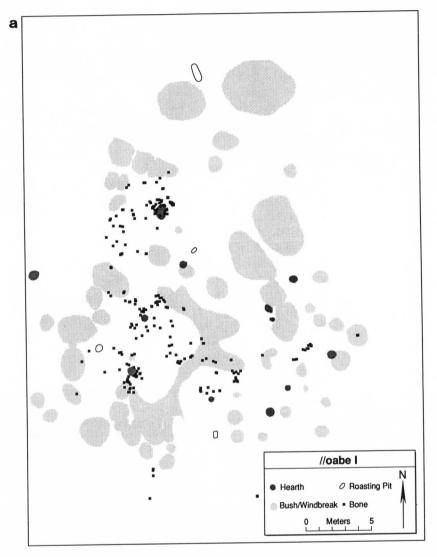

Figure 14. //oabe I: Distribution of bones less than or equal to 48 mm in length (14a) and those greater than 48 mm (14b). The median length of the plotted bone specimens is 48 mm.

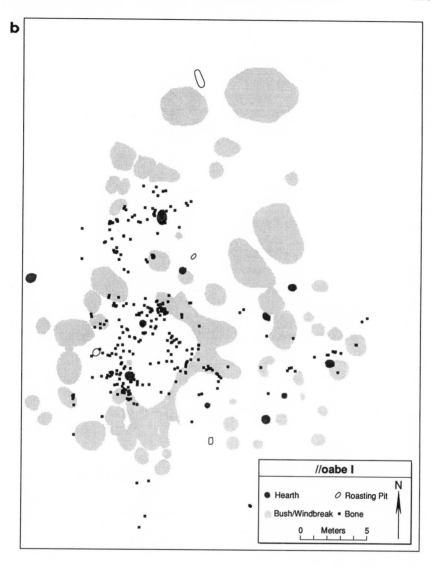

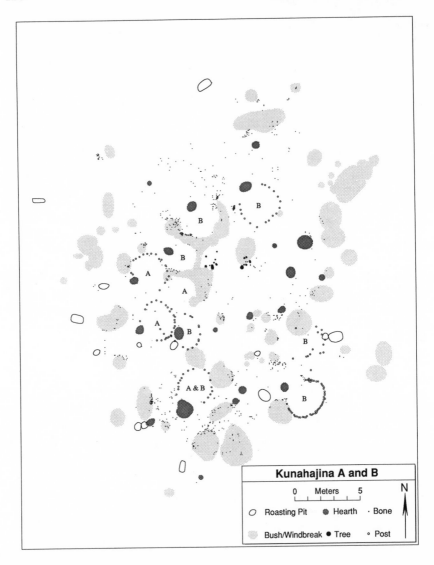

Figure 15. Kunahajina, cool dry season 1986. Kunahajina A and B are explained in the text.

parts of at least 21 mammal carcasses introduced into the camp during its second occupation; the majority of the bone illustrated in the figures dates to this time. For clarity, Figures 16a to 16c illustrate the camp's bone refuse plotted over maps of structures, bushes, and hearths, respectively.

Bone refuse at this camp was found both in clusters and in diffuse scatters. In Figure 16a, it is evident that clusters of bone were located both in and/or next to the windbreaks and huts, especially near their openings. Bones were located in some peripheral locations as well. Figure 16b shows that many of the clusters were located in and on the margins of bushes. Figure 16c shows only one kind of clear association of bone refuse and hearths/roasting pits. Next to each primary nuclear area hearth (1 to 4), there is a clearly visible band of bone refuse on each of two sides of the hearth at a distance of about 1 to 2 meters. Near Hearths 1 and 2, the clusters are the same ones that were mentioned before in association with the windbreak. For the third and fourth hearths, the bone distribution is better understood by the positions of the bushes illustrated in Figure 16b, as will be discussed.

Scatters, the other pattern of bone distribution, were more common than clusters. These were often found within 2 to 3 meters of hut or windbreak openings (Figure 16a). When present, they were often located just beyond a relatively refuse-free area immediately in front of the structures. Examples of this can be seen in Figure 16a. It is clear that some of the huts exhibited more associated bone refuse than others, making the scatters more apparent.

The distributional variability just outlined can be explained as follows. Within the nuclear areas, bone clusters are principally associated with areas of food consumption. Many of the bones were discarded as primary refuse either in the structures themselves or in bushes near these areas. If discarded in the structures, the bones were principally restricted to the ends of the windbreak near the opening or by the doorposts of a hut. Figure 16b also reveals that many of the clusters are associated with bushes, which are themselves adjacent to nuclear household areas or to the communal area. Once again the bushes in these places were used as targets for primary refuse, and the side of the bush most easily accessible from the household nuclear area is where most of the clusters are found. This same behavior pattern is what accounted for the bones in the bushes in the communal area; diners would consume the meat from the bones and then simply toss them into the nearest bush. The communal area was otherwise free of bones. Thus primary bone refuse at this camp is found adjacent to nuclear and communal areas, out of traffic zones, in bushes, and at the margins of structures.

As secondary refuse, bone was found primarily in diffuse scatters. Many of these scatters were located in front or off to one side of the openings of huts or windbreaks (Figure 16a). This kind of bone distribution is the result of periodic sweeping of the various nuclear areas with grass "brooms." Interestingly, not all of the huts and windbreaks exhibit the diffuse scatters in front of them, but the

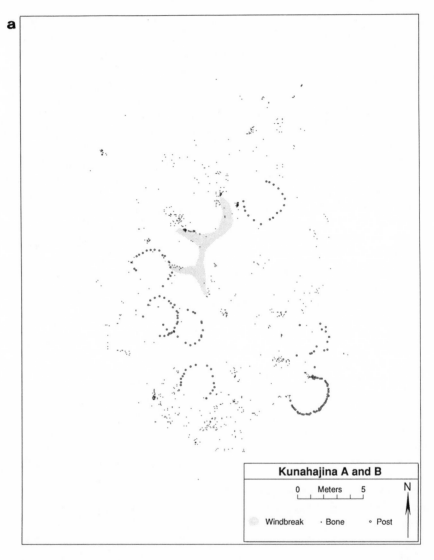

Figure 16. Kunahajina, cool dry season 1986: Distributions of bones and structures (16a), bones and vegetation (16b), bones and cooking facilities (16c).

b

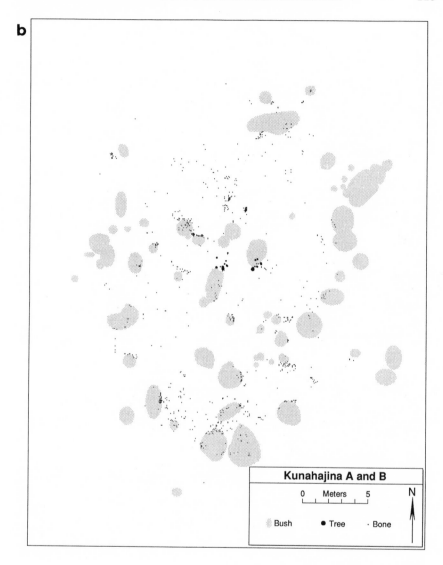

Kunahajina A and B

0   Meters   5   N

Bush   ● Tree   · Bone

C

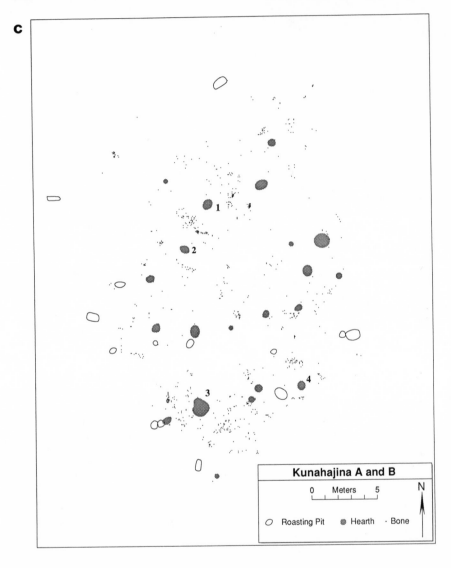

Kunahajina A and B

0   Meters   5   N

○ Roasting Pit   ● Hearth   · Bone

ones that do have them correspond to the longest occupied structures. Sweeping was the principal means of dealing with the accumulation of refuse in nuclear areas, but in one case a hut (the southwesternmost hut associated with Hearth 3) was abandoned and rebuilt nearby (the southeasternmost hut associated with Hearth 4) because of the overaccumulation of refuse in the nuclear area of the original structure. Ashdumps were not observed at this camp, despite its span of occupation.

The overall pattern of bone refuse at Kunahajina reflects the location of the most frequently used consumption areas. The spatial redundancy of bone-generating activities ensured that the locations of the longest occupied nuclear areas were emphasized, even to the extent of mimicking the outlines of the associated structure. The practice of placing bones fragments at the margins of the windbreaks or against the inside walls of huts accounted for this structural outlining. This pattern is due in part to the large number of bones discarded at the camp, but more importantly to the relative lack of effort expended in secondary refuse disposal. Where present, secondary disposal took the form of sweeping, so that disruption of the pattern was minimal. As Figure 16c illustrates, however, little bone refuse was left to indicate the positions of the structures that were occupied for only a short time.

4.4. Special-Purpose Camps and Special-Purpose Locations

Among the Kua, special-purpose camps were rarely the result of logistically organized subsistence strategies (Binford 1980), although camps resulting from such a strategy are certainly not unknown among foragers (Brooks and Yellen 1987:66–67). "Biltong hunts" (Silberbauer 1981:209–210, 214, 219; 1981:478) or "expedition hunts" (Hitchcock 1982:198, 258–260) are examples of logistical tactics employed occasionally by the Kua. In our observations, however, these techniques were only practiced by the sedentary cattle post groups who hunted eland, giraffe, and hartebeest from horseback with spears. This method of transport was available only by arrangement with the stockowners or herdsmen at cattle posts and therefore was unavailable to most of the Kua we observed. The large quantities of meat obtained in this manner were transported to residential locations on the backs of donkeys or horses (Masakazu 1984).

Instead, the special-purpose camps that we observed were primarily created as a consequence of recovering a single large antelope. In instances where the transport considerations discussed earlier (e.g., distance to camp, etc.) were immediately manageable, carcasses were returned to the base camp with a minimum of processing, and an overnight stay at the kill site was unnecessary. Alternatively, the party might process the meat into biltong in order to reduce the weight and bulk before carrying it (Binford 1984:49). If the carcass provided quantities of meat exceeding the immediate carrying abilities of the field party, however, the meat (in the form of biltong) was temporarily cached for later retrieval. In rare instances, the base camp was moved to the kill, but this was practiced exclusively during rainy and cool dry seasons when group sizes were smaller.

All special-purpose death-site camps appeared with little advance planning because their specific location was determined mainly by where the animal fell. Because the hunter could not reliably predict the position of the camp relative to other necessary resources (e.g., water-bearing melons), the hunter and his party collected melons while tracking to ensure at least some fluids at the camp. This kind of camp was not occupied any longer than necessary; because of the hunter's obligation to share the meat of the animal with a larger group, the tendency was to hurry up and abandon the special-purpose camps as soon as possible. Thus these camps could be the site of a wide range of carcass-processing activities, from hasty disarticulation to more elaborate drying, bundling, and subsequent storage of meat. Although not discussed here, another sort of special purpose camp we observed (Table 2) was the special purpose "reconnaissance camp," one occupied solely for the purpose of gathering information about the kinds and quantities of resources in an area.

Figure 17a shows an example of a special-purpose camp called Dutara. The Dutara camp was created in late June by a Kua hunter and his nuclear family. The group had been living in a series of cool dry season camps with another family from whom they had recently parted. On a foraging trip from one of these last camps, the hunter shot a large male eland with a poisoned arrow. Feeling that his chances were good for finding the animal, he returned to collect his family, and together they tracked the eland. They discovered the animal alive in the early evening at Dutara, and after dispatching it with a spear and skinning it, they cooked the liver and the meat from some of the ribs in a hearth next to the carcass. That evening they built a small windbreak, to the east of the carcass (WB1 in Figure 17a), in which they spent the night. The windbreak was built by the light provided by a fire set in the upper branches of a fallen tree nearby. At the opening of the windbreak, they roasted the eland's head in a pit dug for the purpose.

For the next day and night, they stayed at Dutara, while they processed the carcass for transport by filleting the meat off of the bones and drying it on the rack shown in Figure 17a. They packed the biltong into bundles bound with strips of the animal's hide. All of the filleted limb bones were taken to a new windbreak (WB2 in Figure 17a), constructed to the east because of bothersome insects in the first structure. Here the bones were roasted and cracked for marrow next to a hearth in the opening of the windbreak. The resulting fragments were discarded on the north side of the windbreak adjacent to where the marrow was eaten (shown in Figure 17a as a dense cluster just outside the second windbreak). They also consumed some of the meat and cracked all of the marrow bones that were discarded at the camp.

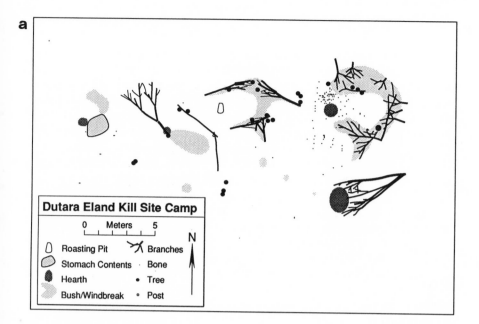

a

Dutara Eland Kill Site Camp

0   Meters   5

N

◊   Roasting Pit   ✗ Branches

◯   Stomach Contents   · Bone

●   Hearth   • Tree

░   Bush/Windbreak   ○ Post

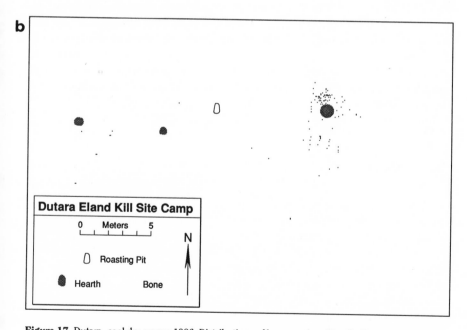

b

Dutara Eland Kill Site Camp

0   Meters   5

N

◊   Roasting Pit

●   Hearth   Bone

Figure 17. Dutara, cool dry season 1986. Distributions of bones and cooking facilities with (17a) and without (17b) structures and vegetation. WB1 and WB2 refer to the first and second windbreaks occupied at the camp, respectively. WB2 was formed mainly by the still connected branches of a single fallen tree.

The following day, a storage platform was built in a tree to hold the meat until the hunter could return with others to help carry the meat back to relatives at Kani//am/odi. The only location suitable for the construction of the platform was in a group of trees a full kilometer away; no suitable tree could be found in the grove where the animal fell. After the platform was complete, the bundles of biltong were carried to the tree, and the entire structure was covered with logs, branches, and grass to keep out vultures and other scavengers.

After abandonment, the bones remaining on the ground at Dutara camp were scavenged by brown hyenas and vultures before we had an opportunity to map it. This was immediately apparent upon our return to the camp when we encountered abundant vulture feathers and hyena feces. Figure 17b shows the bone distribution as mapped with the structures removed from view.

Interestingly, the hyenas had a far greater effect on the skeletal part composition of the bone assemblage than on the integrity of its primary spatial patterning. The hyenas preferentially removed limb ends from the camp, taking them beyond the limits of our search (we recovered both of the eland's horns, which had been dragged a distance of 106 meters from our mapping station), choosing them because of the adhering tissue and the grease that was contained in the cancellous epiphyses. The more numerous limb shaft fragments, however, remained undisturbed in the clusters where they had been deposited as primary refuse. Thus the hyenas did not seriously distort the original spatial patterning of the bones at the camp and did not impede the identification of behaviorally meaningful clusters, which were still visible as areas of primary refuse. The most significant of these clusters was located at the place where the marrow bones were cracked (Bunn and Kroll 1988).

4.5. Transient Camps

As noted, these camps were associated with travel between rainy season camps or between cool dry season camps. Their bone assemblages reflected carcass portions transported from other camps (where complementary portions of the same carcass were abandoned), as well as bones from smaller animals obtained en route. These camps invariably consisted of a windbreak and a hearth or two, but little else. Bones were restricted to the primary refuse locations discussed, that is, immediately in front of the windbreak opening and adjacent to hearths. Because of their ephemeral human occupation, these camps were frequently the targets of scavenging carnivores who found the bond refuse still attractive after abandonment.

5. DISCUSSION

5.1. Camp Comparisons

Now that the basic characteristics of the varaious types of Kua camps have been reviewed, we can compare the sizes, facilities and structures, locations of activities, and distributions of bone refuse.

5.1a. Camp Size

As measured by Yellen's absolute limit of scatter (Yellen 1977a:103), hot dry season camps are an order of magnitude larger than all other camp types. (Please note that in Table 2 the ALS areas for Kani//am/odi are listed by household group; the camp's total area is much larger than the sum of the individual areas.) Size differences exist among the other camp types, too, but intratype variability is large. When additional quantitative analyses have been conducted on all of the camps, we may find that other measures (e.g., Yellen 1977a:103–105) will discriminate among them; indeed, preliminary analyses indicate that there are significant correlations between ALS area and occupation length for camps of the same type.

Overall, special purpose and transient camps are small (< 100 m²), consisting of no more than a single structure or two, and usually less than half a dozen or so other features. Rainy season and cool dry season base camps most often are larger (averaging 250–500 m²), reflecting longer occupancy and larger populations. Only slightly larger are the component household groups of hot dry season camps (which average slightly over 400 m²). The difference between the latter two types is small, reflecting their similar population sizes and social composition. However, it must be kept in mind that dry season household groups were not individual camps *per se*; rather they were constituent parts of a larger camp of vastly greater extent.

5.1b. Facilities and Structures

The preceding examples illustrate that despite variations in occupation length, number of residents, primary function, and season of occupation, all Kua camps share many structural components.

With respect to residential structures, windbreaks were present at all camp types and with the exception of transient camps, so were huts. However, among special-purpose camps, huts were present only at those from the rainy season.

The arrangement of residential structures at Kua camps (and within household groups) was frequently linear. This layout was observed at virtually all camps where windbreaks were the primary shelter (e.g., Kani//am/odi HHG-7), and almost invariably, the windbreaks opened to the west. This western orientation provided more light for evening activities in the windbreak and kept the direct sun off of the residents for a bit longer in the morning. However, where huts were the predominant dwelling (as at many rainy season camps), conformation to this pattern was not as consistent (e.g., Kunahajina). Hitchcock, Kroll, and Bunn mapped a rainy season camp occupied by many of the same Kua in April 1978, which had a linear arrangement of windbreaks Kroll (n. d.). The linear camp plan observed for the Kua complements the "ring model" of camp structure long documented among southern African foragers (e.g., Schapera 1930:87 and references therein) and extensively analyzed by Yellen for !Kung camps (1977a).

Because of their many essential roles of subsistence activities, hearths and roasting pits were ubiquitous among all types of camps, but they varied in their frequency as a function of occupation length. We observed only two kinds of facilities that were unique to an individual camp type, that is, storage platforms and ashdumps, which were present only at hot dry season camps. Their presence could potentially identify dry season camps archaeologically.

Thus the limited range of facilities present at camps of many types precludes the archaeological recognition of camp types on the simple presence or absence of particular facilities, except perhaps for the occurrence of storage platforms and ashdumps, although there is no reason to expect them not to occur whenever a camp is occupied long enough to require secondary refuse disposal or additional storage areas.

5.1c. Locations of Activities

We have shown that for the hot dry season base camps such as HHG-7 at Kani//am/odi and for the rainy season base camps such as //oabe I, the positioning of activities was controlled principally by the distribution of midday and afternoon shade over the camp. During the occupation of both of these hot season camps, activities shifted daily between morning and midday/afternoon areas, so that at Kani//am/odi HHG-7, the activity space was essentially bilateral along the axis of the windbreak. At //oabe I, more shade to the north provided an additional area for afternoon activities, including butcheries. At cool dry season base camps like Kunahajina, the same daily shift was less pronounced. Here, the midday shift was often to the shaded communal area, but this shift was not as predictable as in the hot dry season camps where shade was desperately sought. On some cool days at Kunahajina, inhabitants sat until early afternoon in the direct sunlight of the eastern side of the windbreaks. Again, this could have a possible bearing on determinations of seasonality of certain archaeological sites. At the special-purpose and transient camps, activities were restricted to a few principal areas immediately adjacent to the shade-producing structures.

5.1d. Bone Distribution

Differences in the distribution of bone refuse over the surface of the camps reflected three factors:

1. The positioning of activities generating bone refuse (i.e., processing, consumption, and discard).
2. The intensity of secondary disposal activities.
3. The intensity of other taphonomic factors (trampling and children's play, dogs, and postoccupational scavenging).

As stated, the location of consumption areas was the most important factor determining the location of primary bone refuse. Consumption areas, in turn, most often conformed with the windbreak or hut openings in nuclear areas and less frequently with shaded afternoon communal areas. Closer examination revealed that these primary discard loci often coincided with bushes near the consumption areas, the interior margins of windbreak structures (especially near the openings), and the zone of about 1 to 3 meters in front of the opening of the structure. At //oabe I (Figure 10a), a concentration of primary bone refuse extended from the nuclear area of the windbreak to about 2.5 meters out from the hearths in the windbreak opening. Butchery and marrow-cracking areas were also represented by primary bone refuse, but they accounted for less of the apparent patterning. Also at this camp, where bone identifications have been completed, there was patterning evident in the relative distribution of the bones of individual carcasses that were discarded early in the camp's depositional history, and there were differences in the distribution of axial and appendicular elements that reflected the relative effort required to get the meat off of the bones.

Primary bone refuse was also likely to be preserved *in situ* in those nuclear areas that had only been occupied a short time before camp abandonment (see Stevenson, Chapter 9 this volume), even though by that time much of the remaining bone refuse at the camp was in secondary context. An example of this is presented by Kani//am/odi HHG-7 (Figure 9a), where, in front of Hut 2, a bone cluster in a primary nuclear area was present in front of one of the last structures built before abandonment. Further work with the Kua data will delimit the range where bone densities in nuclear areas were deemed unacceptable, so that steps were taken to remove it to secondary dumps.

Secondary discard took two forms at Kua camps. The first, sweeping of bone refuse away from primary discard locations, was a less effective but more frequently employed means. This is illustrated well by Kunahajina where, for example, at the northernmost windbreak (Hearth 1 in Figure 16c) and the south-westernmost hut (Hearth 3 in Figure 16c), the areas immediately adjacent to the nuclear area hearths were relatively free of bone refuse but beyond lay diffuse scatters of bone. In contrast to the distribution at //oabe I (Figure 10a), at the hot dry season camp of Kani//am/odi HHG-7 (Figure 9a), there was a light scatter of bone immediately in front of the windbreak opening, but an additional band of secondary bone refuse is present in a less trafficked location 6 to 8 meters out from the windbreak opening. This band was created by periodic sweeping up and dumping of the same kind of primary refuse observed *in situ* at //oabe I. This suggests that the distribution pattern of bone at //oabe I is analogous to an earlier stage in the evolution of the nuclear area debris pattern of HHG-7 (see Stevenson, Chapter 9 this volume).

Thus aside from their size and unique facilities, camp types were distinguished from one another by their ratios of secondary to primary bone refuse. Kunahajina and Kani//am/odi HHG-7 exhibit increasingly larger proportions of secondary bone refuse, respectively, unlike //oabe I (Figures 10 to 13) and Dutara (Figure 17), which illustrate relatively undisturbed primary bone refuse patterning. This is in part related to adjustments in attitudes about camp maintenance at the more sedentary camps. Similarly, Hitchcock (1982:364–369, 1987) has noted pronounced differences in bone refuse disposal patterns between the Kua sites he observed in the Western Sandveld and the sedentary camps of Tyua Basarwa along the Nata River:

> In the case of the Nata sites. . . . First of all, people remove bones so they will not attract predators and vermin. Second, bones are removed because people do not like stepping on them; one result is a size sorting of bones, with smaller ones being trampled into the sandy substrate of the site. A third reason for the cleanup of bones is that people are afraid that game scouts will find out they have been involved in illegal hunting. Fourth, bones are collected and taken to a central place for purposes of later pickup and sale to the bonemeal factory in Francistown. . . . Finally, bones of specific species of animals are removed from the sites and buried, one example being the bones of warthogs which are believed to be bad for dogs. (1987:416)

At the hot dry season camps like Kani//am/odi, the first three of Hitchcock's reasons motivated the disposal of secondary refuse. Secondary refuse disposal at other types of Kua camps, however, seemed to be primarily in the form of sweeping and pushing of hearth contents away from the centers of nuclear areas and was again prompted by the first and second reasons offered by Hitchcock.

Other taphonomic factors, like trampling and children's play, dogs, and postoccupational scavenging, resulted in differences in the distribution of refuse. The effects of trampling were most evident at longer occupations where we frequently recovered buried bones, especially in nuclear areas. Bones were not buried intentionally by the Kua but instead as the result of domestic activity and play in nuclear and communal areas. Dogs were most destructive to bones at camps where they were the hungriest, that is, at the hot dry season camps. Further examination of the positions of gnawed bone at the camps may show that the highest frequencies are on the camp margins, to which the dogs retreated for a peaceful chew. Postoccupational scavenging by hyenas and jackals had little effect on the distribution of bone at the camps. Instead, as illustrated by the Dutara camp (Figure 17a), they primarily affected the skeletal part composition of the assemblage, through their selective removal of grease- or tissue-bearing bones. What is important is that the evidence we encountered indicated that brown hyenas removed the bones from the camp entirely, perhaps taking them to dens or other sheltered locations. Alternatively, hyenas may have ingested some of the missing bones. Despite lengthy searches for outlying bones, we were rarely successful in finding their choices.

5.2. Archaeological Implications

We have focused our attention in this chapter on the spatial patterning in faunal remains from the Kua camps. Archaeological interpretation should proceed using as many independent lines of evidence as are available (see Carr, Chapter 7 this volume). Although it would be myopic to restrict the analysis of prehistoric hunter–gatherer sites to spatial patterning in faunal remains (as we have done here), it would be unrealistic to hope to base identifications of distinct intrasite areas on materials that are perishable in most archaeological contexts. When the evidence likely to be preserved from the Kua camps is examined as an archaeologist might see it, we come face to face with the interpretive challenge, and the faunal remains form one of the most significant classes of information available. Without the aid of ethnoarachaeological documentary evidence, the patterns obvious to one observing their formation revert to ambiguity. Some of the main points for archaeological analyses are summarized next.

5.2a. Site Size and Scales of Observation

The Kua camps described here are among the largest available sets of data on which to test approaches to reconstructing social and residential units. To date some of the largest excavations at spatially significant prehistoric hunter–gatherer sites are on the order of 100 to 300 m² (e.g., FxJj50 [Bunn et al. 1980], FLK-Zinjanthropus [Leakey 1971], Pincevent [Leroi-Gourhan and Brézillon 1966], and Meer [Van Noten 1978]). The camp-size data presented in Table 2 suggest that only the absolute limit of scatter of the smallest Kua camps or a single household group at a hot dry season camp would be completely exposed by archaeological excavations of comparable sizes.

This point reinforces previous assertions by O'Connell (1987:104 and O'Connell *et al.*, Chapter 3 this volume) that most archaeological excavations have been too small to cover the area of discard from all but the smallest ethnoarchaeologically documented camps. This fact inhibits the possibility of testing the innovative approaches for explaining variability in camp size and intracamp household spacing suggested by several workers (e.g., Gargett and Hayden, Chapter 1 this volume; Gould and Yellen 1987; Kent 1987, Chapter 2 this volume; O'Connell 1987; Whitelaw 1983). The extensive sharing of meat among household groups played an important role in maintaining good community relations at Kua hot dry season camps. In fact, the importance of small carcasses as food among such a large group was diminished in comparison with its social role. The archaeological consequence of this behavior was to distribute carcass parts to distant discard locations at widely spaced household groups. The occurrence of spatially extensive sharing underscores the need for horizontal archaeological excavations on a scale not previously attempted. Additionally, it is easy to see from this example how summary statistics (e.g., minimum number of individuals) computed for the bone assemblages from individual household groups where this kind of sharing was practiced would seriously overrepresent the amount of meat available to the residents. Special effort given to conjoining bone fragments of identical skeletal parts and rearticulating elements from individual carcasses can help to reduce errors of this kind.

5.2b. Site Structure

Hitchcock (1982:338) has identified four variables that determine the organization of space within hunter–gatherer camps: intensity of use of a place, site population, type of activity conducted, and anticipated length of stay (see Kent, Chapter 2 this volume). To his list, we would add the physical characteristics of the space itself (e.g., shaded or unshaded, obstructed or cleared), which we have demonstrated have a strong influence on the subsequent positioning of structures and activities.

Monitoring the effects of these variables in ethnoarchaeological contexts will be useful to the understanding of prehistoric sites at low to mid latitudes where the presence of shade during hot seasons may have been a powerful attractant (e.g., Gould 1980; Hayden 1979; O'Connell 1987; Yellen 1977a). The daily shift in the use of space documented at many Kua camps has serious implications for studies of archaeological site patterning in sub-Saharan Africa and other tropical environments. Though the location of shade is seasonally of critical importance in determining the position of major structural elements in the camp framework, the framework itself, once established, is of greater importance than the shade in determining the primary refuse distribution patterns. The concept of a "nuclear area" may need to be reconsidered in terms of the bilateral symmetry of activity performance at HHG-7 and //oabe I.

Kua residential camps present an alternative camp structure to the "ring model" proposed by Yellen (1977a) as a basis for the interpretation of camp structure among Kalahari foragers. Unlike !Kung rainy season camps, most Kua camps exhibited a linear structure (although some rainy season camps with huts were an exception to this pattern). Here we have not presented the numerical relationships between various camp measurements (e.g., Yellen 1977a) and occupation length or number of households, but it is clear that analytical transformations based on these measurements need to be reevaluated when the fundamental layout of the camp is altered (e.g., linear vs. circular plans).

There is reason to expect that certain archaeologically recognizable structures or features may be indicative in themselves of certain camp types, such as the storage platforms and ashdumps present only at dry season Kua camps. The factors accounting for their presence can also be expected to have operated prehistorically with similar results. However, discerning contemporaneity among structures and features presents a particularly difficult challenge. We have shown that multiple hearths were used simultaneously by individual households, yet the primary nuclear area hearths were restricted to one or two per household. These could be identified by their size and density of associated bone refuse, if secondary disposal had not altered their contents and the contents of the associated nuclear area scatters. Here, the conjoining of bone specimens offers a means of establishing that secondary refuse disposal areas were derived from specific nuclear areas and also which particular nuclear areas were occupied simultaneously.

Morphology and orientation of residential structures offers additional archaeological food for thought. Brooks and Yellen (1987:96–98) remark that the arcuate stone structures from Sampson's excavations at Orangia I (Sampson 1968) may in fact represent prehistoric examples of water-margin hunting blinds, rather than residential camps as interpreted by Sampson. Aside from the site's location, which in itself is persuasive evidence for a hunting venue, formal similarities in size, shape, and orientation to Kua brush windbreak structures lead us to consider other lines of evidence before we accept Brooks and Yellen's interpretation of the structures.

Confirming the predictions of some archaeologists (e.g., Schiffer 1972), Gifford (1980:98–100) has documented a relationship between occupation length and the proportion of secondary to primary refuse in her ethnoarchaeological examination of Dassanetch *gal dies* camps. Our preliminary analysis of the Kua data lend further support to this belief. However, the issue of how to discriminate primary versus secondary bone refuse deposits must now be addressed. Indeed, much of the variability among the camps discussed here has been couched in terms of these two classes of refuse. Distinguishing them archaeologically might be possible by first identifying other aspects of the site that would lead one to expect the presence of secondary refuse, for example, large site areas, substantial residential structures, or high-density deposits of refuse located in peripheral positions to the rest of the site's structures.

5.2c. Bone Refuse Patterning

Because of the potential for bone preservation in archaeological sites, we ask the question, "Can the different types of Kua camps be discriminated archaeologically via bone food refuse?" To help see the challenge these camps present as archaeological sites, we illustrated four of the camps with only the most likely features of the camp to survive, that is, their bone refuse, hearths, and roasting pits (Figures 9b, 10b, 16c, and 17b).[3]

A number of hypotheses for further testing are suggested by our preliminary look at the bone refuse from the Kua camps presented here:

1. The most frequently performed refuse-generating activities will leave their signature far more indelibly in the bone refuse than those that occur at the same location but less frequently. The repeated use of butchery and consumption locations is of primary importance in the accumulation of dense concentrations of bone refuse (also see Brooks and Yellen 1987; O'Connell 1987).

2. Even in relatively short-term occupations, the bones of a single carcass are likely to be distributed over much of a camp but will occur prominently as primary refuse in household and communal consumption areas. Among the Kua, the size of a carcass is relatively unimportant in terms of the probability that it will be shared.

3. Axial parts in primary context may be more useful as indicators of secondary consumption loci than appendicular parts. We suggested that this is due to the increased processing requirements of axial parts.

4. Alternatively, limb elements (long bones) in primary context are more likely to be distributed at both primary (butchery) consumption loci and secondary (nuclear) consumption loci because many of these bones are frequently cracked and their marrow eaten during the butchery process itself.

5. Clusters comprised primarily of limb shafts probably represent the location of marrow-cracking activities, and these areas are likely to remain distinct despite postoccupational scavenging, as illustrated at Dutara.

6. Isolated clusters of bone composed of diverse elements from diverse taxa on the periphery of occupations probably represent secondary disposal areas (e.g., ashdumps or middens).

7. The possibility of transporting large quantities of meat (in the form of biltong) without attached bone renders numerical transformations of

---

[3]It should be noted, however, that Kalahari weathering environments are generally harsh and would in most cases preclude the preservation of unburied, and perhaps even buried bone, at open air sites not immediately adjacent to pans (Yellen 1977a, b; Denbow and Wilmsen 1986; Brooks and Yellen 1987).

bone refuse into available meat from rainy and cool dry season base camps minimum estimates at best, whereas the complementary kill/processing sites associated with this behavior would accurately reflect this.

It is likely that much of the patterning evident in bone refuse can only be understood in terms of features that are unlikely to be archaeologically detectable. However, the presence of these features may sometimes be inferred from ethnoarchaeologically documented patterns of association in categories of features and artifacts more likely to be preserved, for example, hearths, ashdumps, or evidence of structures (stones, postmolds, etc.).

6. CONCLUSIONS

In order to be useful to archaeologists, ethnoarchaeological research must provide the means for generating valid inferences from the preserved traces of human/hominid occupation of a site. Archaeologists have long recognized the potential of animal bones for preserving behavioral traces from the past, and thus this constitutes an obvious focus for the ethnoarchaeologist seeking to identify behavioral processes to link the observable present with the unobservable past. Through work among contemporary people who generate bone-food refuse, ethnoarchaeology is in a unique position to pursue avenues of research that promise to identify the archaeological issues approachable with these data and provide archaeologists with the tools to resolve them. We hope that this preliminary look at some of the processes that condition the spatial configurations of bone refuse at contemporary Kua camps can help guide our inferences about spatial patterning in bone assemblages from the prehistoric world.

ACKNOWLEDGMENTS

Financial support for our research among the Kua was provided by the National Science Foundation and by the Institute for International Education's Fulbright Program. We thank the Office of the President, Republic of Botswana, and Mr. C. Mogotse for permission to conduct fieldwork in Central District, and Robert Hitchcock for introducing us to the field area. In Gaborone, Alec Campbell, James Denbow, Angier Peavey, and Ruby Apsler provided much needed advice and assistance. We are especially grateful to Keith Whitelock, general manager of Debswana Mining Pty. Ltd., Orapa, and Irene Whitelock for endless logistical support and extraordinary kindness. We thank Kgatiso Gabatswane and Keikantsemang "Shakes" Tshikhinya for their translations between English and Kua, and Lisanne Bartram, Christian Gurney, and Marty Jakobs for their conscientious and enthusiastic assistance in the field and laboratory. Finally, we extend our gratitude to the Kua themselves for their tolerance, good humor, and friendship during our stay.

7. REFERENCES

Bartram, L. E., n. d., *An Ethnoarchaeological Analysis of Kua San Bone Food Refuse*. Dissertation in progress, Department of Anthropology, University of Wisconsin, Madison.

Behrensmeyer, A. K., 1978, Taphonomic and Ecologic Information from Bone Weathering, *Paleobiology* 4(2):150–162.

Behrensmeyer, A. K., Gordon, K. D., and Yanagi, G. T., 1986, Trampling as a Cause of Bone Surface Damage and Pseudo Cut Marks, *Nature* 319(6056):768–771.

Binford, L. R., and Bertram, J. B., 1977, Bone Frequencies—and Attritional Processes. In *For Theory Building in Archaeology: Essays on Faunal Remains, Aquatic Resources, Spatial Analysis, and Systemic Modeling* (L. R. Binford, ed.), Academic Press, New York. pp. 77–153.

Binford, L. R., 1978a, Organization and Formation Processes: Looking at Curated Technologies, *Journal of Anthropological Research* 35(3):255–273.

Binford, L. R., 1978b, *Nunamiut Ethnoarchaeology*, Academic Press, New York.

Binford, L. R., 1980, Willow Smoke and Dog's Tails: Hunter–Gatherer Settlement Systems and Archaeological Site Formation, *American Antiquity* 45:4–20.

Binford, L. R., 1981, *Bones: Ancient Men and Modern Myths*, Academic Press, New York.

Binford, L. R., 1982, The Archaeology of Place, *Journal of Anthropological Archarology* 1(1):5–31.

Binford, L. R., 1983, *In Pursuit of the Past: Decoding the Archaeological Record*, Thames and Hudson, London.

Binford, L. R., 1984, *Faunal Remains from Klasies River Mouth*, Academic Press, New York.

Binford, L. R., and Binford, S. R., 1966, A Preliminary Analysis of Functional Variability in the Mousterian of Levallois Facies, *American Anthropologist* 68(2):238–295.

Bleek, D. F., 1956, *A Bushman Dictionary*, American Oriental Society, New Haven. Zellig S. Harris, vol. ed., American Oriental Series, 41.

Blumenschine, R. J., 1987, Characteristics of An Early Hominid Scavenging Niche, *Current Anthropology* 28(4):383–407.

Boaz, N. T., and Behrensmeyer, A. K., 1976, Hominid Taphonomy: Transport of Human Skeletal Parts in An Artificial Fluviatile Environment, *American Journal of Physical Anthropology* 45:53–60.

Bonnichsen, R., and Sorg, M., (Eds.), 1990, *Bone Modification*. Center for the Study of Early Man, Orono, Maine.

Bonnichsen, R., 1973, Some Operational Aspects of Human and Animal Bone Alteration. In *Mammalian Osteo-Archaeology: North Amrica* (B. Miles Gilbert, ed.), Missouri Archaeological Society, Columbia, pp. 9–24.

Brain, C. K., 1967, Bone Weathering and the Problem of Bone Pseudo-Tools, *South African Journal of Science* 63:97–99.

Brain, C. K., 1969, The Contribution of Namib Desert Hottentots to an Understanding of Australopithecine Bone Accumulations, *Scientific Papers of the Namib Desert Research Station* 39:13–22.

Brain, C. K., 1980, *Some Criteria for the Recognition of Bone-Collecting Agencies*. Fossils in the Making, University of Chicago Press, Chicago.

Brain, C. K., 1981, *The Hunters or the Hunted? An Introduction to African Cave Taphonomy*, University of Chicago Press, Chicago.

Brooks, A., and Yellen, J.E., 1987, The Preservation of Activity Areas in the Archaeological Record: Ethnoarchaeological and Archaeological Work in Northwest Ngamiland, Botswana. In *Method and Theory for Activity Area Reasearch: An Ethnoarchaeological Approach*, (S. Kent, ed.), Columbia University Press, New York, pp. 63–106.

Bunn, H. T., 1982, Animal Bones and Archaeological Inference. Review of *Bones: Ancient Men and Modern Myths*, by L. R. Binford, *Science* 215(4532):494–495.

Bunn, H. T., 1983a, Evidence on the Diet and Subsistence Patterns of Plio-Pleistocene Hominids at Koobi Fora, Kenya, and Olduvai Gorge, Tanzania. In *Animals and Archaeology: 1. Hunters and Their Prey*. (J. Clutton-Brock and C. Grigson, eds.), British Archaeological Reports (International Series) 163, pp. 21–30.

Bunn, H. T., 1983b, Comparative Analysis of Modern Bone Assemblages from a San Hunter–Gatherer Camp in the Kalahari Desert, Botswana, and from a Spotted Hyena den near Nairobi, Kenya. In *Animals and Archaeology: 1. Hunters and their Prey* (J. Clutton-Brock an C. Grigson, eds.), British Archaeological Reports (International Series) 163, pp. 143–148.

Bunn, H. T., Harris, J. W. K., Isaac, G., Kaufulu, Z., Kroll, E. M., Schick, K., Toth, N., and Behrensmeyer, A. K., 1980, FxJj 50: An Early Pleistcene Site in Northern Kenya. *World Archaeology* 12:109–136.

Bunn, H. T., Bartram, L. E., and Kroll, E. M., 1988, Variability in Bone Assemblage Formation from Hadza Hunting, Scavenging, and Carcass Processing, *Journal of Anthropological Archaeology* 7(4):412–457.

Bunn, H. T., and Kroll, E. M., 1986, Systematic Butchery by Plio-Pleistocene Hominids at Olduvai Gorge, Tanzania, *Current Anthropology* 27(5):431–52.

Bunn, H. T., and Kroll, E. M., 1988, Reply to 'Fact and Fiction about the Zinjanthropus Floor. Data, Arguments, and Interpretation', by Lewis Binford, *Current Anthropology* 29(1):135–149.

Campbell, A. C., 1968, Some Notes on Ngwaketse Divination, *Botswana Notes and Records* 1:9.

Campbell, A. C., and Hitchcock, R., 1985, Some Setswana Names of Woody Plants, *Botswana Notes and Records* 17:117–129.

Cooke, H. J., 1982, The Physical Environment of Botswana. In *Settlement in Botswana: The Historical Development of a Human Landscape*, (R. Renée Hitchcock and Mary R. Smith, eds.), Marshalltown, South Africa. *Heinemann Educational Books and the Botswana Society*, pp. 1–12.

Crader, D., 1974, The Effects of Scavengers on Bone Material from a Large Mammal: An Experiment Conducted among the Bisa of the Luangwa Valley, Zambia, (C. B. Donnan and C. W. Clewlow, eds.), U. C. L. A. Institute of Archaeology, Monograph 4. pp. 161–173.

Crader, D., 1983, Contemporary Single-Carcass Butchery Scatters and the Problem of Butchery Sites in the Archaeological Record. In *Animals and Archaeology: 1. Hunters and their Prey*. (J. Clutton-Brock and C. Grigson, eds.). Oxford, British Archaeological Reports (International Series) 163, pp. 107–141.

Denbow, J. R., and Wilmsen, E. N., 1986, Advent and Course of Pastoralism in the Kalahari, *Science* 234:1509–1515.

Elphick, R., 1977, *Khoikhoi and the Founding of White South Africa*, Ravan Press, Johannesburg.

Fisher, J. W., Jr., 1987, Pygmies of the Ituri: An Ethnoarchaeological Exploration, *Anthro Notes* (National Museum of Natural History Newsletter for Teachers), 9(3):1–6.

Gifford, D. P., 1977, *Observations of Modern Human Settlements as an Aid to Archaeological Interpretation*. Unpublished Ph.D. Dissertation, Department of Anthropology, University of California–Berkeley.

Gifford, D. P., 1978, Ethnoarchaeological Observations on Natural Processes Affecting Cultural Materials. In *Explorations in Ethnoarchaeology*, University of New Mexico Press, (R. A. Gould, ed.), Albuquerque, pp. 77–101.

Gifford, D. P., 1980, Ethnoarchaeological Contributions to the Taphonomy of Human Sites. In *Fossils in the Making*, (A. K. Behrensmeyer and A. Hill, eds.), University of Chicago Press, Chicago, pp. 93–106.

LAURENCE E. BARTRAM ET AL.

Gifford, D. P., 1981, Taphonomy and Paleoecology: A Critical Review of Archaeology's Sister Disciplines. *Advances in Archaeological Method and Theory* 4:77–101.

Gifford, D. P., and Behrensmeyer, A. K., 1977, Observed Formation and Burial of a Recent Occupation Site in Kenya. *Quaternary Research* 8(2):245–266.

Gould, R. A., 1980, *Living Archaeology*, Cambridge University Press, Cambridge.

Gould, R. A., and Yellen, J. E., 1987, Man the Hunted: Determinants of Household Spacing in Desert and Tropical Foraging Societies, *Journal of Anthropological Archaeology* 6(1):77–103.

Hanson, C. B., 1980, Fluvial Taphonomic Processes: Models and Experiments. In *Fossils in the Making*, (A. K. Behrensmeyer and A. Hill, eds.), University of Chicago Press, Chicago, pp. 156–181.

Hayden, B., 1979, *Paleolithic Reflections: Lithic Technology and Ethnographic Excavation among Australian Aborigines*, Australian Institute of Aboriginal Studies, Canberra.

Haynes, G., 1983, A Guide for Differentiating Mammalian Carnivore Taxa Responsible for Gnaw Damage to Herbivore Limb Bones, *Paleobiology* 9(2):164–172.

Hill, A., 1979, Disarticulation and Scattering of Mammal Skeletons, *Paleobiology* 5:261–274.

Hitchcock, R. K., 1978a, *Kalahari Cattle Posts: A Regional Study of Hunter–Gatherers, Pastoralists, and Agriculturalists in the Western Sandveld Region, Central District, Botswana*, Ministry of Local Government and Lands, Gaborone.

Hitchcock, R. K., 1978b, A Socio-Economic Survey of the Eastern Kalahari Cattle Post: A Note, (1979) *Botswana Notes and Records* 10(11):137.

Hitchcock, R. K., 1980, Tradition, Social Justice, and Land Reform in Central Botswana, *Journal of African Law* 24:1–34.

Hitchcock, R. K., 1982, *The Ethnoarchaeology of Sedentism: Mobility Strategies and Site Structure among Foraging and Food Producing Populations in the Eastern Kalahari Desert, Botswana*. Unpublished Ph.D. Dissertation, Department of Anthropology, University of New Mexico.

Hitchcock, R. K., 1985, Patterns of Sedentism among the Basarwa of Eastern Botswana. In *Politics and Leadership in Band Societies* (E. Leacock and R. Lee, eds.), Cambridge University Press, Cambridge, pp. 223–267.

Hitchcock, R. K., 1987, Sedentism and Site Structure: Organizational Changes in Kalahari Basarwa Residential Locations. In *Method and Theory for Activity Area Research: An Ethnoarchaeological Approach* (Susan Kent, ed.), Columbia University Press, New York, pp. 374–423.

Isaac, G. Ll., 1967, Toward the Interpretation of Occupation Debris: Some Experiments and Observations, *Kroeber Anthropological Society Papers* 37:31–57.

Johnson, E., 1985, Current Developments in Bone Technology, *Advances in Archaeological Method and Theory* 8:157–235.

Kroll, E. M., n. d., *The Anthropological Meaning of Spatial Configurations at Plio-Pleistocene Archaeological sites in East Africa*, Ph.D. Dissertation, Department of Anthropology, University of California, Berkeley.

Leakey, M. D., 1971, *Olduvai Gorge, Vol. 3. Excavations in Beds I and II, 1960–1963*, Cambridge University Press, Cambridge.

Lee, R. B., 1979, *The !Kung San: Men, Women, and Work in a Foraging Society*, Cambridge University Press, Cambridge.

Lee, R. B., and DeVore, I. (eds.), 1976, *Kalahari Hunter–Gatherers: Studies of the !Kung San and their Neighbors*. Harvard University Press, Cambridge.

Leroi-Gourhan, A., and Brézillon, M., 1966, L'habitation magdalenienne no. 1 de Pincevent pres Montereau (Seine-et-Marne), *Gallia Prehistorie* 9(2):263–385.

Marks, S. A., 1976, *Large Mammals and a Brave people: Subsistence Hunters in Zambia*, University of Washington Press, Seattle.

Marshall, L., 1976, *The !Kung of Nyae Nyae*, Harvard University Press, Cambridge.

Masakazu, O., 1984, The Social Influence of Change in Hunting Technique among the Central

CAMP STRUCTURE AND BONE FOOD REFUSE PATTERNING 147

Kalahari San. *African Study Monographs* 5:49–62, The Research Committee for African Area Studies, Kyoto University.

Morlan, R. E., 1980, Taphonomy and Archaeology in the Upper Pleistocene of the Northern Yukon Territory: A Glimpse of the Peopling of the New World. National Museum of Man, Ottawa, *Archaeological Survey of Canada Paper*, No. 89.

Noe-Nygaard, N., 1977, Butchering and Marrow Fracturing as a Taphonomic Factor in Archaeological Deposits. *Paleobiology* 3:218–237.

O'Connell, J. F., 1987, Alyawara Site Structure and Its Archaeological Implications, *American Antiquity* 52(1):74–108.

Pike, J. G., 1971, Rainfall over Botswana, *Botswana Notes and Records*, Special Ed. No. 1:69–76. Proceedings of the Conference on Sustained Production from Semi-Arid Areas.

Richardson, P. R. K., 1980, Carnivore Damage to Antelope Bones and Its Archaeological Implications, *Paleontologica Africana* 23:109–125.

Sampson, C. G., 1968, The Middle Stone Age Industries of the Orange River Scheme Area. *Memoirs of the National Musuem at Bloemfontein*, No. 4. Orange Free State, Bloemfontein.

Schapera, I., 1930, *The Khoisan Peoples of South Africa*, Routledge & Kegan Paul, London.

Schiffer, M. B., 1972, Archaeological Context and Systemic Context, *American Antiquity* 37:156–165.

Schiffer, M. B., 1983, Toward the Identification of Formation Processes, *American Antiquity* 48:675–706.

Silberbauer, G. B., 1972, The G/wi Bushmen. In *Hunters and Gatherers Today*, (M. G. Bicchieri, ed.), Holt Rinehart, & Winston, New York, pp. 271–326.

Silberbauer, G. B., 1981, *Hunter and Habitat in the Central Kalahari Desert*, Cambridge University Press, Cambridge.

Smithers, R. H. N., 1971, The Mammals of Botswana. *Mus. Mem. Natl. Mus. Monum. Rhodesia* 4:1–340.

Smithers, R. H. N., 1983, *The Mammals of the Southern African Subregion*, University of Pretoria Press, Pretoria.

Spurling, B., and Hayden, B., 1984, Ethnoarchaeology and Intrasite Spatial Analysis: A Case Study from the Australian Western Desert. In *Intrasite Spatial Analysis in Archaeology* (H. Hietala, ed.), Cambridge University Press, Cambridge, pp. 224–241.

Sutcliffe, A. J., 1970, Spotted Hyaena: Crusher, Gnawer, Digester, and Collector of Bones, *Nature* 227(5263):1110–1113.

Tobias, P. V., (Ed.), 1978, *The Bushmen: San Hunters and Herders of Southern Africa* Human & Rosseau, Cape Town.

Traill, A., 1978, Preliminary Report on the Linguistic Situation amongst the Kua Basarwa Living on the Cattle Posts Bae, Motsetlharobega, Metsimonate in the Central District. Appendix 28 in *Kalahari Cattle Posts* (R. K. Hitchcock, ed.), Republic of Botswana, Ministry of Local Government and Lands, Gaborone, pp. 252–260.

Van Noten, F., 1978, *Les Chasseurs de Meer*, Dissertationes Archaeologicae Gandenses, De Tempel, Brugge.

Vierich, H. I. D., and Hitchcock, R. K., 1978, Some Economically Important Plant Species in the Kalahari: Description and Use, Appendix 6 in *Kalahari Cattle Posts*, by R. K. Hitchcock, Republic of Botswana, Ministry of Local Government and Lands, Gaborone, pp. 42–54.

Vrba, E. S., 1980, The Significance of Bovid Remains as Indicators of Environment and Predation Patterns. In *Fossils in the Making* (A. K. Behrensmeyer and A. P. Hill, eds.), University of Chicago Press, Chicago, pp. 247–271.

Westphal, E. O. J., 1979, Languages of Southern Africa. In *Perspectives on the Southern African Past* (C. C. Saunders, C. de B. Webb, and M. West, eds.), University of Cape Town, Centre for African Studies, Cape Town, pp. 37–68.

Whitelaw, T., 1983, People and Space in Hunter–Gatherer Camps: A Generalizing Approach in

Ethnoarchaeology, *Archaeological Review from Cambridge* 2(2):48–66.

Winter, M. C., 1976, The Archaeological Household Cluster in the Valley of Oaxaca. In *The Early Mesoamerican Village* (Kent V. Flannery, ed.), Academic Press, New York, pp. 25–312.

Wollard, J., 1986, The Active Chemical Components of the Basarwa Arrow Poison, *Botswana Notes and Records* 18:139–141.

Yellen, J. E., 1974, *The !Kung Settlement Pattern: An Archaeological Perspective*, Department of Anthropology, Harvard University, Cambridge.

Yellen, J. E., 1977a, *Archaeological Approaches to the Present: Models for Reconstructing the Past*, Academic Press, New York.

Yellen, J. E., 1977b, Cultural Patterning in Faunal Remains: Evidence from the !Kung Bushmen. In *Experimental Archaeology* (D. W. Ingersoll, J. E. Yellen, and W. MacDonald, eds.), Columbia University Press, New York, pp. 271–331.

Yellen, J. E., 1985, The Process of Basarwa Assimilation in Botswana, *Botswana Notes and Records* 17:15–23.

Chapter 5

Linking Ethnoarchaeological Interpretation and Archaeological Data

The Sensitivity of Spatial Analytical Methods to Postdepositional Disturbance

SUSAN A. GREGG, KEITH W. KINTIGH,
AND ROBERT WHALLON

1. INTRODUCTION

In this chapter we examine the extent to which archaeological techniques of spatial analysis produce satisfactory results when applied to an ethnographically recorded hunter–gatherer site, and we explore the degree to which useful results can be obtained after simulated disturbance of the site. We believe we have gained some insights into methods of spatial analysis and clarified our understanding of their strengths and limitations through this study. John Yellen's (1977) ethnoarchaeological study of !Kung sites in Botswana was selected to provide the basis

SUSAN A. GREGG • Center for Archaeological Investigations, Southern Illinois University, Carbondale, Illinois 62901.   KEITH W. KINTIGH • Department of Anthropology, Arizona State University, Tempe, Arizona 85287.   ROBERT WHALLON • Museum of Anthropology, University of Michigan, Ann Arbor, Michigan 48109.

for this investigation. Yellen's data were selected because we were curious to test the validity of our quantitative methods of spatial analysis with ethnoarchaeological data. His study provided a data set comparable to those from open-air sites of mobile hunter–gatherers on which such methods most commonly are applied archaeologically.

This chapter is a portion of a larger study in which we analyzed a series of Yellen's camps (see acknowledgments). Here we present a synopsis of three components of our inquiry using his Camp 14. First is a quantitative spatial analysis of the material distributions recorded for Camp 14. Second, we simulate the transformation of this ethnographic camp into three "archaeological sites." Third, we analyze each simulated archaeological site using the same techniques we had used for analyzing the undisturbed ethnographic data, and we compare the results with those of the original analysis.

2. ANALYSIS OF THE ETHNOGRAPHICALLY RECORDED CAMP

2.1. The Ethnographic Context

The data collected by Yellen provide a productive context in which to test the utility of quantitative methods of spatial analysis. His ethnographic observations of the camps include the number of inhabitants, the social relationships among the members of the different households, the length of occupation, and the locations and types of activities that took place. Because the camps were recorded only a short time after abandonment, Yellen's maps show the locations of the materials and features left by the inhabitants.

These maps clearly illustrate aspects of hunter–gatherer open-air sites that are easily overlooked by archaeologists. First, the distribution of remains over each of the camps is diffuse. Dense concentrations of cultural remains simply did not accumulate during the relatively brief period that each camp was occupied. Second, as Yellen points out, individuals cared for prized tools; they were rarely discarded (Yellen 1977:88). Material remains of the ethnographic occupation consisted, at the time of abandonment, of a scatter of organic materials as well as hearths, postholes, and expedient tools such as nut-cracking stones. Of course, under normal conditions, most of the floral debris would decompose quickly, so at best archaeologists would find features, postholes, charred floral remains, and faunal materials—but few formal tools. Sites with materials like these appear to comprise the bulk of open-air hunter–gatherer sites in prehistory. Thus Yellen's data provide a good opportunity to test the validity and robusticity of spatial analytical methods on the kind of hunter–gatherer sites we are most likely to encounter archaeologically.

Yellen developed an interpretive model in which he divided the ethnographic camps into a series of nested rings (Figure 1). The extreme extent of cultural remains at the camp defined the outer ring, the *absolute limit of scatter*. The inner ring, or *limit of nuclear area total*, was defined by what he called a "hut circle"— the hearths and their associated huts. Within this inner ring, the nuclear area

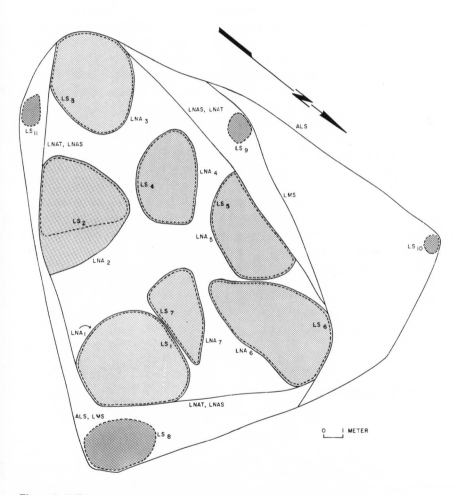

Figure 1. Yellen's model of !Kung camp organization applied to Camp 14 (redrawn from Yellen 1977).

used by a social unit, the *limit of scatter: nuclear area* was defined by the presence of a hearth and a scatter of debris. Yellen's model lends itself nicely to comparison with the results of a quantitative spatial analysis. If his model holds, our expectations are (1) nuclear areas should be identifiable by discrete clustering of materials, and (2) similar patterns of domestic activities should be identifiable within each nuclear area.

2.2. Alternative Approaches to Spatial Analysis

In conducting analyses of spatial distributions, archaeologists must consider two fundamental problems. First, the nature of the spatial structure at a site must be defined and described. Is material clustered throughout, or is it evenly distributed over the site—and what criteria have been used to identify the site structure? Second, the presence or absence of clustering must be interpreted. In particular, the degree to which clustering is due to natural agencies—including a host of taphonomic, chemical, biological, and physical factors—must be established, and the behavioral activities of the human inhabitants must be evaluated.

The problem of identifying spatial structure can be approached from two related perspectives, which we have called a pure locational approach and an assemblage composition approach. The pure locational approach first identifies the spatial structure at the site by evaluating the physical distribution of structures and material remains. Then, if clustering is present, discrete clusters are defined. Finally, the contents of each cluster are examined as a basis for interpreting the cluster's significance. The assemblage composition approach considers the problem from a slightly different perspective. This approach calls for determining whether clearly definable differences in assemblage composition exist. If so, sets of similar material remains are located and plotted. The composition and distribution of these assemblages provide the basis for the interpretation.

The two approaches are concerned with interrelated but different problems in defining and describing site structure. In essence, each approach analytically takes most into account what the other ignores. They therefore provide different, but complementary, results that mutually corroborate one another. The application of these approaches, however, does not provide an interpretation. This must be derived from multiple lines of evidence that, when they show concordance, give us confidence in our ideas.

The analyses presented here are aimed at determining whether Yellen's ring model—which he based on ethnographic observations as well as on his maps—can be replicated using objective, quantitative approaches. Yellen identified seven social groups at Camp 14, each with a hut and a hearth, as well as the anthropologist's campsite. In addition to these social units, an isolated hearth lies to the northwest of the huts, and activities took place in the shade of a tree to the northeast. Because the camp was mapped shortly after abandonment, it is assumed here that major postdepositional disturbances of the material remains did not occur. As discussed, if the ring model holds, the spatial analysis should reveal seven discrete clusterings indicating the social units, and each should have evidence of similar activity patterns.

2.3. Pure Locational Analysis

For the pure locational approach we used the method proposed by Kintigh and Ammerman (1982), which involves the use of k-means, nonhierarchical clustering. In contrast to some more common hierarchical clustering techniques, such as average linkage clustering, k-means analysis is driven by the global criterion of minimizing the within-cluster variation (which simultaneously maximizes the variation among clusters). The sum-squared-error (SSE) statistic is the measure of within-cluster variation that the analysis attempts to minimize, and this statistic is used in interpreting the k-means results. As the number of clusters increases, it is a mathematical necessity that within-cluster variation (SSE) decrease. As with any clustering routine, there is always a question of what defines a "significant" cluster that warrants further investigation. We used two methods for identifying the significant clustering levels, and both entailed using the SSE statistic. The easiest method is to plot the $\log_{10}$ %SSE against the clustering stage and to examine the resulting curve for negative inflection points. These points tend to indicate stages that produce more "economical" clustering, and these clusters should be further examined.

An independent method, which we also used, entails comparing the difference between the $\log_{10}$ %SSE statistic from the input data and the $\log_{10}$ %SSE statistics from the analysis of randomized versions of the input data. The plots of the $\log_{10}$ %SSE from both the normal run and the random runs are plotted against clustering stage. If the normal data plots within the range of the randomized data, then no significant clustering is indicated. Conversely, significant clustering is indicated where there is strong divergence between the real input and the random data. In conducting the k-means clustering, we specified that two random runs be completed. We then calculated the average $\log_{10}$ %SSE statistic for the two random runs and plotted the difference between this and the $\log_{10}$ %SSE statistic for the input data by clustering step. Peaks in the graph indicate clusters of the input data that diverge from the random data. The visual inspection of both the $\log_{10}$ %SSE plotted against clustering step and the difference between the average random clustering and the original data mutually reinforce one another.

To perform a pure locational analysis, the X and Y coordinates of all artifacts and features (excluding the separate scatter associated with Yellen's tent) were recorded from the map of the camp (Figure 2). (In terms of true compass orientation, these represent southwest–northeast [X] and southeast–northwest

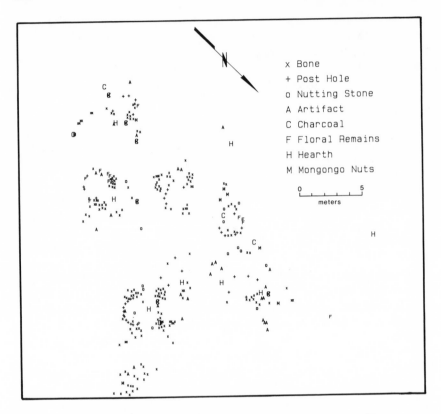

Figure 2. The distribution of materials recorded by Yellen at Camp 14.

[Y] directions.) The coordinates then were clustered using a k-means program written by Kintigh and Ammerman (1982). The plot of $\log_{10}$ %SSE against cluster step first shows a divergence from the random runs at Step 3, and thereafter the curve flows smoothly until Step 7, where it begins to flatten (Figure 3). A plot of the difference between the average random clustering and the original data (Figure 4) also shows that significant clustering occurs at Clusters 3 and 7. The assignment of each point in the three- and seven-cluster solutions is shown in Figures 5 and 6, respectively.

The three-cluster solution divides the site distinctly into Cluster 1 in the south, Cluster 3 to the west, and Cluster 2 to the north. Table 1 shows the material composition of each cluster. Faunal remains predominate in each cluster, followed by postholes. All other material classes are represented in relatively low proportions in Cluster 1, and similarly, all classes except floral debris occur in relatively low proportions in Cluster 2. Cluster 3 differs slightly in its relatively

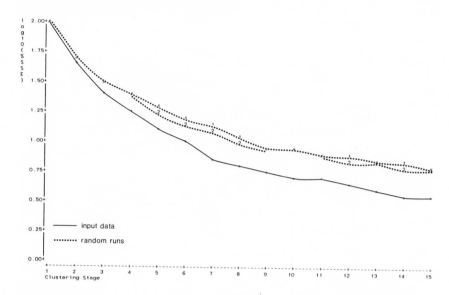

Figure 3. Plot of $\log_{10}$ %SSE for k-means clustering of Camp 14—Yellen's data; comparing runs of input and randomized data.

high percentage of nutting stones and logs. Virtually all artifact classes are present in every cluster, so at the grossest level, three basic living groups can be identified. How, then, does the seven-cluster solution differ from the three-cluster solution?

The frequencies of the various material classes represented in each cluster (Table 2) show that for Clusters 1–3, 5, and 7, faunal remains are the dominant material class, followed once again by postholes. As before, the remaining material classes occur in relatively small proportions, with the exception of mongongo nuts in Clusters 5 and 7, charcoal scatters in Cluster 5, and nutting stones and logs in Cluster 7. Either a hearth or a charcoal scatter (or both) are present in each of the aforementioned clusters. In conformity with Yellen's nuclear area construct, the content of the clusters suggests that similar activities occurred in every cluster. Cluster 6 stands out because faunal remains are overwhelmingly dominant in the assemblage, and neither charcoal scatters nor hearths are present. It would thus appear that a different range of activities occurred in Cluster 6. Because the cluster is located on the periphery of the site and is dominated by faunal remains, Cluster 6 seems to represent either a special activity area or a dump, whereas each of the remaining clusters represents the nucleus of a common suite of domestic activities.

Visually, the results of the seven-cluster solution (Figure 6) conform remarkably well with Yellen's behaviorally based interpretation; six of the clusters

Table 1. Camp 14: Counts and Percentages of Material Classes for Three-Cluster K-Means Solution

Cluster	1	2	3
N^a	136	117	72
Bones	91	81	27
%	66.9	69.2	37.5
Mongongo nuts	6	3	6
%	4.4	2.6	8.3
Nutting stones	3	4	8
%	2.2	3.4	11.1
Logs	7	4	11
%	5.1	3.4	15.3
Charcoal	6	2	3
%	4.4	1.7	4.2
Hearths	3	2	3
%	2.2	1.7	4.2
Postholes	14	18	12
%	10.3	15.4	16.7
Artifacts	3	3	1
%	2.2	2.6	1.4
Floral	3	0	1
%	2.2		1.4

[a] Number of items in cluster.

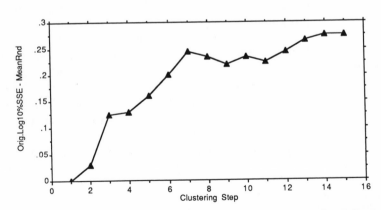

Figure 4. Plot of the difference between $\log_{10}$ %SSE and the mean $\log_{10}$ %SSE for random runs of Camp 14—Yellen's data.

Table 2. Camp 14: Counts and Percentages of Material Classes for Seven-Cluster K-Means Solution

Cluster	1	2	3	4	5	6	7
N^a	51	92	46	35	39	25	37
Bones	34	59	37	13	20	22	14
%	66.7	64.1	80.4	37.1	51.3	88.0	37.8
Mongongo nuts	1	2	0	2	5	1	4
%	2.0	2.2		5.7	12. 8	4.0	10.8
Nutting stones	3	4	0	2	0	0	6
%	5.9	4.3		5.7			16.2
Logs	2	4	3	7	2	0	4
%	3.9	4.3	6.5	20.0	5.1		10.8
Charcoal	1	2	0	1	5	0	2
%	2.0	2.2		2.9	12.8		5.4
Hearths	1	2	1	3	1	0	0
%	2.0	2.2	2.2	8.6	2.6		
Postholes	4	18	5	5	5	0	7
%	7.8	19.6	10.9	14.3	12.8		18.9
Artifacts	2	1	0	1	1	2	0
%	3.9	1.1		2.9	2.6	8.0	
Floral	3	0	0	1	0	0	0
%	5.9			2.9			

[a]Number of items in cluster.

correspond closely with household areas identified by Yellen (Figure 1). The only significant difference is that our Cluster 2 combines Yellen's Hut 1 and Hut 7, the households of two brothers, one of whom is not married. But as Yellen noted, the unmarried man spent so much of his time at his brother's hearth that he probably should not be considered to represent a separate social unit. Thus the locational analysis may actually mirror the reality of the situation. The locational analysis also identified, as a separate cluster, a concentration of material remains northeast of the hut area. The pure locational analysis at the seven-cluster solution confirms one level of Yellen's ring model, although, with the exception of the concentration of faunal debris, it does not highlight patterning of spatially distinct activities. This may be derived through an analysis emphasizing assemblage composition.

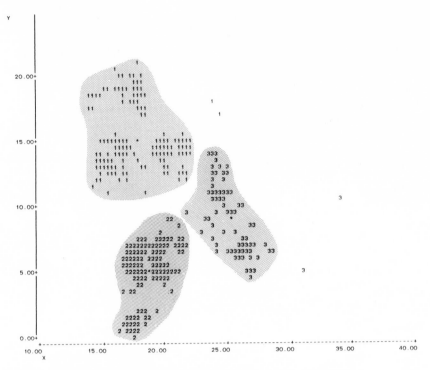

Figure 5. Distribution of three k-means clusters, Camp 14—Yellen's data.

2.4. Assemblage Composition Analysis of Camp 14

The same data from Yellen's Camp 14 were analyzed for significant spatial variation and patterning in assemblage composition using the "unconstrained clustering" approach proposed by Whallon (1984). This approach begins with the calculation of smoothed density contours for each artifact class over the area under analysis.

As pointed out in the original article on unconstrained clustering, the approach is quite sensitive to the spatial scale at which the smoothing and calculation of density contours is carried out, but the critical importance of smoothing was not made adequately clear in the original article. If spatial data are not smoothed, they tend to reflect, often rather strongly, small-scale irregularities that usually are introduced by the standard use of a grid or series of templates to define densities over the area under analysis. Smoothing, that is, using a *moving* template, eliminates the small-scale vagaries and provides a more general and interpretable picture of density variation over a site. However, caution is needed

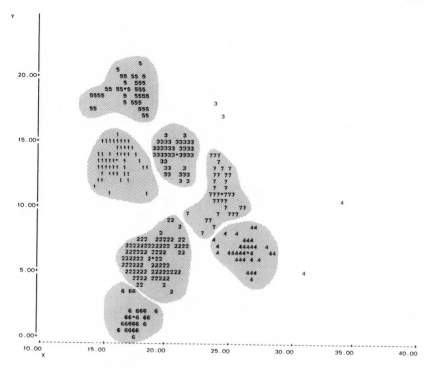

Figure 6. Distribution of seven k-means clusters, Camp 14—Yellen's data.

in selecting template size because a large-scale template may smooth the data excessively. This results in a picture of relatively bland uniformity of material distribution that obliterates the very patterns that might be attributable to the various formation processes—in particular, any cultural/behavioral formation processes—that created the site under investigation. As a general rule of thumb, it seems reasonable to smooth the data initially at a relatively small scale, not much more than is necessary to eliminate excessively frequent, sharp changes in density, which lead to a highly irregular or "choppy" picture of density distribution. Any final choice of the degree to which spatial data are smoothed for analysis will be based, of course, not only on the nature of the data itself but also very much on the questions and interpretive framework in the mind of the analyst.

For Camp 14, after some experimentation, the spatial data were smoothed using a 1-m moving template (i.e., a circular template with a 1-m radius and displacement). At each move, densities for all classes of materials within the circle were determined and assigned to its center point. Smoothing thus occurs through the overlapping of templates in adjacent positions. Densities for all material classes then were calculated at each item location by interpolation from the smoothed densities.

Following the unconstrained clustering approach, the absolute densities of all material classes were summed at each point and then divided by this sum to create "relative" or proportional densities. These relative densities comprised the data for clustering the item points in terms of the similarities and differences in the density composition of the material assemblages in their near vicinities. Unconstrained clustering disregards completely the physical locations of the points at this step. Because the single material class of bones overwhelmingly outnumbered all others at the camp (comprising over 60% of all items), we decided to standardize the relative densities of each material class in order to weight them all equally in the cluster analysis and to prevent bone densities from dominating the results. Clustering was done using Ward's method (minimization of within-group variance).

The plot of the clustering criterion (sum of squared errors) as groups of item points are formed on the basis of the similarities in standardized relative densities show a single sharp and clear inflection at eight clusters (Figure 7), which is the solution examined here. The assemblage composition of each defined cluster is best expressed by the means and standard deviations of the relative densities of all material classes over the item points included in each cluster (Table 3). A material class was considered significant in the characterization of a cluster if its mean relative density was greater than its standard deviation. Within the group of significant material classes, particular attention was then paid to those whose mean relative densities were greater than 10%. Evaluated in this manner, the clusters defined by the analysis can be characterized as follows:

> *Cluster 1* is by far the largest, containing over two-thirds of all the data points in the analysis. In composition, it represents an assemblage made up largely of bones (an average of over 75% relative density), with only a small, insignificant smattering of other material classes. This corresponds well with the dominance of bones in the materials scattered over the camp, which manifests itself in this cluster in spite of the standardization of the variables in the cluster analysis to avoid an undue influence of the bones in defining assemblage composition clusters. Clearly, a bone-dominated assemblage is characteristic of much of the camp. It is worth noting that every other material class is represented to some extent in this cluster, although their means are invariably low and in every case the standard deviations are greater than the means, indicating extreme variability of occurrence.
>
> This is true also of *Cluster 3*. The major difference between Cluster 3 and Cluster 1 is that postholes are very common in Cluster 3, reaching their highest relative density (a mean of *ca.* 44%) in this cluster. Mean relative bone density is reduced accordingly, and most other material classes occur in trace frequencies only. However, nutting stones occur consistently, as

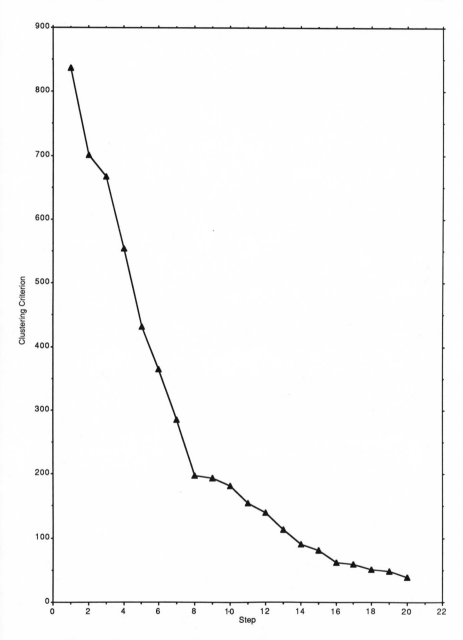

Figure 7. Plot of clustering criterion for unconstrained clustering of Camp 14.

Table 3.   Camp 14: Means and Standard Deviations of Relative Densities by Unconstrained Cluster

Cluster	1	2	3	4	5	6	7	8
N^a	219	1	48	15	6	25	9	2
Bones	76.5 ±14.3	0	46.9 ±11.2	42.4 ±13.6	23.1 ±15.7	35.8 ±12.4	2.0 ±5.6	0
Mongongo nuts	3.1 ±4.6	0	.3 ±1.1	7.5 ±7.1	1.9 ±2.5	28.3 ±12.4	.3 ±0.9	0
Nutting stones	2.0 ±3.5	0	4.5 ±4.1	26.3 ±20.9	11.1 ±15.7	2.7 ±5.0	4.8 ±4.3	0
Logs	4.6 ±6.9	0	.8 ±3.9	1.6 ±6.0	4.9 ±8.1	7.9 ±11.0	86.8 ±12.9	15.2 ±21.4
Charcoal	2.1 ±3.3	0	.5 ±1.1	6.6 ±3.7	.5 ±1.3	19.9 ±15.8	.2 ±0.5	0
Hearths	2.4 ±4.2	0	.5 ±0.9	0	.1 ±0.3	1.2 ±2.9	4.6 ±6.8	84.8 ±21.4
Postholes	6.7 ±8.0	0	44.2 ±7.7	15.6 ±7.8	23.0 ±9.0	4.0 ±9.9	1.4 ±3.0	0
Artifacts	1.4 ±4.0	0	1.9 ±2.4	0	33.2 ±10.8	.3 ±0.6	0	0
Floral	1.0 ±2.9	100	.3 ±1.6	0	2.1 ±2.6	0	0	0

^{a}Number of items in cluster.

indicated by a standard deviation even lower than their low mean relative density.

Cluster 4 is similar in contents if not in precise proportions. It has high densities of bones, nutting stones, and postholes, in that order.

Cluster 5 also is characterized by relatively high densities of bones and postholes but adds a strong component of "artifacts" (tools).

Cluster 6 shows high relative densities of bones, mongongo nuts, and charcoal. Postholes are not represented in significant densities.

Cluster 2 represents a single, isolated fragment of floral debris (a water root in this case); *Cluster 8* consists only of two isolated hearths; and *Cluster 7* is made up of groups of logs, relatively separated from other material debris.

Inspection of the composition of these clusters along with their spatial distributions plotted over Camp 14 (Figure 8) suggests a relatively clear interpretation in standard archaeological and behavioral terms, which can be compared to ethnographic reality as recorded by Yellen. Thus one might identify Clusters 1, 3, 4, 5, and 6 as constellations of debris left from various "domestic" activities, deposited either *in situ* or as a result of sweeping, cleaning, and/or dumping. The differences among these clusters and their spatial distributions lead to a more detailed reconstruction. Cluster 1 could represent "core" domestic debris given its comparative frequency of occurrence, its wide and almost ubiquitous distribution over the site, and its composition. Proportionately, the largest component of this debris is bones, whose distribution thus constitutes the "core," but within and beside which examples of all other classes of material at this camp are found in comparatively small and highly variable numbers. Cluster 3 effectively represents the same thing, but in a position adjacent to structures, either as a result of activities in or beside them or by virtue of being swept up or dumped against their edges. Cluster 5 again consists of general debris, also in close association with structures, but with the added "specialization" of high densities of "tools" and nutting stones. It is worth noting that only these three clusters—1, 3, and 5—represent areas in which assemblage composition comprises all material classes recorded at the camp. Clusters 4 and 6 are somewhat more specialized, with 4 exhibiting high densities of nutting stones and propinquity to

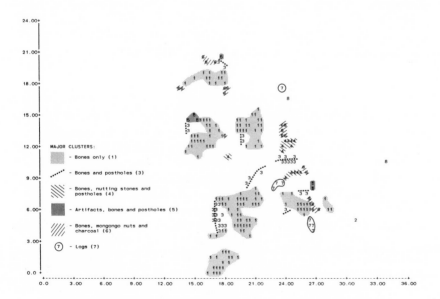

Figure 8. Distribution of eight unconstrained clusters, Camp 14—Yellen's data.

structures (with no associated "tools"), whereas 6 shows a concentration of mongongo nuts and charcoal. The remaining clusters must be interpreted as activity-specific or as isolated events.

These interpretations translate into a picture of camp organization that identifies seven structures (referring to the Y axis, one lies between 17 and 21 meters; three are between 10 and 15 meters; and three are between 3 and 9 meters) with associated materials, most of which are dominated by bones (Figure 8). Each separate indication of a structure generally seems to be linked to its own scatter of debris. These effectively are the "pure locational" clusters defined by the k-means analysis, which is why a direct comparison shows that the clusters defined by the one are subdivided extensively and spread right across the clusters defined by the other, and vice versa (Table 4). The one exception to this, noted before, is the dwelling of the one unmarried man in the group, who appears to share a central area of activities and deposition of debris with the adjacent dwelling of his married brother. An eighth, separate group of item locations, belonging only to Cluster 1, can be seen on the bottom of the map. Its position and composition would seem to argue that it represents simply a small bone dump here.

The more "specialized" clusters (Clusters 4, 6, and to some extent 5), however, are not ubiquitous, and are, in fact, noticeably differentially distributed among the "structural concentrations" seen on the map of the unconstrained clusters. In particular, the distribution of Clusters 4 and 6 and the contrasting distribution of Cluster 1 (and to a lesser extent Clusters 3 and 5) seem to indicate a general organization of the site into two general areas: (1) several "central" concentrations with little or no indication of important processing or consumption of mongongo nuts in comparison to the evidence for consumption of game and (2) an "arc," above and to the right of the "central" area, with evidence for greater use of nuts compared to game. The latter pattern reaches its strongest manifestation in one concentration on the middle right side of the camp that shows no Cluster 1 assemblage (dominated by bone) at all, consisting instead of Clusters 4 and 6 as well as 3. Cluster 4 is highly localized, virtually restricted to this particular concentration, and one normally would interpret its high proportion of nutting stones as indicative of mongongo nut processing, an apparently plausible interpretation, judging from ethnographic observations.

Interestingly, at Camp 14, nutting stones (which, in the context of a Bushman camp, typically are thought of as functionally linked directly to the cracking of mongongo nuts) are consistently and strongly disassociated from mongongo nuts remains themselves. This can be seen in a comparison of the content of Clusters 4 (to a lesser extent 5 as well) and 6 in this analysis, and it holds true at other spatial scales and in the k-means analysis as well. A plausible interpretation eludes us for the spatial segregation of the probable processing equipment and the mongongo nut shell debris supposedly resulting from such processing at this camp.

Table 4. Comparison of K-Means and Unconstrained Clustering of Camp 14

		(1)	(2)	(3)	(4)	(5)	(6)	(7)
					K-means clusters			
Unconstrained		(1)	(2)	(3)	(4)	(5)	(6)	(7)
clusters, $N = 325$		51	92	46	35	39	25	37
Row%		15.7	28.3	14.2	10.8	12.0	7.7	11.4
Column%								
(1)	219	43	66	41	19	25	25	0
Row%		19.6	30.1	18.7	8.7	11.4	11.4	
Column%		67.4	84.3	71.7	89.1	54.3	64.1	100.0
(2)	1	0	0	0	1	0	0	0
Row%					100.0			
Column%	3				2.9			
(3)	48	2	26	3	3	2	0	12
Row%		4.2	54.2	6.3	6.3	4.2		25.0
Column%	14.8	3.9	28.3	6.5	8.6	5.1		32.4
(4)	15	1	0	0	0	0	0	14
Row%		6.7						93.3
Column%	4.6	2.0						37.8
(5)	6	3	0	0	2	1	0	0
Row%		50.0			33.3	16.7		
Column%	1.8	5.9			5.7	2.6		
(6)	25	2	0	0	5	11	0	7
Row%		8.0			20.0	44.0		28.0
Column%	7.7	3.9			14.3	28.2		18.9
(7)	9	0	0	1	4	0	0	4
Row%				11.1	44.4			44.4
Column%	2.8			2.2	11.4			10.8
(8)	2	0	0	1	1	0	0	0
Row%				50.0	50.0			
Column%	.6			2.2	2.9			

Nonetheless, in broad strokes, we reach the same conclusions, interpretations, and reconstruction of the ethnographic camp, treated as if it were an archaeological site, from both a pure locational (k-means) and an assemblage composition (unconstrained clustering) approach. The results from the two techniques mutually reinforce and corroborate each other. This not only gives us increased confidence in both methods and in their results but suggests strongly to us that they are not competing or alternative approaches but rather are best seen and used together as complementary methods for spatial analysis.

3. ANALYSIS OF THE "ARCHAEOLOGICAL SITES"

3.1. Simulation of Archaeological Site Formation

We have shown that quantitative methods of spatial analysis can be used productively on the comparatively low density distributions recorded ethnographically. But to what degree could these results have been obtained from archaeological data? To explore this question, we simulated the process of archaeological site formation for the Camp 14 distributions three separate times, varying the degrees of disturbance each time. Each simulation involved "destroying" a substantial fraction of the floral and faunal remains and randomly moving the remaining artifacts. The first simulated site has a low degree of random artifact movement; in the second, artifacts were moved to a moderate degree; movement in the third was relatively extreme.

Item destruction was governed by a number of factors (Table 5). Each class of materials was assigned an overall probability of surviving in the archaeological record. The probability of a bone's survival was further affected by factors relating to the species, the anatomical part, and the condition of the bone. For example, let us look at the probability of survival of an unbroken gemsbok femur. As a class, bones were accorded a probability of survival of 0.6. The gemsbok (this is a relatively large animal) has a species factor of 0.8 (as compared to a guinea fowl with a species factor of 0.2). A femur has a part factor of 0.8, and because the bone is whole it has a condition factor of 1.0. The simulated probability of survival of that bone is $0.6 \times 0.8 \times 0.8 \times 1.0 = 0.38$.

The original site has 325 artifacts and features, and each was subjected to the item destruction every time the simulation was run. A total of 84 items survived the first run, 94 survived the second run, and 75 survived the third. The artifact and feature compositions for the original and the three "decomposed" camps are given in Table 6. Bones and postholes comprise the two largest material classes in the original data; all other materials are present in relatively low frequencies. The simulated decomposition changes the relationship between material classes.

Table 5. **Abbreviated List of Decomposition Simulation Survival Probabilities, Survival Factors, and Random Walk Factors**

Material	Survival probability	Walk factor	Element survival factors	
Bone	0.60	1.00	Cl: Clavicle	0.50
Mongongo nuts	0.80	1.00	Ca: Carapace	1.00
Hammer stone	1.00	0.80	Cr: Cranium	0.90
Water root	0.10	1.00	F: Femur	0.80
Monkey orange	0.10	1.00	Fi: Fibula	0.60
Spiny melon	0.10	1.00	H: Humerus	0.80
Log	0.10	1.00	Ho: Horn	0.50
Tin can	0.50	1.00	Ri: Rib	0.50
Hut post mold	0.20	0.00	St: Sternum	0.20
Charcoal	0.80	1.00	Te: Tooth	1.00
Raised hearth	0.80	0.00	Ti: Tibia	0.90
Depressed hearth	0.90	0.00	V: Vertebra	0.50
Digging stick	0.10	1.00		
Artifact	0.50	1.00		

Species survival factors		Condition survival factors	
Aw: Aardwolf	0.50	C: Complete	1.00
Dk: Duiker	0.50	Fr: Fragmentary	0.50
Gb: Gemsbok	0.80		
Gf: Guinea fowl	0.20		
Gi: Giraffe	1.00		
Li: Lizard	0.10		
Pc: Porcupine	0.50		
Sp: Springhare	0.50		
To: Tortoise	0.60		

The proportion of bones in the simulated camps drops to roughly 30% and that of postholes falls to between 7% and 10%. Conversely, the proportions of nutting stones, charcoal scatters, and hearths show increases because of the loss of organic materials and the obliteration of features. Furthermore, because some of the botanical materials might have been charred, the proportion of botanical remains also increases in assemblages of the decomposed camps. The loss of organic materials and the obliteration of features has resulted in all three cases in an assemblage composition that is quite dissimilar from the original data.

Table 6.   **Camp 14—Global Counts and Percentages of Material Classes in the Original Data and for All Degrees of Simulated Decomposition**

Artifact class	Original data	Degree of disturbance		
		Minimum	Moderate	Maximum
Bones	199	27	36	21
	61.2%	32.1%	38.3%	28.0%
Mongongo nuts	15	7	13	10
	4.6%	8.3%	13.8%	13.3%
Nutting stones	5	15	15	15
	4.6%	17.9%	16.0%	20.0%
Logs	22	6	1	3
	6.8%	7.1%	1.1%	4.0%
Charcoal scatters	11	11	11	8
	3.4%	13.1%	1.7%	10.7%
Hearths	8	7	7	7
	2.5%	8.3%	7.4%	9.3%
Postholes	44	7	7	8
	13.5%	8.3%	7.4%	10.7%
Artifacts	7	2	3	2
	2.2%	2.4%	3.2%	2.7%
Miscellaneous floral	4	2	1	1
	1.2%	2.4%	1.1%	1.3%
Total	325	84	94	75

The loss of major portions of analytical classes presents a significant obstacle for archaeologists to surmount in their interpretations; however, it is compounded by the postdepositional disturbance of materials at the site. To simulate this disturbance, each surviving item was individually subjected to physical disturbance, which was simulated by a "random walk." The movement of an artifact was determined by the maximum length of a walk step, the number of steps, a material-dependent walk factor, and by the slope. The walk factor was a measure of the degree to which a specific material might move. It ranges from 0 (no movement—for postholes) to 1 (for most organic remains). The direction of the walk step is chosen at random. The distance of a given walk step is the product of a randomly generated number from 0 to 1, the maximum step length, and the

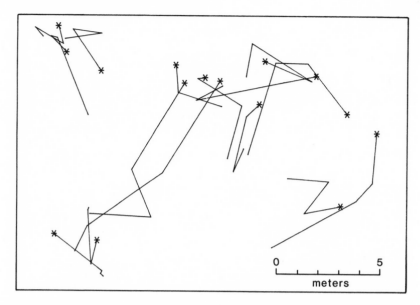

Figure 9. Displacement of nutting stones by random walk at the level of maximum disturbance.

item's material walk factor. In addition, a simulated slope has the effect of lengthening movement if the direction is downslope and shortening movement if the direction is upslope. The effect of extreme disturbance on one class of artifacts, nut-cracking stones, which have a walk factor of 0.8, is shown in Figure 9. Materials with a higher walk factor move further than the nutting stones, whereas those with a lower walk factor move a correspondingly shorter distance.

The parameters controlling step length and number of steps were varied for each run (Table 7). As Figures 10a–d show, the spatial patterning of the original

Table 7. Parameters Characterizing Simulated Decompositions of Camp 14

Camp decomposition	Program parameters			Program results	
	Slope (%)	Random walks	Maximum step length (cm)	Average move (cm)	Number of objects
14a Minimum	5	3	50	35	84
14b Moderate	20	3	100	71	94
14c Extreme	50	3	400	282	75

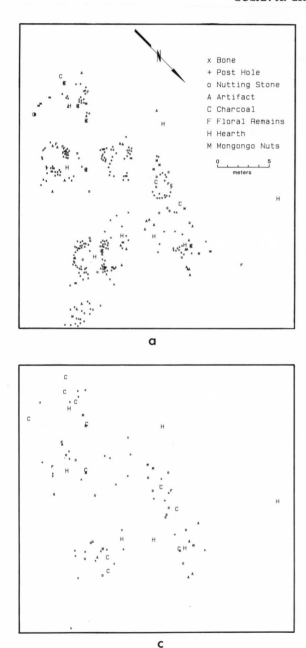

Figure 10. The distributions of original and "decomposed" data for Camp 14: a—original distribution; b—minimum decomposition; c—moderate decomposition; d—maximum decomposition.

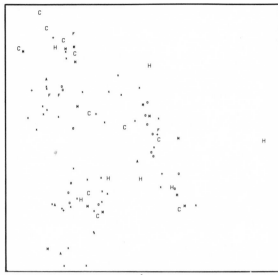

b

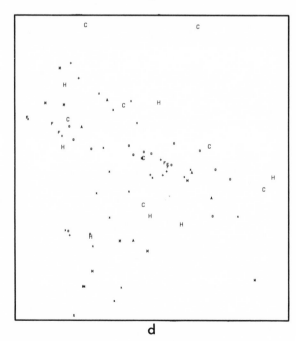

d

data (Figure 10a) becomes blurred as the degree of disturbance increases (Figures 10b–d). Some of the original patterning is visible in the minimum and moderate levels of disturbance, but virtually all patterning is lost to the eye at the extreme level. To what degree would the results of locational and compositional analyses of the disturbed data (particularly the maximum level) conform to the results obtained with the original data?

3.2. Pure Locational Analysis of the Simulated Sites

K-means clustering of the artifact and feature coordinates was performed for each simulated camp just as it had been for the original camp. The plots of the $\log_{10}$ %SSE and the differences between the input data and the average of randomized data clustering were also plotted. The three simulated camps are discussed in turn.

3.2.1. Minimum Disturbance (Figure 10b)

The plot of the $\log_{10}$ %SSE (Figure 11) shows a rather steep drop from the two- to the three-cluster solutions, but the four- and five-cluster levels differ little from the randomized data. The drop from the fifth to the sixth step is fairly steep. The curve flattens at the seventh step and makes another relatively steep drop to

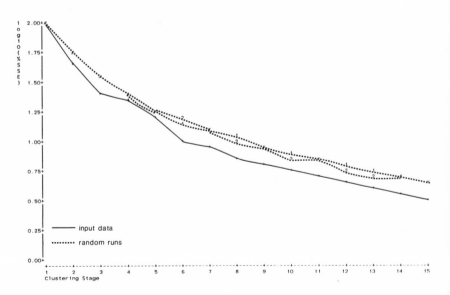

Figure 11. Plot of $\log_{10}$ %SSE for k-means clustering of Camp 14—minimum "decomposition," comparing runs of input and randomized data.

the eighth step. Thereafter the plot is a straight line. The $\log_{10}$ %SSE graph suggests that Clusters 3 and 6, 7, or 8 are potentially interesting. A plot of the difference between the average $\log_{10}$ %SSE of the random runs and the input data against clustering step (Figure 12) confirms that Cluster 3 warrants further inspection, and it vividly shows that Cluster 8 is of interest. A plot of the cluster assignments for the three-cluster solution (Figure 13) shows the same three clusters that were obtained with the original Camp 14 data. The composition of each cluster (Table 8) is dominated by bones. Nutting stones and mongongo nuts are the other primary components of each cluster, and both hearths and charcoal scatters are present in each. The three clusters appear to reflect a similar set of processes and/or activities, which would probably be interpreted as representing three basic residential areas containing multiple family units.

The map of the eight-cluster solution (Figure 14) is not simply a subdivision of the clusters defined at the third level. Instead, it represents a division of some clusters and the recombination of others. First, an isolated feature to the west of the site was split off to form its own cluster (Cluster 4). Second, portions of Clusters 1 and 3 were combined to form Cluster 8. Finally, parts of Clusters 3 and 2 were split off to form new clusters. The table of cluster compositions (Table 9) shows that bones dominate Clusters 1, 2, 6, 7, and 8, and either hearths or charcoal scatters are found in all but Cluster 6. Mongongo nuts occur in Clusters 1–3, 5, 7, and 8. Nutting stones occurs in Clusters 1, 2, and 5. Clusters 1–3, 5, 7, and 8 appear to represent a wide range of activities that archaeologists normally would interpret at representing individual living areas. Clusters 4 and 6, however, have strikingly different artifact assemblages. Cluster 6 consists exclusively of

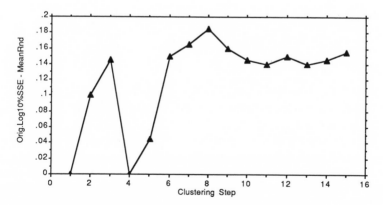

Figure 12. Plot of the difference between $\log_{10}$ %SSE and the mean $\log_{10}$ %SSE for random runs, Camp 14—minimum "decomposition."

Table 8. Camp 14—Minimum "Decomposition":
Counts and Percentages of Material Classes for Three-
Cluster K-Means Solution

Cluster	1	2	3
N^a	36	20	28
Bones	14	9	4
%	38.9	45.0	14.3
Mongongo nuts	3	1	3
%	8.3	5.0	10.7
Nutting stones	4	5	6
%	11.1	25.0	21.4
Logs	2	1	3
%	5.6	5.0	10.7
Charcoal	7	2	2
%	19.4	10.0	7.1
Hearths	1	1	5
%	2.8	5.0	17.9
Postholes	3	1	3
%	8.3	5.0	10.7
Artifacts	1	0	1
%	2.8		3.6
Floral	1	0	1
%	2.8		3.6

[a]Number of items in cluster.

bone, which suggests that it represents either a special activity area, such as a butchering area, or a garbage dump. Cluster 4 is an isolated hearth.

The eight-cluster solution provides a more refined picture of the spatial structuring at the site than was obtained by the three-cluster solution. Clearly, the site is comprised of three fundamental units that can be subdivided and recombined into what might be interpreted as six household groups and two special activity areas. The results obtained from the k-means analysis of the minimally disturbed camp conform surprisingly well with the original data.

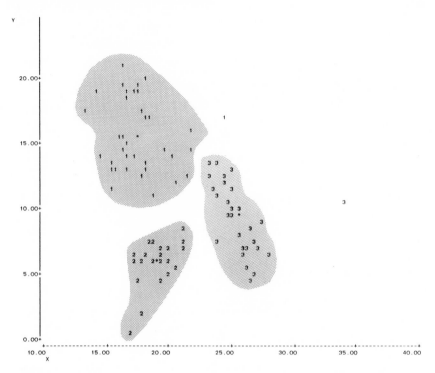

Figure 13. Distribution of three k-means clusters, Camp 14—minimum "decomposition."

3.2.2. Moderate Disturbance (Figure 10c)

The $\log_{10}$ %SSE plot (Figure 15) shows that at the one- and two-cluster levels, there is virtually no difference between the input and the randomized data. Differences, however, do exist from the three-cluster solution onwards. Once again, there is a rather steep drop from the six-to the seven-cluster solution; the curve flattens slightly at the eight-cluster solution and drops relatively steeply to the nine-cluster level. Thereafter the plot forms a straight line until an inflection occurs at the 14-cluster solution. The site has 94 artifacts and features, so each of the clusters in this solution could be expected to contain only six or seven items. Even though the negative inflection at that level on the $\log_{10}$ %SSE plot indicates significant improvement in clustering, common sense eliminates the 14-cluster solution from further consideration. The plot of the difference between average random clustering and the input date (Figure 16) shows a plateau at the 3- and 4-cluster levels and peaks at the 8- and 10-cluster levels. Once again the 3- and 8-cluster solutions appear to warrant further examination.

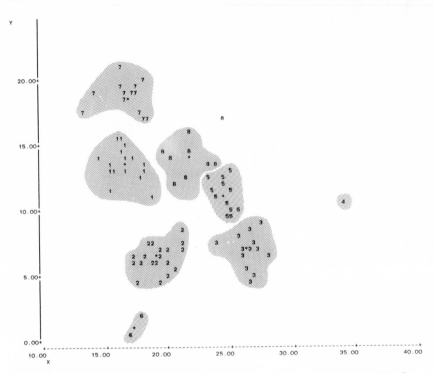

Figure 14. Distribution of eight k-means clusters, Camp 14—minimum "decomposition."

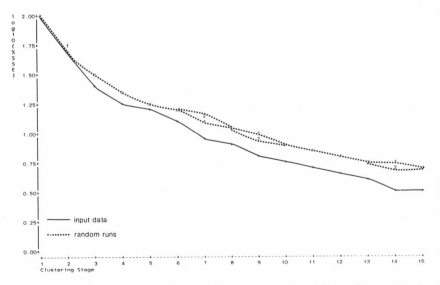

Figure 15. Plot of $\log_{10}$ %SSE for k-means clustering of Camp 14—moderate "decomposition."

Table 9.   Camp 14—Minimum "Decomposition": Counts and Percentages of Material Classes for Eight-Cluster K-Means Solution

Cluster	1	2	3	4	5	6	7	8
N^a	16	18	13	1	12	2	13	9
Bones	5	7	2	0	2	2	3	6
%	31.3	38.9	15.4		16.7	100.0	23.1	66.7
Mongongo nuts	1	1	1	0	1	0	2	1
%	6.3	5.6	7.7		8.3		15.4	11.1
Nutting stones	4	5	0	0	6	0	0	0
%	25.0	27.8			50.0			
Logs	2	1	3	0	0	0	0	0
%	12.5	5.6	23.1					
Charcoal	2	2	2	0	0	0	5	0
%	12.5	11.1	15.4				38.5	
Hearths	0	1	2	1	1	0	0	2
%		5.6	15.4	100.0	8.3			22.2
Postholes	1	1	1	0	2	0	2	0
%	6.3	5.6	7.7		16.7		15.4	
Artifacts	0	0	1	0	0	0	1	0
%	0			7.7			7.7	
Floral	1	0	1	0	0	0	0	0
%	6.3		7.7					

^{a}Number of items in cluster.

The map of the cluster assignments for the three-cluster level (Figure 17) agrees with the three-cluster solutions obtained for the original camp and for the minimally disturbed camp. Bones dominate the composition of Clusters 1 and 3 (Table 10), but nutting stones are the most frequent type of material in Cluster 2. Logs occur only in Cluster 2; miscellaneous floral remains appear only in Cluster 3, and artifacts are found in both Clusters 1 and 3. The mapped cluster assignments for the eight-cluster solution (Figure 18) shows basically the same results as obtained earlier. The cluster compositions (Table 11) again show that bones, mongongo nuts, nutting stones, and hearths or charcoal scatters occur in the majority of clusters.

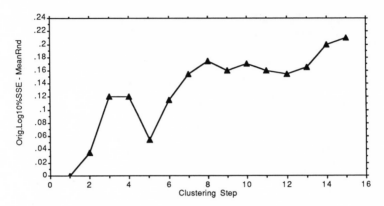

Figure 16. Plot of the difference between $\log_{10}$ %SSE and the mean $\log_{10}$ %SSE for random runs, Camp 14—moderate "decomposition."

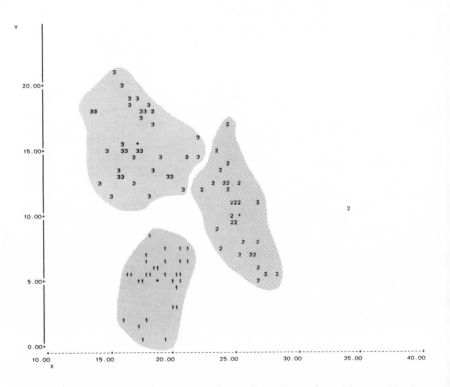

Figure 17. Distribution of three k-means clusters, Camp 14—moderate "decomposition."

Table 10.   Camp 14—Moderate "Decomposition":
Counts and Percentages of Material Classes for Three-
Cluster K-Means Solution

Cluster	1	2	3
N^a	30	29	35
Bones	15	6	15
%	50.0	20.7	42.9
Mongongo nuts	3	5	5
%	10.0	17.2	14.3
Nutting stones	4	8	3
%	13.3	27.6	8.6
Logs	0	1	0
%		3.4	
Charcoal	2	3	6
%	6.7	10.3	17.1
Hearths	2	4	1
%	6.7	13.8	2.9
Postholes	2	2	3
%	6.7	6.9	8.6
Artifacts	2	0	1
%	6.7		2.9
Floral	0	0	1
%			2.9

[a]Number of items in cluster.

Once again the clusters would be interpreted as representing the same polythetic set of processes, most likely those referable to the activities of individual family units. Interpretive problems could arise from the similarities of the compositions of Clusters 3 and 7. Bones dominate both assemblages, neither has a hearth, and Cluster 3 has nutting stones, whereas Cluster 7 has one of the three artifacts. It would appear that both clusters were formed by different processes than those affecting the other clusters. The locational analysis cannot clarify the range of activities that did occur at either of these clusters, nor can it illuminate the degree to which Clusters 3 and 7 are similar to one another. The assemblage composition analysis is very much needed to complement the locational analysis.

Table 11. Camp 14—Moderate "Decomposition": Counts and Percentages of Material Classes for Eight-Cluster K-Means Solution

Cluster	1	2	3	4	5	6	7	8
N^a	23	16	15	10	1	13	7	9
Bones	0	3	8	2	0	2	5	6
%	43.5	18.8	53.3	20.0		15.4	71.4	66.7
Mongongo nuts	2	3	1	2	0	4	1	0
%	8.7	18.8	6.7	20.0		30.8	14.3	
Nutting stones	4	6	3	2	0	0	0	0
%	17.4	37.5	20.0	20.0				
Logs	0	1	0	0	0	0	0	0
%		6.3						
Charcoal	2	2	0	1	0	5	0	1
%	8.7	12.5		10.0		38.5		11.1
Hearths	2	0	0	2	1	1	0	1
%	8.7			20.0	100.0	7.7		11.1
Postholes	2	1	1	1	0	1	0	1
%	8.7	6.3	6.7	10.0		7.7		11.1
Artifacts	1	0	1	0	0	0	1	0
%	4.3		6.7				14.3	
Floral	0	0	1	0	0	0	0	0
%			6.7					

[a] Number of items in cluster.

3.2.3. Maximum Decomposition (Figure 10d)

The plot of the $\log_{10}$ %SSE of the input data does not vary to a large extent from the plots of the random runs (Figure 19). Only at the 4-cluster level does there appear to be a significant divergence between the input and the randomized data. The plot of the difference between the average random clustering and the original input data (Figure 20) confirms that significant patterning is obtained with the 4-cluster solution; furthermore it shows a peak at the 11-cluster solution.

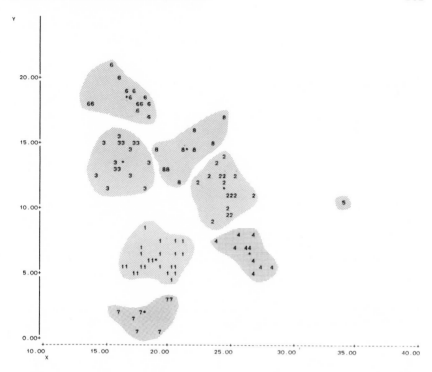

Figure 18. Distribution of eight k-means clusters, Camp 14—moderate "decomposition."

The mapped cluster assignments for the 4-cluster solution (Figure 21) differ from the results obtained for the previous analyses. The displacement of the materials along the northwestern side of the site is responsible for the differences. The composition of the clusters (Table 12) shows that bones dominate Clusters 1–3. Hearths, nutting stones, mongongo nuts, and postholes are also found in these clusters. Clearly, the same set of processes formed Clusters 1 to 3. Cluster 4 differs to some degree from the other three because it does not contain postholes, and it has relatively few bones. Thus, at least three, and possibly four household groups could be identified with the maximally decomposed data. The degree of movement, however, has obliterated the spatial integrity of what might have been identified as individual family units.

Pure locational analysis has proved effective in identifying both the underlying spatial structure of the site as well as the more refined structuring of what we know ethnographically to have been the individual households. At the maximum level of disturbance, even though virtually all of the spatial structuring of

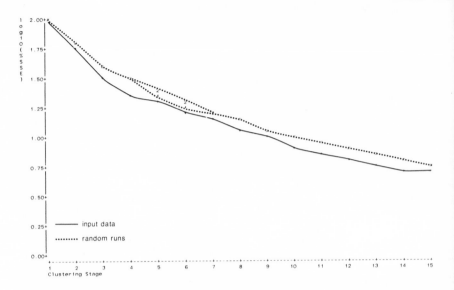

Figure 19. Plot of $\log_{10}$ %SSE for k-means clustering of Camp 14—maximum "decomposition," comparing runs of input and randomized data.

the original site had been obscured to the eye, the locational analysis was still able to identify the underlying structure of three units. In all instances, however, a pure locational analysis was not able to identify co-occurring sets of artifacts and features that might illuminate processes that occurred at the site. The compositional analysis was directed at determining whether spatial differences within the artifact assemblage could be identified.

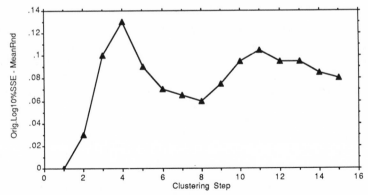

Figure 20. Plot of the difference between $\log_{10}$ %SSE and the mean $\log_{10}$ %SSE for random runs, Camp 14—maximum "decomposition."

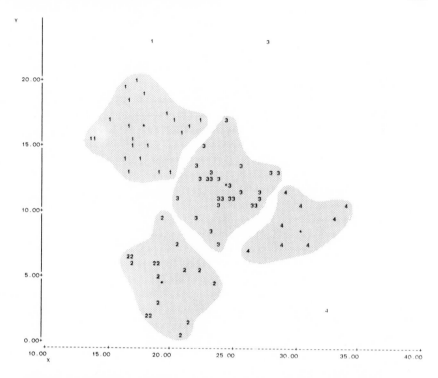

Figure 21. Distribution of four k-means clusters, Camp 14—maximum "decomposition."

3.3. Assemblage Composition Analysis of "Decomposed" Camp 14

The artifact distributions for the minimum, moderate, and maximum simulated "decompositions" of Camp 14 were analyzed using an unconstrained clustering approach in the same way as the original data. The only modification in an otherwise identical procedure was to use a 1.5-m moving template to generate the smoothed density contours for the maximally decomposed data, rather than a 1-m template as was used for the original camp and the other, less extensively decomposed sets of data. This was necessary in order to smooth adequately the small-scale, local variations in the comparatively low-density scatter of material resulting from the maximal decomposition of the camp, following the general rule of thumb discussed briefly above.

The clustering of item points based on standardized relative densities in the minimally decomposed data showed a rather clear break at seven clusters (Figure 22). Clustering of points for the moderate and the maximum decompositions of Camp 14 both revealed marked and unmistakable breaks at a nine-cluster solution (Figures 23–24).

Table 12. Camp 14—Maximum "Decomposition": Counts
and Percentages of Material Classes for Four-Cluster K-Means
Solution

Cluster	1	2	3	4
N^a	22	17	27	9
Bones	6	8	6	1
%	27.3	47.1	22.2	11.1
Mongongo nuts	3	4	2	1
%	13.6	23.5	7.4	11.1
Nutting stones	3	2	7	3
%	13.6	11.8	25.9	33.3
Logs	1	1	1	0
%	4.5	5.9	3.7	
Charcoal	3	0	4	1
%	13.6		14.8	11.1
Hearths	2	1	2	2
%	9.1	5.9	7.4	22.2
Postholes	2	1	5	0
%	9.1	5.9	18.5	
Artifacts	1	0	0	1
%	4.5			11.1
Floral	1	0	0	0
%	1.3			4.5

^{a}Number of items in cluster.

The compositions of the clusters so defined are presented in Tables 13 to 15, and they can be compared directly with Table 3, which has the results for the original, undecomposed data from the camp. A number of similarities strike one on the first inspection of theses tables, but their evaluation is much easier when the material classes significantly represented and characteristic of each cluster are listed in a comparative table, where the clusters that appear to be most alike among the four different analyses are aligned as well as possible, and distinctively different clusters are separated and allowed to stand apart.

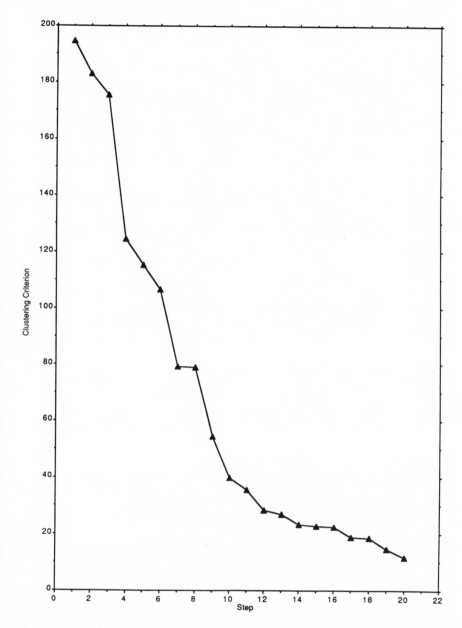

Figure 22. Plot of clustering criterion for unconstrained clustering of Camp 14—minimum "decomposition."

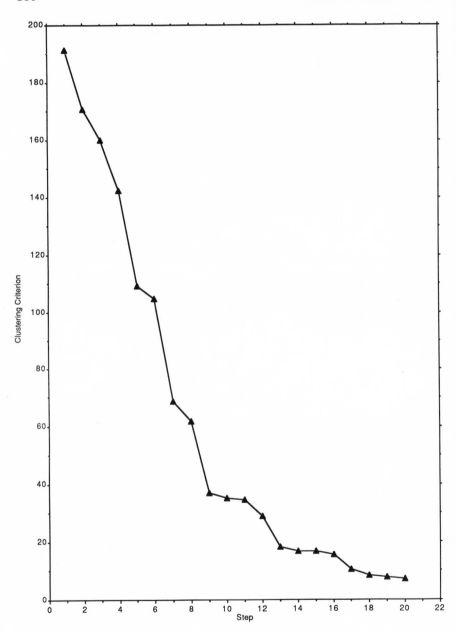

Figure 23. Plot of clustering criterion for unconstrained clustering of Camp 14—moderate "decomposition."

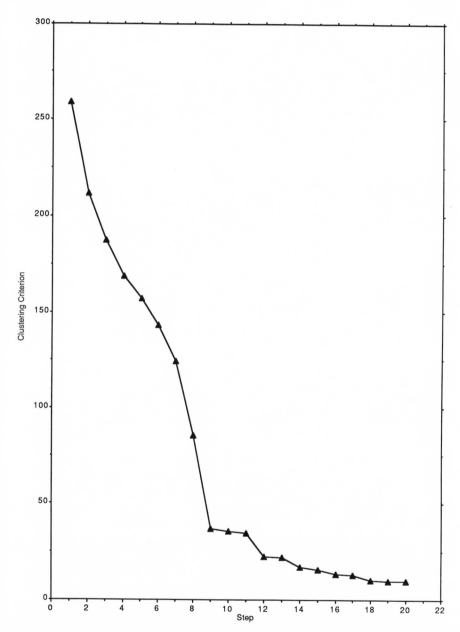

Figure 24. Plot of clustering criterion for unconstrained clustering of Camp 14—maximum "decomposition."

Table 13.   Camp 14—Minimum "Decomposition": Means and Standard Deviations of Relative Densities by Unconstrained Cluster

Cluster	1	2	3	4	5	6	7
N^a	32	6	27	9	3	4	3
Bones	57.8 ±28.3	5.2 ±5.6	23.0 ±18.8	1.6 ±4.9	0	42.4 ±22.8	14.3 ±12.6
Mongongo nuts	7.5 ±12.0	58.4 ±15.8	1.4 ±3.1	6.5 ±12.3	0	0	2.0 ±3.5
Nutting stones	4.4 ±9.2	16.8 ±21.5	38.8 ±22.1	7.2 ±8.9	0	1.4 ±2.7	26.7 ±9.4
Logs	2.3 ±5.5	0	3.8 ±8.3	57.6 ±25.7	0	3.1 ±3.9	2.0 ±3.5
Charcoal	19.4 ±23.2	18.9 ±19.7	9.5 ±12.2	10.8 ±11.8	0	0	0
Hearths	5.9 ±10.5	.7 ±1.8	4.8 ±12.7	15.8 ±12.6	100 ±0	5.4 ±4.3	0
Postholes	.7 ±2.5	0	18.0 ±16.9	.5 ±1.5	0	18.2 ±28.5	0
Artifacts	.9 ±3.5	0	.4 ±1.4	0	0	0	36.8 ±12.1
Floral	1.1 ±3.7	0	.2 ±1.0	0	0	29.6 ±3.2	18.0 ±15.8

^{a}Number of items in cluster.

This systematic comparison (Table 16) seems to us to show a substantial degree of overall similarity in the assemblage composition of the clusters defined for the original and all degrees of "decomposed" data. One cluster that consistently appears in every analysis is composed only of a high proportion of bones. This is also the numerically dominant cluster for all but the maximum degree of decomposition, where it is displaced by two clusters characterized by postholes, nutting stones, and bones, and by nutting stones and bones, respectively (compare Table 15 to Tables 3, 13, and 14). These latter two clusters also find one or two counterparts in all other analyses, indicating that some combination or

Table 14.   Camp 14—Moderate "Decomposition": Means and Standard Deviations of Relative Densities by Unconstrained Cluster

Cluster	1	2	3	4	5	6	7	8	9
N^a	24	8	11	18	23	3	3	3	1
Bones	84.8 ±15.4	48.9 ±13.7	23.8 ±23.6	15.6 ±11.8	25.7 ±15.8	6.3 ±11.0	0	8.1 ±7.3	4.5 ±0
Mongongo nuts	3.8 ±9.2	0	7.4 ±11.5	16.9 ±18.6	40.5 ±22.2	0	0	.8 ±1.4	0
Nutting stones	4.2 ±8.6	5.1 ±5.9	13.1 ±14.3	53.4 ±22.8	5.9 ±7.8	0	0	58.9 ±11.7	45.3 ±0
Logs	0	0	0	.5 ±1.5	0	0	0	0	50.2 ±0
Charcoal	2.1 ±5.0	0	19.6 ±16.9	4.3 ±7.1	22.9 ±7.1	91.5 ±12.9	0 ±9.7	0	0
Hearths	3.5 ±9	.2 ±0.4	4.9 ±9.3	6.0 ±9.6	4.3 ±7.9	1.1 ±1.9	100 ±0	0	0
Postholes	.3 ±1.2	15.2 ±16.5	30.8 ±12.9	2.8 ±4.7	.7 ±1.8	1.1 ±1.9	0	0	0
Artifacts	1.2 ±4.1	30.7 ±10.3	.3 ±0.9	.5 ±1.4	0	0	0	1.0 ±1.7	0
Floral	0	0	0	0	0	0	0	31.3 ±3.5	0

^{a}Number of items in cluster.

combinations of proportions of nutting stones and bones, in association with structural remains (postholes) or not, is typical of the spatial organization of the debris scattered over Camp 14 and of the simulated "decompositions" of this camp.

Another common pattern of assemblage composition in all of the analyses comprises clusters with important proportions of mongongo nuts, either alone or in association with significant amounts of bones and charcoal or logs. A cluster characterized by bones and "artifacts" (tools) is found in three out of four analyses, as is a cluster dominated by logs, but with variable secondary contents.

Table 15.   Camp 14—Maximum "Decomposition": Means and Standard Deviations of Relative Densities by Unconstrained Cluster

Cluster	1	2	3	4	5	6	7	8	9
N^a	10	6	2	7	6	16	20	6	2
Bones	83.1	39.4	49.7	25	33.1	20.8	12.6	9.6	0
	±18.8	±29.8	±5.6	±23.9	±16.9	±13.3	±10.7	±16.1	
Mongongo nuts	1.0	0	1.4	66.3	28.2	2.9	10.2	0	0
	±2.1		±1.9	±18.5	±20.6	±5.6	±11.5		
Nutting stones	6.0	19.5	0	0	9.2	46.9	26.4	0	0
	±10.2	±30.9			±11.2	±15.4	±16.2		
Logs	.5	.5	0	2.6	26.1	7.9	0	0	0
	±1.6	±0.8		±6.8	±6.9	±9.3	±0.1		
Charcoal	5.0	10.2	0	4.9	.7	11.0	3.9	34.3	100
	±10.7	±9.3		±12.2	±1.0	±13.5	±5.0	±28.2	±0
Hearths	2.2	0	0	1.0	0	7.5	5.8	56.1	0
	±5.2			±2.0		±10.7	±10.5	±23.8	
Postholes	1.6	0	0	.2	2.0	1.7	41.2	0	0
	±5.1			±0.4	±4.3	±3.5	±14		
Artifacts	.6	30.4	0	0	.7	1.3	0	0	0
	±1.9	±11.9			±1.1	±3.5			
Floral	0	0	48.9	0	0	0	0	0	0
			±7.5						

^{a}Number of items in cluster.

Finally, hearths along define a cluster of three of the analyses and combine with a secondary component of charcoal in the fourth. These broad similarities among all the analyses account for virtually all of the clusters defined, leaving less than a half-dozen clusters that do not recur in at least three of four cases, and no cluster that does not have a possible counterpart identifiable in another analysis.

In spite of the apparently substantial uniformity in results with both the undecomposed and decomposed data, there are some noticeable differences that demonstrate a gradual degradation in the resolution of the reconstructed picture of the spatial organization of the camp as the original data are subjected to increasing degrees of disturbance and attrition. One can see this degradation

Table 16. Comparison of Cluster Compositions for Unconstrained Clustering Analysis of Camp 14, Original and "Decomposed" Data[a]

Undecomposed	Decomposed		
	Minimum	Moderate	Maximum
1. Bones	**1.** Bones	**1.** Bones	**1.** Bones
3. Bones Postholes (Nutting stones)		**3.** Postholes Bones Charcoal	**7.** Postholes Nutting stones
4. Bones Nutting stones Postholes (Mongongo nuts) (Charcoal)	**3.** Nutting stones Bones Postholes	**4.** Nutting stones Bones	**6.** Nutting stones Bones
2. Floral[b]	7. Artifacts Nutting stones Floral Bones	8. Nutting stones Floral Bones	
	6. Bones Floral (Hearth)		3. Bones Floral
5. Artifacts Bones Postholes		**2.** Bones Artifacts	**2.** Bones Artifacts Charcoal
	2. Mongongo nuts		**4.** Mongongo nuts
6. Bones Mongongo nuts Charcoal		**5.** Mongongo nuts Bones Charcoal	**5.** Bones Mongongo nuts Logs
7. Logs (Nutting stones)	4. Logs Hearths	9. Logs Nutting stones (Bones)	
8. Hearth[b]	5. Hearth[b]	7. Hearth[b]	**8.** Hearths Charcoal
		6. Charcoal	9. Charcoal

[a]Bold numbers = clusters with more than five members; nonbold numbers = clusters with five or fewer members; parentheses = item classes with mean relative densities below 10%, although this value is greater than its standard deviation.
[b]Isolated.

when the assemblages defined by unconstrained clustering are characterized by their content and seen in their distribution over the site area, plotted to produce a picture of the spatial organization of the "decomposed" camps that can be compared to that obtained from the original data. This picture of overall spatial organization normally would represent, in this approach, the final analytical results that would constitute the basis on which interpretations—archaeological, geological, and the like—might be made.

Because there is a good deal of similarity in the clustering results across all four analyses, we generally can characterize the different scatters of material assemblages commonly, in terms of five main assemblage types, plus a few minor clusters, as follows: (1) an assemblage dominated only by bones, (2) bones and postholes, separately or in various combinations with (3) nutting stones and bones, (4) bones and "artifacts" (tools), and (5) mongongo nuts, either alone or with bones and charcoal or logs, followed by (a) concentrations of logs, (b) isolated hearths, (c) isolated patches of charcoal, and (d) mixed assemblages with significant proportions of floral remains as secondary components. When these assemblages are plotted over the camp area, a picture of spatial organization very similar to that in the original data, but in one respect increasingly less detailed, is evident in all the decomposed camps.

At every level of decomposition, we easily can see that the various defined assemblages (clusters) are organized in spatial groups, each of which exhibits evidence for structural remains in the form of an important component of postholes in one or more clusters, plus patches of most of the other clusters defined in the analysis (Figures 25–27). These are the sorts of spatial groups that an archaeologist very likely would tend to identify as "domestic" or "residential" locations, and which, in the undisturbed, original data, replicated the ethno-graphically observed seven dwellings with their associated debris at this site. They are also the spatial groupings that tend to be identified by a pure locational (k-means) approach to spatial analysis, leading to a close complementarity be-tween these two analytical approaches.

However, as simulated "decomposition" increasingly disturbs the original data, both through a high level of attribution and through physical movement, the number of these spatial groupings gradually declines, and the distinction of a core area with little evidence for processing of mongongo nuts, as against a periphery in which such evidence is relatively abundant, disappears. In the orig-inal camp, seven such spatial groups were identified (Figure 8). The number declines to five for minimal decomposition (Figure 25) or six for moderate decomposition (Figure 26) and drops sharply to three for the maximum level of simulated disturbance (Figure 27). The general restriction of significant evidence for mongongo nut processing to the peripheries of the site disappears in all the decomposed camps. Evidence for the small dumping area on the southern edge

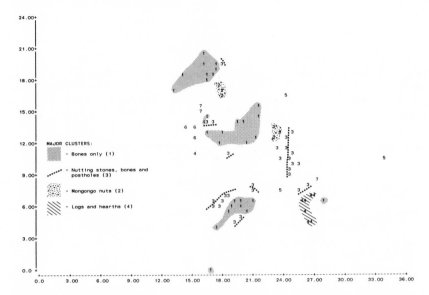

Figure 25. Distribution of seven unconstrained clusters, Camp 14—minimum "decomposition."

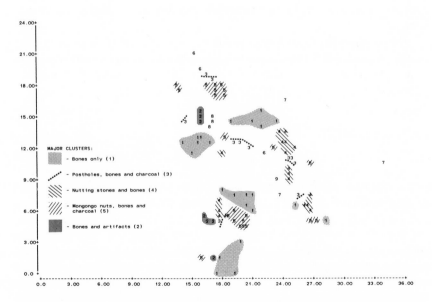

Figure 26. Distribution of nine unconstrained clusters, Camp 14—moderate "decomposition."

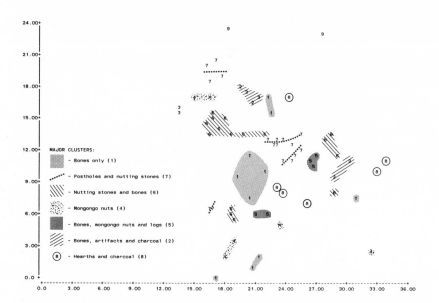

Figure 27. Distribution of nine unconstrained clusters, Camp 14—maximum "decomposition."

of the site is present only in the moderately disturbed data, and equivocally even there.

However, the clear spatial segregation of mongongo nut remains themselves and the nutting stones presumably used in their processing is maintained consistently and clearly at all scales and in all analyses. This is rather striking and suggests strongly that this pattern is very real at this camp.

4. CONCLUSIONS

What then can we conclude from this project? Yellen based his ring model on the repeated observation that the San conceptually divide themselves into identical units (Yellen 1977:131). The pure locational analysis confirmed that the spatial distributions of materials and features accurately reflect Yellen's observation that six or seven social units were present at the site. The assemblage composition analysis showed that a consistent pattern of activities occurred throughout the site and that hearths were the focus of specific activities. The combination of the pure locational and the activity-based methods produced objective results that correspond well with the results of Yellen's subjective analysis. In at least this instance, these methods have provided an objective means for identifying the structure and patterns of variability inherent in the ethnographic record.

All of the patterns revealed in the data by our analyses, including of course all the specifics of assemblage composition and spatial organization, are simply demonstrated, not explained. Although in any practical application, the steps of description and interpretation of analytical results typically are closely linked, frequently blending right into each other, they are in fact logically quite independent. Quantitative spatial analysis provides a rigorous description of data structure on a site; it is up to the archaeologist to interpret this description using whatever analogies, interpretive principles, additional data, and the like that he or she sees fit in any particular case.

However, we have seen two things in the comparison of the assemblage composition spatial analyses of original and "decomposed" data from Yellen's Camp 14: (1) a great robustness of both site structure and the analytical approach employed to define and describe it, and (2) a gradual loss of resolution of absolute spatial location while maintaining general integrity of the assemblage composition and pattern of distribution over the site.

The conclusions we can draw from these results seem to us generally positive. The original spatial organization of a human site may be maintained in large part, though probably with some generalization or loss of resolution, through the relatively extensive attrition and physical disturbance that may occur during the process of its transformation into an archaeological location. Relatively simple approaches and methods of quantitative spatial analysis now available to us can, particularly when used together in a complementary fashion, adequately reveal this organiztion and make it available for archaeological consideration and interpretation.

ACKNOWLEDGMENTS

Research conducted for this chapter grew directly out of a more comprehensive study conducted as part of a graduate seminar in analytical methods taught by Robert Whallon at the University of Michigan. Seminar participants— including Michael Blake, C. Wesley Cowan, Susan Gregg, Keith Kintigh, Jocelyn Moore, William Parry, Katherine Spielmann, Thomas Rocek, and Tristine Smart—shared an equal role in establishing a computerized data bank for all 16 camps and in developing approaches for analyzing the ethnographic and simulated archaeological data. Results presented in this chapter are a refinement of the approaches developed by all of the seminar participants. Last, but far from least, we would like to thank John Yellen for the comments and advice he has provided throughout the project. Yellen was willing not only to allow a seminar of critical graduate students to reanalyze his data; he also met with the seminar to discuss our results. Since the seminar, Yellen's comments and suggestions have allowed us to refine our techniques.

5. REFERENCES

Kintigh, K. W., and Ammerman, A., 1982, Heuristic Approaches to Spatial Analysis in Archaeology, *American Antiquity* 47:31–63.

Whallon, R., 1984, Unconstrained Clustering for the Analysis of Spatial Distributions in Archaeology. In *Intrasite Spatial Analysis in Archaeology* (H. J. Hietala, ed.), Cambridge University Press, Cambridge, pp. 242–277.

Yellen, J. E., 1977, *Archaeological Approaches to the Present: Models for Reconstructing the Past*, Academic Press, New York.

Part II

Spatial Analysis of Archaeological Sites

The "Stone Age" sites that are examined in this part of the volume are separated by thousands of both years and miles. Nevertheless, the archaeological approaches to understanding the spatial patterning present at each are similar. Current archaeological studies, including the intrasite spatial analyses discussed in this part, must incorporate the results of ethnoarchaeological and experimental research. Some of the conclusions from actualistic observations during the past 10 years are (1) concentrations of functionally associated artifacts or tool kits were not regularly discarded where they were used in single-purpose activity areas; (2) hearths commonly represent a focal point for a variety of domestic, maintenance, and special-purpose activities; (3) size sorting of refuse can be an important means for distinguishing locations where refuse-producing activities actually occurred; and (4) a variety of natural processes can rearrange the refuse generated by human activities. However, the implications of these findings only now are appearing in published archaeological research.

Examples of such ethnographically informed studies include the following four chapters. The chapters in this part share an appreciation of the multifarious processes that might have formed the spatial patterns at archaeological sites ranging from tens of thousands to a few hundred years old, in France and northern Canada. These chapters share the goal of reconstructing the human activities and behaviors—technological, subsistence, and social—that contributed to the deposition of the sites.

The chapters avoid simplistic assumptions that the spatial patterns at the sites were formed directly or only from human activities. All of the chapters consider alternative interpretations of how the recognized spatial patterns might have formed. Three (Carr, Keeley, Stevenson) emphasize the impact of human activities, ranging from the conscious or deliberate to the unconscious or incidental arranging of refuse. The fourth focuses on the impact of natural processes that can rearrange refuse, including the impact of nonhuman predators on distributions of bone refuse (Rigaud and Simek).

In assessing alternative interpretations of a particular spatial pattern, the authors succeed in examining a variety of spatial evidence—the distributions of stone artifacts of different size, morphological and technological type, and function based on microwear, as well as core reduction sequences based on refitting; the distributions of bones of different taxa, skeletal parts, and size, and having surface modifications including cut and gnaw marks; the distributions of artifactual and faunal refuse relative to hearths; the distributions of other refuse including ocher—as well as the implications of additional evidence, such as assemblage composition, paleoenvironment, and the geological context of the site.

By raising further challenges for future actualistic research, the chapters in this part highlight the interactive relationship between actualistic and archaeological spatial studies. As future actualistic studies provide further insights into the formation of archaeological spatial patterning, the interpretations proposed in the chapters in this part probably will be reassessed. Meanwhile, by examining the available lines of evidence, each of the chapters offers a balanced interpretation of the spatial evidence at a major Stone Age archaeological site.

Chapter 6

Interpreting Spatial Patterns at the Grotte XV

A Multiple-Method Approach

JEAN-PHILIPPE RIGAUD AND JAN F. SIMEK

1. INTRODUCTION

Since the early 1970s the analysis of the spatial distribution of artifacts has been an important research concern for many archaeologists. In particular, techniques for mathematically defining spatial patterns within archaeological sites have received much attention. Methods employed to investigate spatial patterning were selected because of *a priori* notions concerning the primary cause of the patterning. Thus anticipated interpretations determined the technique used to examine the patterns, and explanation was in some ways predetermined.

More recently, archaeologists have come to admit that site formation is a complex phenomenon that may involve many different causes (Schiffer 1983, 1987). In this chapter, we attempt to show how an understanding of multiple site formation processes, acting to produce spatial patterns within a site, can be obtained by using several analytic techniques applied together in heuristic fashion. Both quantitative and nonquantitative means for investigating spatial processes will be applied in a case study of complex cave deposits containing Mousterian artifacts at the Grotte XV (also known as the Grotte Vaufrey) in

JEAN-PHILIPPE RIGAUD • Direction des Antiquites Préhistoriques d'Aquitaine, 6 bis Cours de Gourgue, 33074 Bordeaux, France. JAN F. SIMEK • Department of Anthropology, University of Tennessee, Knoxville, Tennessee 37996-0720.

199

southwestern France. We shall illustrate how several lines of evidence, each provoking a rather limited kind of interpretation, together produce a richer, more textured view of site formation.

2. BACKGROUND

The choice of method in spatial analysis has long been determined by preconceptions about the spatial distribution of artifacts in a site. By far the most prevalent concept has been the "activity area," a place within a site where a relatively limited set of tasks was performed with a limited set of artifacts (e.g., Binford 1978; Carr 1984; Dacey 1973). Identifying activity variation was seen as important for two reasons. First, there was a growing interest among archaeologists in reconstructing past lifeways that, in fact, led to the initial development of spatial archaeology (Clarke 1968, 1977; Whallon 1973, 1974; Hodder and Orton 1976). Second, ethnographic research indicated that people often, but not always, organize their tasks spatially when they occupy a place (e.g., Binford 1964, 1978, 1979; Binford et al. 1970; Gould 1977; Schiffer 1972, 1976; Yellen 1977).

Activity organization was seen as the primary source of artifact spatial patterning, and this expectation for patterning led archaeologists to seek analytic techniques that could successfully identify activity areas. Because activity areas had two relevant dimensions of variation—spatial discreteness and content—the analytic problem was to simultaneously define areas within sites where individual activities had occurred and to detect the specific artifact class associations that reflected tool kits employed in specific tasks. It was assumed that because tasks were distributed differentially in space, the tools employed in those activities would also have patterned distributions. In other words, artifact concentrations would "map" activity areas. Guided by these notions, quantitative techniques were either borrowed (especially from geography and plant ecology) or, more recently, invented to permit both pattern recognition and content analysis simultaneously (e.g., Carr 1984; Dacey 1973; Hietala and Stevens 1977; Whallon 1974, 1984).

In the past few years, however, an expanding array of actualistic, ethnographic, and archaeological studies have shown that many different factors can and do influence archaeological spatial distributions. These include geological processes (e.g., Laville 1975; Laville et al. 1980; Rigaud and Simek 1987; Stein 1983), local topography (Rigaud 1978; Simek 1987), social structure (Yellen 1977), and nonhuman animal site use (Binford 1981, 1984; Binford and Bertram 1978). Moreover, it is evident that more than one process can act on a deposit (Schiffer 1972, 1983, 1987). It would seem obvious that single-method approaches to spatial data oversimplify artifact distributions prior to interpretation, especially when guided by a desire to define activity areas (cf. Whallon 1984).

The contribution of nonhuman site occupatants to site formation is of particular interest to us here, because (as will be seen), the Grotte XV was used by at least one other carnivore in addition to humans. Animal behavior in and around archaeological sites has been studied in detail for some species, and their importance in site formation has been demonstrated (e.g., Binford 1981, 1984, 1985; Brain 1981). Some see animals as primary contributors to observed patterning in the archaeological record, especially in early time periods (e.g.. Binford 1981). Others (e.g., Bunn *et al.* 1980; Bunn and Kroll 1987) see human behavior as most important in many contexts where both animals and humans have been identified as site occupants. A variety of means have been employed to detect the nature and extent of nonhuman impact on archaeological sites; most often, these comprise characteristics marks left on bones, bone fragmentation, and body part frequency profiles (Binford 1981, 1984; Bunn and Kroll 1987). Little attention has been paid to the spatial effects of human- versus nonhuman agents. We hope to illustrate how spatial data can help in identifying complex site formation processes, in particular, the impact of nonhuman animals on the Grotte XV artifact distribution.

3. A STUDY OF THE GROTTE XV

3.1. The Approach

Our study of Grotte XV artifact distributions utilizes several analytic techniques: (1) Visual inspection of artifact distributions and content variation over space allows the definition of obvious patterns and also allows maximum integration of the excavator's knowledge into the pattern recognition process. (2) A k-means cluster analysis of artifact locations identifies statistically significant clusters. Separate statistical analysis of cluster contents enables rather specific interpretations of pattern formation. (3) Refitting studies indicate patterned relations (or lack thereof) among clusters within the site. We argue that multiple approaches to spatial analysis are required if interpretation of archaeological spatial patterning is to account for the complex posibilities of site formation. No single technique, quantitative or qualitative, is inherently preferable for identifying spatial patterns. We attempt to integrate results from these three analytic techniques into a general interpretation of site formation in the Grotte XV.

3.2. The Site

The Grotte XV is a very large, deeply stratified cave located in the massive Le Conte Cliffs near Castelnaud, Dordogne, France (Figure 1). The site, one of at least

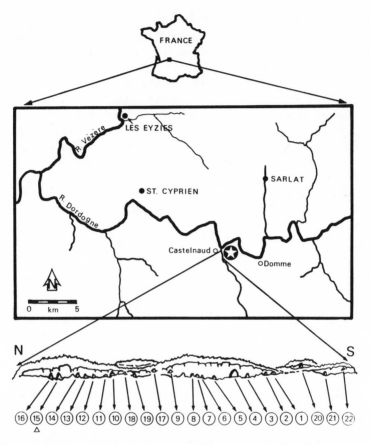

Figure 1. Map showing the location of the Grotte XV (a.k.a. Vaufrey Cave) in the Le Conte Cliffs, Dordogne, France.

22 in the Le Conte karst, was excavated between 1965 and 1983 by teams under the direction of J-Ph. Rigaud (1982). A detailed monograph on the site (Rigaud 1988), provides the stratigraphy and cultural sequence.

This chapter considers archaeological materials from a single layer at the Grotte XV: a fine-grained sedimentary unit called Couche VIII. The layer contained a Typical Mousterian stone tool assemblage deposited sometime during the penultimate (Riss) glaciation. Couche VIII varies in depth between 50 and 70 cm and was probably deposited rather slowly and regularly under moderate climatic conditions (Laville and Kervazo 1988). Artifacts and animal bones were scattered throughout this accumulation in lenticular arrangements, and no clear evidence could be seen for expansive individual occupation floors within Couche VIII (Rigaud and Geneste 1988).

A total of 4,658 specimens was recorded with Cartesian coordinate locations in Couche VIII, including 3,503 whole and fragmented bones and 1,155 flaked stone artifacts. F. Delpech's analysis of the faunal assemblage shows that 830 bones could be identified as to species and that 23 different animal species are represented; the red deer (*Cervus elaphus*) is by far the most common animal, with 573 identifiable specimens having precise locational data (Delpech 1988). Binford (1988) observed that some bone fragments were gnawed, although he provides a count only for red deer (26 of the 150 bones he identified as belonging to this species had tooth marks). Delpech found a few bones showing traces of cutting, whereas Binford asserts that no cutmarks were in evidence (1985:317–18). Thus the faunal assemblage was produced and/or affected by several agents. The agents responsible for the lithic assemblage, one assumes, were human. Six general classes of flaked stone artifacts were defined for this study, including generalized tool classes and debitage. Table 1 lists frequencies for each animal species identified, for unidentified bones, and for the lithic classes defined for spatial analysis.

3.3. Analytic Techniques

This chapter deals primarily with the interpretation of spatial patterns rather than with the description of analytic techniques. Our study is accomplished using three primary modes of analysis: visual inspection, quantitative analysis, and refitting. All three approaches have received much attention in the literature. Rather than review them here, we shall simply provide references to technical articles dealing with the methods.

Perhaps the oldest form of analysis involves visual assessment of spatial patterning and artifact class co-occurrence (e.g., Deplorte 1968; Leroi-Gourhan and Brézillon 1966, 1972; Rigaud 1978). Given adequate time and data that can be graphically displayed, this is a very satisfying and successful mode of spatial analysis. Here, we describe data using simple density maps as visual aids.

Our quantitative approach has two parts (Simek 1984a, 1988). First, we apply a k-means clustering algorithm (Kintigh and Ammerman 1982) as our basic pattern recognition technique (Simek 1984a). We then use a variety of statistical techniques to examine spatial relations among different artifact classes (Simek 1987); pattern elements recognized in the first stage serve as units within which artifact class association is assessed in the second (e.g., Kintigh and Ammerman 1982; Simek 1984a, 1987, 1988; Simek and Larick 1983).

Refitting of the Grotte XV lithics was perfomed by J-M. Geneste (1985). A certain number of bones were also refitted from Couche VIII by F. Delpech in the course of her faunal analysis. In the New World, lithic refitting has most often been employed to examine technological characteristics of an assemblage, but in the Old World the technique has also been applied to spatial analysis (e.g., Bunn

Table 1. Artifact Classes Considered in Grotte XV Couche VIII Analyses (NISP is number of identifiable specimens per taxon)

Class	NISP
Cattle/bison	13
Red deer	573
Horse	46
Bear	13
Beaver	17
Rhinoceros	2
Lynx	13
Dog (*Cuon sp.*)	35
Thar	94
Chamois	5
Elephant	1
Roe deer	3
Badger	1
Unidentifiable	2,673
Total fauna	3,503
Levallois pieces	41
Points	9
Sidescrapers	49
Knives	15
Notches and denticulates	20
Miscellaneous retouched	12
Debitage	995
Unanalyzed	14
Total lithics	1,155

et al. 1980; Cahen *et al.* 1979; Leroi-Gourhan and Brézillon 1972). However, until now, the results of refitting have been used alone to infer spatial patterning and are rarely integrated with quantitative analyses.

4. RESULTS OF ANALYSES

4.1. Visual Inspection

Visual examination of artifact distributions at Grotte XV first considered the contextual elements that might have affected artifact deposition and dispersal—those unchangeable characteristics of the cave itself that constitute what Delporte (1968) has termed "structural givens." These included internal cave topography, dominated by a large pile of boulders fallen from the roof prior to the deposition of Couche VIII. Fireplaces and related features would normally be considered contextual elements (Simek 1984b), but no identifiable fireplace was found during the course of excavation (Simek 1987; Rigaud and Geneste 1988).

The first artifacts to be examined, worked lithics and burnt stones, were attributed to human agents of deposition (Figure 2). When patterns of artifact frequency are examined (Figure 3), three principle areas ("zones") can be defined: (1) a dense concentration of materials at the southwest edge of the excavated area within the large block mass, (2) a narrow band of accumulation further east toward the back of the cave, and (3) a dispersed concentration in the large open area north of the rock mass.

Based on visual analysis of the distributions of various stone tool classes (Figure 4), the three zones can be characterized in terms of content. Zone 1 has the densest deposit of material and contains a wide range of artifact classes: burnt materials, tools, debitage, and the like. The accumulation is generally concentric, is bounded by large rocks, and covers around 7 m² of area. Zone 2 contains a more limited set of artifact classes. Debitage dominates, although there are small clusters of stone tools and burnt matter. Zone 3 is dispersed and seems to be composed of two somewhat discrete concentrations of burnt material, each associated with a few tools, connected by a scatter of debitage. It should be noted that all lithic artifact classes are present in all three zones; certain classes, however, have distinct spatial patterns within each of the three concentration areas. This suggests different introduction patterns for lithic artifacts in the three accumulation zones.

Faunal remains are essentially coincident in space with lithic materials (Figure 5). The few bone tools found at the site are located toward the back part of the cavity.

Explanation of the patterns defined by visual examination varies by zone. Interior cave topography is an important influence on the shape and form of Zone

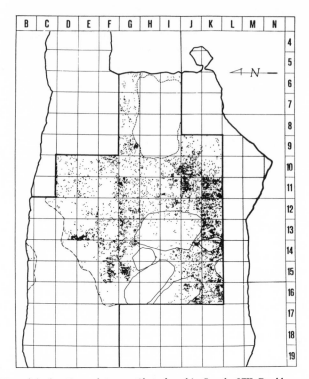

Figure 2. Map of the locations of stone artifacts found in Couche VIII. Boulders are shown as light solid outlines; light broken line shows outline of clandestine excavation. Punctuated line shows limits of eroded area at mouth of cave.

1. The Zone 1 spatial configuration clearly was constrained by rock boundaries. The range of activities represented is less clear. Zone contents may reflect the material products of a variety of activities overlapping in the same location *because* they were deposited among the rocks where horizontal dispersal was constrained. Zones 2 and 3, on the other hand, have no apparent topographic constraints determining their dispersion. Artifact classes either form dense, structured accumulations (as in Zone 2) or scattered, rather sparse concentrations (as in Zone 3). The nature and variability of these unconstrained zones suggests that they represent deposits produced by fewer or more limited activities than Zone 1.

4.2. Quantitative Analysis

Our quantitative treatment of the Couche VIII data involves several analytic steps. First, we employ a k-means cluster analysis to define several levels of artifact

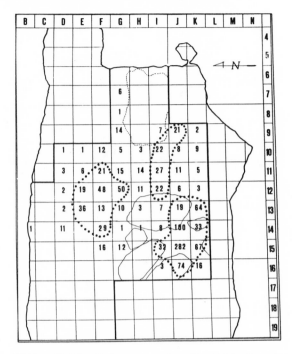

Figure 3. Map of lithic artifact density by square meter grid unit (after Rigaud and Geneste 1988). Heavy dotted line shows boundaries of visually-defined artifact concentrations.

clustering; this technique locates clusters in space, identifies all individual members of each cluster, and gives measures of cluster size (Kintigh and Ammerman 1982). To analyze cluster contents, the results of cluster analysis are used as data for principal components extracation and factor analysis. The goal of this second analytic step is to examine artifact class relationships over space.

K-means cluster analysis of the Couche VIII artifacts was performed separately for bones and stones because there was no *a priori* reason to expect coincident patterns (or causation) for these materials (see Simek 1987, 1988). The first step in a k-means analysis—comparison of the observed distribution to randomized data patterns—indicated that bones are nonrandomly distributed. Three optimal clustering solutions were identified. (1) The lowest scale solution identifies three bone clusters that coincide with the three accumulation zones identified visually (Figure 6a). (2) A five-cluster pattern refines the basic structure of bone cluster distributions (Figure 6b). The large rock mass is a basic topographic constraint conditioning the dispersal of four of the clusters. The two richest clusters lie to the south of the rocks along the wall, one within and one

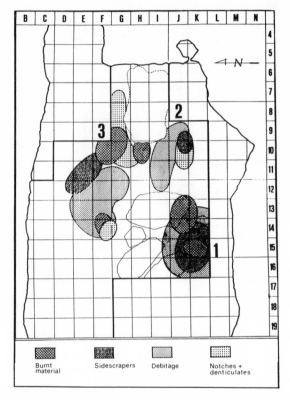

Figure 4. Density patterns for various Couche VIII artifact classes (after Rigaud and Geneste 1988).

east of the rock circle. Two less dense clusters are positioned north of the blocks. A fifth cluster, not very rich and rather dispersed, is located further north of the four dense accumulations. (3) Figure 7a shows the highest-scale solutions for bone and stone materials, overlain on a single map. For bones, 11 clusters are defined at the highest scale, all relatively small in size. Three rich clusters are located along the southern side of the excavated area. North of the blocks 4 similarly sized clusters arc around the rock mass. Four very sparse bone clusters are scattered across the northern part of the cave floor.

According to k-means analysis, lithic artifacts also have a nonrandom distribution. In contrast to bones, however, only a single optimal pattern composed of 10 clusters characterizes the distribution. Small, rich clusters are located at the southern edge of the excavated area, within and east of the rocks. The densest lithic accumulations are located within the rock circle. Five less dense clusters are scattered around the northern edge of the rocks. Three sparse clusters are scattered across the open part of the cave toward the north wall.

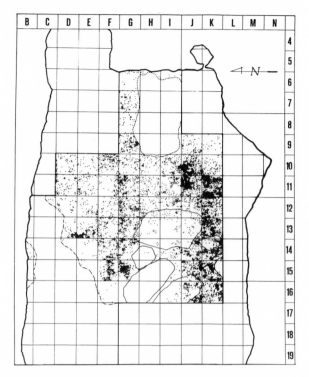

Figure 5. Map of the locations of bones and bone fragments found in Couche VIII.

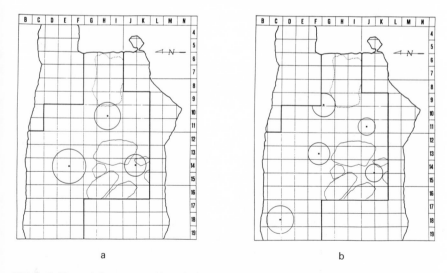

a

b

Figure 6. Maps of cluster centroids and RMS Radii for k-means analyses of Couche VIII bones: A shows three-cluster pattern; B shows five-cluster solution (Simek 1987).

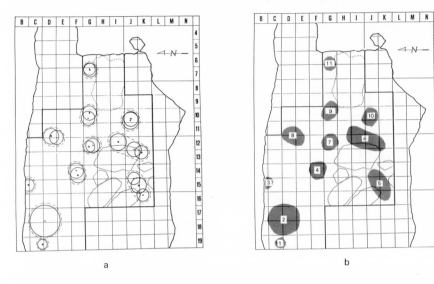

a   b

Figure 7. Maps of k-means cluster solutions and cluster zones defined for Couche VIII lithics and bones: A shows 10 cluster lithic pattern (triangles) overlaid with 11 cluster bone pattern (squares); B shows cluster zones used in factor analysis of cluster content (Simek 1987).

When the highest scale k-means solutions for bones and the only solution for stones are compared, clusters overlap in most cases; however, in the northern areas of the cave (Zone 3), bone and stone clusters are separate. Within the rock circle, overlapping sets of three and four clusters are present. In the deposits just north of the rocks, bone and stone clusters are paired. Overall, in the south and central part of the cave, the two distributions are remarkably coincident. Observed patterns of intercluster overlap can be used to define 11 "cluster zones" (see Simek 1984a, 1987) for use in content analyses of the Couche VIII data. These are illustrated in Figure 7b.

Table 2 shows the results of a factor analysis of artifact counts for each of 11 cluster zones indicated in Figure 7b. The rotated factor solution accounts for over 85% of the common variance in the matrix. A Kendall's tau correlation matrix was generated, based on raw artifact counts (Simek 1987). These coefficients were used as the initial similarity matrix for extraction of principal components. This approach was chosen because assumptions underlying parametric correlation statistics, upon which factor analyses are usually based, are not met by these data.

Three things should be noted concerning the factor solution for Couche VIII spatial zones. First, nearly all stone tool classes and the most abundant animal species are highly correlated with Factor 1. That so many classes exhibit spatial interrelationships suggests a rather uniform and redundant distribution of most

Table 2.   Varimax Rotated Factor Pattern Produced from Kendall's Tau
Correlation Matrix for Couche VIII Artifact Classes by Cluster Zone (Simek 1987)

| | Factor | | | | | |
Class	1	2	3	4	5	6
Levallois pieces	.79	.37	−.03	.17	.01	.10
Points	.41	.65	.51	−.13	−.13	−.10
Sidescrapers	.78	.33	.30	.15	.03	−.15
Knives	.65	.03	.64	.14	.01	.06
Notches and denticulates	.91	.00	.00	−.04	−.09	−.23
Miscellaneous retouched	.61	.51	−.05	−.37	.02	−.22
Debitage	.86	.03	.01	−.03	−.13	−.01
Cattle/bison	.54	.12	.23	−.33	−.27	−.50
Red deer	.78	.21	.28	−.01	.26	.21
Horse	.80	.18	.26	−.09	.32	.07
Bear	.66	.45	−.10	−.30	.31	.19
Beaver	−.02	.13	.18	.24	.03	.81
Rhinoceros	.36	.86	.20	−.11	.06	.14
Lynx	.22	.40	−.05	.15	−.27	.69
Dog (*Cuon sp.*)	.75	.37	.06	−.13	.23	.04
Thar	.68	.27	.45	.15	.21	.18
Chamois	.02	.15	.28	−.11	.78	.10
Elephant	.36	−.42	−.15	−.31	−.35	.52
Roe deer	.33	.71	.15	.52	−.01	.20
Badger	.38	−.35	−.16	−.02	.67	−.20
Unidentifiable	.27	.07	−.15	−.15	.76	−.15
% variance explained	39	15	10	10	9	9

artifact classes over the cluster zones defined. Second, each of the first three
factors has some kind of high loading for stone tools. Because these rotated
factors are orthogonal, this indicates several statistically independent depositional
contexts for human artifacts. Finally, three factors have no high loadings for lithic
materials; these independent axes show that at least some aspects of bone accumulation lack positive spatial association with human artifacts.

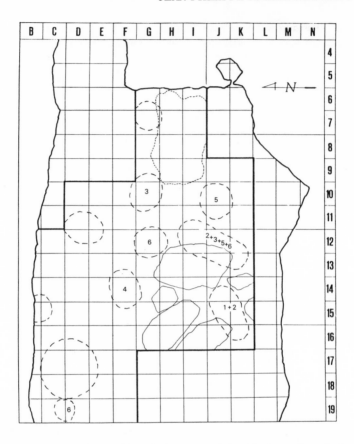

Figure 8. Map of cluster zones defined by k-means analysis with content factor loadings shown in zone areas. Factor numbers correspond to Table 2. Factor scores are given in Table 3.

In general, a high percentage of common variance is accounted for by the six factors. The distribution of that variance among the factors is instructive. Factor 1, correlating most of the cultural artifact classes and many of the bone classes, accounts for 39% of the sample common variance. Thus much of the common variation in the cluster content can be attributed to one independent dimension that involves most of the human artifact classes recovered from Couche VIII. If the common variance contributed by the second and third factors is considered, then 64% of the total is accounted for by factors showing high loadings for stone artifacts. The last three factors have no high loadings for stone artifacts; they may be the products of human activity, or they may reflect the activities of nonhuman site occupants. However, these factors collectively account for very little of the sample common variance (28%).

The spatial distribution of independent content factors can be examined by scoring each of the 11 cluster zones according to the rotated factor solution (Table 3). High scores (≥1) are mapped at cluster locations in Figure 8. Note that the two densest cluster zones, both located at the southern edge of the excavation near and within the rock circle, are complex accumulations of several independent content vectors. Cluster zones in the central part of the site show content profiles of a single factor. Dispersed northern clusters contain no distinctive content profile in terms of the six-factor solution.

4.3. Refitting

Geneste's refitting of lithic materials reveals a general lack of relation between the three important sectors of the site defined both visually and by quantitative analysis (Geneste 1985). Lithics could be joined *within* zones (Figure 9). However, not a single refit links any of the separate zones. Moreover, distinct raw materials were conjoined within each zone, although materials were varied in all areas.

Delpech (1988) found a more complicated pattern in bone refits (Figure 10). Zones 1 and 2 could be related by a series of refitted bone fragments, whereas

Table 3. Factor Scores for Contents of 11 Cluster Zones Defined by K-Means Analysis of Couche VIII (Simek 1987) (Zones were defined as illustrated in Figure 5. Positive factor scores greater than 1 are mapped on Figure 8.)

Cluster zone	Factor					
	1	2	3	4	5	6
1	−.93	.05	−.46	−.33	−.37	1.71
2	−.89	−.19	−.33	−.21	−.13	−.21
3	−1.06	−.17	−.02	−.26	.21	−.05
4	−.09	−.05	−.26	2.78	−.33	−.05
5	1.87	1.77	−.55	.10	−1.32	−1.07
6	.49	1.30	1.82	−.42	2.11	1.73
7	.52	−1.17	−.32	−.86	−.96	1.15
8	−.33	.23	−1.05	−.42	.42	−.66
9	.12	−.79	2.02	−.32	−.99	−1.29
10	.78	−1.00	−.34	.16	1.89	−.52
11	−.47	.00	−.52	−.21	−.53	−.75

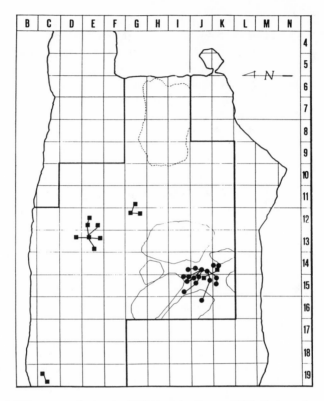

Figure 9. Refitting pattern for Couche VIII lithics (after Geneste 1985). Circles and squares represent distinct raw material types.

Zone 3 had no links to the other two artifact concentrations. In sum, refitting reveals a discordance between the stone and bone distributions from Couche VIII.

5. DISCUSSION AND CONCLUSIONS

In concluding this chapter we would like to address two concerns. First, we will formulate an interpretation of the Couche VIII deposit. Second, we would like to outline what we feel are the interpretive strengths and weaknesses of each analytic technique applied to the Grotte XV data. We hope to show the benefit of using a variety of spatial techniques to enrich inferences about site formation processes.

The Couche VIII distribution has three major components, two of which are related and a third that may or may not be linked to the other two. Zone 1, the

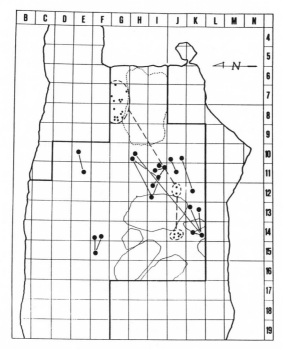

Figure 10. Refitting pattern for Couche VIII bones (after Delpech 1988; Rigaud and Geneste 1988). Dashed lines enclose fragments of single bones; these were joined between areas by a single piece from each group.

densest artifact accumulation, is sheltered within a large rock mass and is composed of a variety of artifact classes. Content analysis, both visual and quantitative, confirms the diverse character of this accumulation. The products of several activities defined by visual study and two different statistical factors are present in this area. Both quantitative factors (statistically independent of each other) have stone tool associations.

Given topographic constraints on deposition in Zone 1 (as discussed), it is unclear whether one or several activities or even occupations are reflected in this area. Examination of another zone sheds light on this problem. Zone 2, located to the east of Zone 1, is unconstrained by interior cave topography. In this area, visual examination shows a more dispersed set of materials than represented in Zone 1. Quantitative techniques show that Zone 2 groups two bone clusters with a lithic cluster and that a number of independent statistical factors contribute to the accumulation contents. Factors with stone tool correlations, probably related to human activity, are present. However, other statistical dimensions lacking tool correlations also occur in this zone, and these may reflect the activities of nonhuman site occupants. Refitting shows a series of links among bone fragments between Zones 1 and 2, but no lithics could be joined. Thus bones seem to have moved between zones whereas stones did not. According to Binford (1988), most of the bones showing carnivore gnawing occur in these two zones. Yet, quantitative analyses show that bone and stone distributions correspond rather well in Zones 1 and 2.

These distributional, content, and refitting patterns allow the recognition of certain formation processes. It seems likely that accumulation Zones 1 and 2 were produced by human action because stone tools are important components of each area. It may be that humans manipulated stone and bone materials at both locations, or the accumulations may be secondary dumps. In either case, some agent, perhaps wild scavenging dogs (evidenced by the presence of *Cuon sp.*) picked over the bones associated with the lithics after deposition by humans, gnawing some fragments and possibly moving individual pieces from one area to the other. This scenario seems more probable than the opposite sequence—humans picking over two separate dog accumulations—because various human activities, including stone tool production and burning, also occurred in both areas (witnessed by the presence of cores, debitage, and burnt stone materials).

Zone 3, a scatter of lithic debitage concentrations and bone accumulations, reflects varied and discrete deposits over the northern part of the cave. Here, single statistical factors lacking stone tool associations, or no factors at all, account for cluster contents. Theses accumulations may represent specialized human activities (e.g., knapping or napping) and/or the formation of small bone accumulations through nonhuman carnivore activity. In any case, the formation of Zone 3 accumulations produced a distinct kind of spatial structure from that in Zones 1 and 2. Even if similar activities were performed in all three areas, Zone 3 deposits would reflect horizontally dispersed concentrations like those layered into the denser southern accumulations because of internal cave topography.

Overall, these studies seem to indicate that human occupation of the Grotte XV was important in the formation of Couche VIII and that a range of activities were performed by human visitors involving stone tools and animal carcasses. Yet the presence of carnivore bones and evidence for bone gnawing on some of the bone fragments from Couche VIII indicate that at last part of the observed patterning was produced by nonhuman agents. Binford (1988) has analyzed both the taphonomy of the bone assemblage and the spatial distribution of certain carnivore-affected elements, and he has argued that wild canids were the most important influence on the Couche VIII bone artifacts (e.g., Binford 1985). Our analyses, however, suggest that humans were the primary agents of deposition during the formation of Couche VIII and that carnivores worked over the remains of human occupations.

Although it seems probable that humans were largely responsible for the spatial patterning of materials in Couche VIII, this is not to say that humans organized their activities in space. Lithic reduction, the use of notched tools and sidescrapers, the manipulation of fire, and certain consumption activities probably represent discrete activities in the usual sense of that concept. However, our analyses show that material residues of such activities occur together in space. This kind of patterning illustrates an important methodological problem. The traditional concept of "activity area," although perhaps useful in terms of observable activity performance (e.g., in an ethnographic context), is not necessarily a valid concept in terms of deposition. Simply put, people might well perform "activities" in "areas," but there is no reason to expect them to map those areas with their garbage; material products of activities may often be collected in dump locations along with the products of other activities performed in other areas, although this may not always be the case (e.g., Binford 1978). Couche VIII seems to comprise artifacts resulting from a variety of activities, perhaps executed in spatially discrete areas, deposited into a series of palimpsests of variable intensity.

In conclusion, we would like to offer some thoughts on the efficacy of the three techniques used here to examine archaeological spatial patterns. Each method offers insight into the complexity and richness of the phenomena being observed, whereas each also has a limited view of the data. The visual technique allows the recognition of clear-cut and fundamental patterning; moreover, observed patterning can easily be integrated with other kinds of knowledge, for example, topographic conditions. Once spatial patterns have been identified, artifact class co-occurrence can be assessed, but this is best accomplished in the context of general and basic patterns. Quantitative techniques are not necessarily preferable to visual analysis when clear patterning is present, but the former can often recognize finer scale patterns within large-scale configurations.

Quantitative means for analyzing cluster contents are adept at assessing multivariate patterns of artifact class co-occurrence; visual techniques normally deal best with bivariate assessments. Both techniques are most useful when they employ the results of artifact distribution studies and do not try to accomplish both spatial and content studies simultaneously (Simek 1984a).

Refitting is an important addition to spatial analyses of all kinds because it provides an objective means to relate spatially discrete material accumulations, although the *meaning* of refit links is often unclear. In Couche VIII, refitting of bones links Zones 1 and 2, although those deposits with the most variable content profiles (the northern or Zone 3 deposits) have no demonstrable relations with the southern zones. Results of refitting here, as in many cases, are more easily understood when considered in light of other analytic findings (e.g., content profiles, bone taphonomy, etc.). As we have suggested, the observed refit pattern indicates that some bones deposited together with stones were moved; given that some bones were gnawed in some areas, this may reflect carnivore alteration of a human spatial pattern.

In conclusion, the deposition of archaeological materials during the formation of Couche VIII from Grotte XV comprised a series of processes involving both human and nonhuman animal occupations of the cave. Although humans were probably the primary agent responsible for the artifact distribution, they were probably not the only one. The nature of some of the deposits (especially Zone 1 with its several content components and topographic context) suggests that correspondence between the deposits today and the locations of ancient human or animal *activities* may not be very precise. This is surely a complicated and, from a reconstuctionist point of view, unsatisfying picture of human behavior at the site. However, spatial data may not always hold the kinds of information reconstruction demands. Using a single analytic technique, it would be rather easy to interpret the deposit too simplistically. Only when the analytic convergence and deviation of several techniques is examined can the true complexity of site formation be appreciated.

ACKNOWLEDGMENTS

Any archaeological excavation and analysis project involves a team effort of huge proportions. Our synthetic work on spatial patterning at the Cave XV relies heavily on studies performed by various scholars whose work appears in the site monograph. F. Delpech and J-M. Geneste provided especially important data derived from their unpublished analyses of site materials. Computer analyses were performed at the University of Tennessee Computer Center with the support of the Department of Anthropology. Of course, the results of our synthetic work can only be blamed on us.

6. REFERENCES

Binford, L. R., 1964, A Consideration of Archaeological Research Design, *American Antiquity* 29:425–41.
Binford, L. R., 1978, Dimensional Analysis of Behavior and Site Structure: Learning from an Eskimo Hunting Stand, *American Antiquity* 43:330–61.
Binford, L. R., 1979, *Nunamiut Ethnoarchaeology*, Academic Press, New York.
Binford, L. R., 1981, *Bones: Ancient Men and Modern Myths*, Academic Press, New York.
Binford, L. R., 1984, *Faunal Remains from Klasies River Mouth*, Academic Press, New York.
Binford, L. R., 1985, Human Ancestors: Changing Views of Their Behavior, *Journal of Anthropological Archaeology* 4:292–327.
Binford, L. R., 1988, Etude Taphonomique des Restes Fauniques de la Grotte Vaufrey, Couche VIII. In *La Grotte Vaufrey: Paleoenvironnement, Chronologie, Activites Humaines* (J-Ph. Rigaud, ed.), Memoires de la Societe Prehistoriques Francaise, Tome 19, C.N.R.S., Paris, pp. 535–564.
Binford, L. R. and Bertram, J., 1977, Bone Frequencies and Attritional Processes. In *Background for Theory Building* (L. R. Binford, ed.), Academic Press, New York, pp. 77–153.

Binford, L. R., Binford, S., Whallon, R., and Hardin, M., 1970, Archaeology at Hatchery West, *American Antiquity* 35(4):1–91.

Brain, C. K., 1981, *The Hunters or the Hunted? An Introduction to American Cave Tephonomy*, University of Chicago Press, Chicago.

Bunn, H., Harris, J., Isaac, G., Kaufulu, Z., Kroll, E., Schick, K., Toth, N., and Behrensmeyer, A., 1980, FxJj50: An Early Pleistocene site in Northern Kenya, *World Archaeology* 12:109–36.

Bunn, H., and Kroll, E. 1987, On Inferences from the Zhoukoudian Fauna, *Current Anthropology* 28:199–201.

Cahen, D., Keeley, L., and Van Noten, F., 1979, Stone tools, Toolkits, and Human Behavior in Prehistory, *Current Anthropology* 20:661–72.

Carr, C., 1984, The Nature of Organization of Intrasite Archaeological Records and Spatial Analytic Approaches to Their Investigation, *Advances in Archaeological Method and Theory* 7:103–222.

Clarke, D., 1968, *Analytic Archaeology*, Methuen, London.

Clarke, D., 1977, Spatial Information in Archaeology. In *Spatial Archaeology* (D. Clarke, ed.), Academic Press, New York, pp. 1–32.

Dacey, M., 1973, Statistical Tests of Spatial Association in the Locations of Tool Types, *American Antiquity* 38:320–28.

Delpech, F., 1988, Les Grandes Mammiferes de la Grotte Vaufrey a l'Exception des Ursides. In *La Grotte Vaufrey: Paleoenvironnement, Chronologie, Activities Humaines* (J-Ph. Rigaud, ed.), Memoires de la Societe Prehistoriques Francaise, Tome 19, C.N.R.S., Paris, pp. 213–290.

Delporte, H., 1968, L'Abri Facteur a Tursac (Dordogne): Iétude generale, *Galia Préhistoire* 11:1–112.

Geneste, J-M., 1985, *Analyse Lithique d'Industries Moustériennes en Périgord: Une Approache Technologique du Comportement des Groupes Humaines au Paléolithique Moyen*, Thèse du Sciences, Université de Bordeaux I.

Gould, R., 1977, *Living Archaeology*, Cambridge University Press, New York.

Hietala, H., and Stevens, D., 1977, Spatial Analysis: Multiple procedures in pattern recognition studies, *American Antiquity* 42:539–559.

Hodder, I., and Orton, C., 1976, *Spatial Analysis in Archaeology*, Cambridge University Press, New York.

Kintigh, K., and Ammerman, A., 1982, Heuristic Approaches to Spatial Analysis in Archaeology, *American Antiquity* 47:31–63.

Laville, H., 1975, *Climatologie et Chronologie du Paléolithique en Périgord: Étude Sédimentologique de Dépots en Grottes et Sous Abris*, Université de Provence, Aix-en-Provence.

Laville, H., and Kervazo, B., 1988, Etude Stratigraphique et Analyse Physicochimique de la Grotte Vaufrey. In *La Grotte Vaufrey: Paleoenvironnement, Chronologie, Activities Humaines* (J-Ph. Rigaud, ed.), Memoires de la Societe Prehistoriques Francaise, Tome 19, C.N.R.S., Paris, pp. 89–154.

Laville, H., Rigaud, J-Ph., and Sackett, J., 1980, *Rock Shelters of the Perigord*, Academic Press, New York.

Leroi-Gourhan, A., and Brézillon, M., 1966, L'habitation magdalénienne no. 1 de Pincevent près de Montereau (Seine-et-Marne), *Gallia Préhistoire* 9:263–385.

Leroi-Gourhan, A., and Brézillon, M., 1972, *Fouilles de Pincevent: Essai d'Analyse Ethnographique d'un Habitat Magdalénien*, *Gallia Préhistoire*, 7th Supplement, C.N.R.S., Paris.

Rigaud, J-Ph., 1978, The Significance of Variability among Lithic Artifacts: A Specific Case from Southwestern France, *Journal of Anthropological Research* 34:299–310.

Rigaud, J-Ph., 1982, *Le Paléolithique en Périgord: Les Donnees du Sud-Ouest Sarladais et Leurs Implications*, Thèse de Doctorat d'Ètat es Sciences Naturelles No. 737. Université de Bordeaux I.

Rigaud, J-Ph. (ed.), 1988, *La Grotte Vaufrey: Paleoenvironnement, Chronologie, Activities Humaines*, Memoires de la Societe Prehistoriques Francaise, Tome 19, C.N.R.S., Paris.

Rigaud, J-Ph., and Geneste, J-M., 1988, L'Utilization de l'Espace dans la Grotte Vaufrey. In *La Grotte*

Vaufrey: Paleoenvironnement, Chronologie, Activites Humaines (J-Ph. Rigaud, ed.), Memoires de la Societe Prehistoriques Francaise, Tome 19, C.N.R.S., Paris, pp. 593–612.

Rigaud, J-Ph., and Simek, J., 1987, "Arms Too Short to Box with God": Problems and Prospects for Paleolithic Prehistory in Dordogne, Southwestern France. In *The Pleistocene Old World: Regional Perspectives* (O. Soffer, ed.), Plenum Press, New York, pp. 47–61.

Schiffer, M., 1972, Archaeological Context and Systemic Context, *American Antiquity* 37:156–65.

Schiffer, M., 1976, *Behavioral Archaeology*, Academic Press, New York.

Schiffer, M., 1983, Toward the Identification of Formation Processes, *American Antiquity* 48:675–706.

Schiffer, M., 1987, *Formation Processes of the Archaeological Record*, University of New Mexico Press, Albuquerque.

Simek, J. F., 1984a, *A K-Means Approach to the Analysis of Upper Paleolithic Habitation Sites: Le Flageolet I and Pincevent 36*, British Archaeological Reports, Oxford.

Simek, J. F., 1984b, Integrating Pattern and Context in Spatial Archaeology, *Journal of Archaeological Science* 11:405–20.

Simek, J. F., 1987, Spatial Order and Behaviorial Change in the French Paleolithic, *Antiquity* 61:25–40.

Simek, J. F., 1988, Analyse de la Repartition Spatiale des Vestiges de la Couche VIII de la Grotte Vaufrey. In *La Grotte Vaufrey: Paleoenvironnement, Chronologie, Activites Humaines* (J-Ph. Rigaud, ed.), Memoires de la Societe Prehistoriques Francaise, Tome 19, C.N.R.S., Paris, pp. 569–593.

Simek, J. F., and Larick, R. R., 1983, The Recognition of Multiple Spatial Patterns: A Case Study from the French Upper Paleolithic, *Journal of Archaeological Science* 10:165–80.

Stein, J. K., 1983, Earthworm Activity: A Source of Potential Disturbance of Archaeological Sediments, *American Antiquity* 48:277–289.

Whallon, R., 1973, Spatial Analysis of Occupation Floors I: Application of Dimensional Analysis of Variance, *American Antiquity* 38:266–278.

Whallon, R., 1974, Spatial Analysis of Occupation Floors II: The Application of Nearest Neighbor Analysis, *American Antiquity* 39:16–34.

Whallon, R., 1984, Unconstrained Clustering for the Analysis of Spatial Distributions in Archaeology. In *Intrasite Spatial Analysis in Archaeology* (H. Hietala, ed.), Cambridge University Press, Cambridge, pp. 242–277.

Yellen, J., 1977, *Archaeological Approaches to the Present: Models for Reconstructing the Past*, Academic Press, New York.

Chapter 7

Left in the Dust
Contextual Information in Model-Focused Archaeology

CHRISTOPHER CARR

1. INTRODUCTION

Many of the chapters in this volume explore models for identifying and interpreting archaeological intrasite spatial patterns. The purpose of this chapter is not to discuss models, *per se*. Rather, it is to stress the complementary roles of models and contextual data in the scientific process. In the excitement of building, testing, and applying models, there can be a tendency to focus too quickly and unduely on a narrow range of data specified by some model, to the exclusion of a broader arena of relevant contextual information. I will discuss some general problems with this model-focused approach and some advantages of using contextual data.

While exploring this broader topic, four additional points will be made. First is that contextual data become more essential to the process of identifying a phenomenon as its characteristics become more ambiguous—a condition often true of archaeological observations. Second, the attitude and techniques of exploratory data analysis (Tukey 1977), which allow the integration of contextual data, are often critical to accurately identifying and interpreting intrasite spatial patterns. Third is the importance of using multiple, alternative models to identify and interpret patterns. This is one of the basic tenets of exploratory data analysis. Fourth, the process of analysis, which culminates in identification and interpretation, is broader than the process of applying a model deductively to data in

CHRISTOPHER CARR • Department of Anthropology, Arizona State University, Tempe, Arizona 85287.

221

order to identify or interpret a phenomenon. The two processes should not be confused.

Each of these subjects will be illustrated with the problem of identifying spatial patterns at the site of Pincevent habitation no. 1 (Leroi-Gourhan and Brézillon 1966). Pincevent is an Upper Paleolithic reindeer hunting camp in northern France.

Focus will be on the logical process of "identification" rather than "interpretation" (Figure 1), as defined by Binford (1977). Identification is the process of inferring "facts" from primary observations or the patterns found among them. It is accomplished with "middle-range theory" (Binford 1977:6), which relates observations or patterns to their formation processes, and these to some identity.

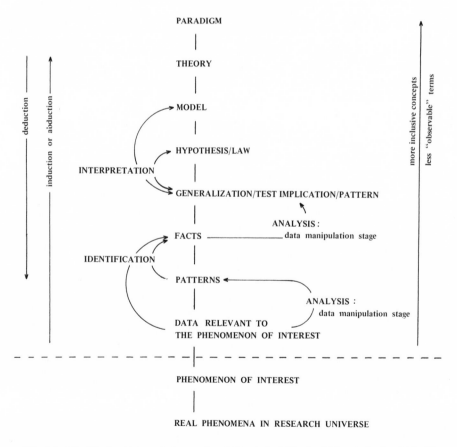

Figure 1. Identification, interpretation, and analytic manipulation in relation to levels of scientific thought and information.

For example, spatial patterns of artifacts around a prehistoric hearth, suggesting their having been tossed and dropped, might be used to identify the hearth as a men's outside hearth rather than an interior one. In contrast, interpretation is the process of explaining a pattern among inferred facts or data by subsuming it under some theoretical framework: explanation in the usual sense (Hemple 1966; Salmon and Salmon 1979). For example, regional spatial distributions of male and female activities—inferred facts—might be found to associate with the seasons of activity—more inferred facts. This pattern might be interpreted using social and economic theory regarding the division of labor. Whereas the process of identification often leads to reconstruction of the states or values taken by variables, which are conditions in the past, the process of interpretation often involves relating variables to each other.

The term *context* has been given many meanings in archaeology (cf. Taylor 1948; Schiffer 1972; Butzer 1982; Hodder 1982). In this chapter, contextual data are defined as those that are relevant to identifying some archaeological observation or pattern, or to interpreting some facts, excluding the data that are used by the one model to make the identification/interpretation. Thus contextual data are not definable in absolute terms, such as environmental contextual data or historical contextual data. Rather, they are defined relative to the phenomenon of interest and the current model being applied to understand it. Data used by a current model can serve as contextual data relative to another model. Contextual data can also be case-specific circumstances that are unlikely to have identifying or interpreting power in general and that consequently are unlikely to be included in models for identifying observations/patterns or interpreting facts.

2. THE IMPORTANCE OF CONTEXTUAL DATA

When making identifications, archaeologists have traditionally used implicit, commonsense models (e.g., Taylor 1948). These contrast with explicit models of formation processes, which are becoming more common in the field today, especially in the United States (e.g., Binford 1978, 1980; Schiffer 1976; Keeley 1977; Yellen 1977).

Explicit models are preferable to the extent that their application permits scrutiny of the logic of identification. However, in moving from intuitive to explicit identifications, there has also been a tendency in American archaeology to narrow the range of exploited data from the diversity of relevant information that is stored in the researcher's mind to many fewer data that are directly specified by middle-range theory. Contextual information, which is often case-specific and cannot be accommodated in theory, is left behind.

This practice of focusing solely on model-specified data rather than on these in conjunction with contextual data is unwise in any scientific endeavor. It can have several negative consequences, as follows.

First, by not letting all of the data speak for themselves, contextual evidence that happens to be strongly supporting or refuting in a specific case may be bypassed for much weaker evidence that is stipulated by the model.

Second, overlooking diverse contextual data and focusing on a limited, model-specified range of information does not encourage the *accurate* identification of observations/patterns. This is especially true when the characteristics of the observations have moderate ambiguity, that is, when the characteristics are not strongly determined by or reflective of unique processes and thus are not good indicators of the observations' identities. The behavioral sciences and sciences of the past, including archaeology, are typified by such data. Here, single characteristics often are unreliable indicators of single processes or else simultaneously reflect multiple processes.

In archaeology, ambiguity results from the degrading, transforming, or pattern-changing effects of cultural and natural formation processes (e.g., Schiffer 1983; Wood and Johnson 1978); from the polythetic nature of behavior and many of the formal properties of material culture (e.g., Carr 1984; Clarke 1968; Goodenough 1965; Williams *et al.* 1973); from the overlapping and indeterminant relations rather than one-to-one mapping between material form, function, behavior, and ideas (e.g., Sackett 1982); and from our lack of knowledge of the full repertoire of past behaviors and technologies.

For ambiguous data, by definition, the probability of determining the correct identity of each kind of relevant observation is unacceptably low when they are considered individually, outside of the context of each other. It is advantageous, instead, to consider multiple kinds of relevant observations *simultaneously*, each as a *context* to the other, and to look for *mutually reinforcing* identifying patterns among them. That is, one asks, "Of all the identifications possibly assignable to each kind of relevant observation on the basis of its characteristics, which identities are shared in common or are logically related to each other?" It is these identities that will have greater prior probabilities of being correct. Thus looking for mutually reinforcing identifying patterns increases the chance of correctly identifying each kind of observation and each observation, on the average.

This approach to using contextual data is analogous to taking a multivariate as opposed to a univariate view of the world. It is similar to using R-mode factor analysis to derive the primary underlying dimensions that commonly structure the characteristics of a set of observations, as opposed to considering each kind of observation by itself for its individual meaning. In semantics, it is analogous to assigning meanings to words in a sentence. Several words may each have multiple meanings, but in the context of each other, their case-specific meanings are constrained to a more limited set and become known with greater certainty.

A detailed example of the strategy of simultaneous identification, where observations have ambiguous meanings and each is used as a context for the other to determine its probable identity, is provided by Carr (1982:218–308).

Here, some kinds of tools and debris in a Middle Woodland base camp in Illinois could not be assigned functions with any certainty on an individual basis. The morphological and raw material characteristics of each such class of items had multiple possible uses. However, based on the spatial associations of the classes and the possible functions that associated classes shared, the probable functional identity of each was constrained to a much more limited set.

Third, and related to the second consequence, overlooking contextual data and focusing on model-specified data during identification does not encourage the building of a *coherent* system of facts from a holistic system of observations. In a model-focused identification strategy, each kind of observation is identified individually with only a small portion of all the data that are available and relevant—those specified by the model. Different kinds of observations are identified sequentially with different models. Attempts may then be made to integrate the identifications—the facts—into a larger picture. However, there is no guarantee that they will fit together, for they have not been inferred in consort as a system.

This is especially true when observations are ambiguous. In this case, the chance of correctly identifying each kind of observation individually is not good. Consequently, the inferred facts have a low probability of coordinating in an integrated system of knowledge. When observations are ambiguous, simultaneous consideration of multiple kinds of observations for their shared or related meanings is a more appropriate procedure. It is more likely to produce correct identifications and logically consistent facts.

Deriving an internally inconsistent set of facts from a system of observations is less likely to be a problem when the ambiguity of individual observations is negligible. In this case, even if different kinds of observations are identified by themselves, each has a high probability of being identified correctly. Inferred facts thus have a good chance of coordinating. Consequently, model-focused identification of individual observations becomes a justifiable procedure. This circumstance often does not pertain, however, to the identification of archaeological observations, which are commonly ambiguous, as described before.

Fourth, by not considering contextual data and instead restricting analysis to the data that pertain to a single model, one reduces the diversity of data that are used in making the reconstruction. This may reduce the plausibility of the argument (Hemple 1966:34).

3. EXPLORATORY DATA ANALYSIS

Consistent with recognizing the importance of contextual data in making archaeological identifications is the philosophy of exploratory data analysis. Exploratory data analysis (EDA) in a strict sense is a set of robust quantitative and visual techniques for recognizing patterns in data (Tukey and Wilk 1970; Tukey 1977). Underlying the application of these techniques, however, is a more general philosophy of how data should be investigated (Tukey 1980). EDA stresses the importance of inductive versus deductive logic. It centers on the question, "What *unanticipated* structures or relationships occur within the data, regardless of expectation?," as opposed to assessing whether a particular structure, stipulated by a model, occurs within them (Tukey and Wilk 1970:371; Hartwig and Dearing 1979:9–10). Thus the philosophy of EDA encourages the use of diverse contextual data, rather than a limited set of model-specified data, in the process of identification.

Although consistent with a context-sensitive approach to identification, EDA is broader. EDA has as its goal the search for patterns regardless of the phenomena to which they pertain. EDA aims at understanding the totality of a data structure in order to generate new ideas, problem areas, and hypotheses (Tukey 1979:122, 1980:23–24). In contrast, the process of identification focuses on understanding a particular phenomenon of interest.

Thus, a context-sensitive approach to identification strictly concords not with EDA but CEDA: constrained exploratory data analysis (Carr 1985a:31–34). CEDA, like EDA, has as its goal the understanding of a data set's total structure. However, this is done in order to isolate those aspects of it that are relevant to one explicitly specified phenomenon of interest, as defined deductively by the larger theoretical framework, paradigm, or problem domain of the researcher. CEDA is an inductive middle step that encourages the researcher to examine a wide range of data from many angles, but within a larger deductive framework that focuses on a single phenomenon. In contrast, EDA is truly an exploratory, unbounded process for initiating inductive analysis. Context-sensitive identification, in evoking a wide range of data but focusing ultimately on a single phenomenon, is consistent with CEDA.

4. USING MULTIPLE, ALTERNATIVE MODELS

One of the basic tenets of EDA and CEDA is that it is preferable to use multiple, alternative models rather than a single model to evaluate data. This holds true for a context-sensitive approach to identification, as well. There are three reasons.

First, usually it is only with multiple models that diverse and contextual data can be accommodated in the identifying process and that mutually reinforcing patterns can be explored. A single model usually pertains to only a narrow range of formation processes and data.

Second, using multiple models as baselines for envisioning data can lead to the discovery of unsuspected data patterns and suggest unexpected identities. The search for hidden data patterns is a primary rationale behind exploratory data analysis and is always a worthwhile endeavor (Tukey and Wilk 1970).

Third, when only one model is used, it becomes difficult to assess the significance of any points of discordance between the data and the model and to evaluate whether the model-specified identification is applicable. Is a 60%, 70%, 80%, or 90% fit between an identifying model and data sufficient for accepting that identity (Hemple 1966:33–34)? Moreover, one is not necessarily guided by the discordances toward any more appropriate model and identity, although this may sometimes be true.

In contrast, when multiple, alternative models are played off against one another, the significance of discordances for different models can be assessed on a relative scale—relative to each other—and the model with the best fit and with the identity that is most probable becomes clear. If the fit of all the models is at best moderate, directionality in their ranking or mutually reinforcing patterns among the residuals from different models may suggest the applicability of other potential models and identities (see later discussion on "abduction"). Rank directionality in the fit of models is especially useful when the casual processes described by the models differ in degree, whereas mutually reinforcing patterns among residuals are useful when the processes differ in kind.

5. MODELING AND ANALYSIS

The final general point of this chapter is that applying a model to a set of data and confirming deductively that the data fit it, in order to identify an observation or pattern, or to interpret a fact, should not be confounded with the process of analysis. Analysis is a broader activity, which if successful, leads to identification or interpretation and includes these as its end products (Figure 1). Analysis includes several kinds of activities: definition, measurement, manipulation, and inference. These respectively pertain to selecting a set of relevant observations and variables; selecting the variables' scale(s) and collecting data with those rules, searching for patterns in data or modeling data, and identification or interpretation. Analysis should not be reduced to the status of determining deductively whether data fit a model.

Analysis requires the use of diverse contextual data as well as explicit models and model-specified data. It also requires data exploration, including inductive and abductive logic (Hanson 1972) as well as model confirmation through deduction (Carr 1985a). These requirements follow directly from the above remarks on EDA. As Tukey (1980) has commented, "We need both exploratory and confirmatory," and by implication, context as well as model.

6. ILLUSTRATION

6.1. Two Views of Pincevent Habitation No. 1

To illustrate these points, let us turn to the site of Pincevent habitation no. 1 (Leroi-Gourhan and Brézillon 1966), a reindeer hunting camp in northern France. Habitation no. 1 dates to the late Magdalenian with radiocarbon assays ranging from 10,760 ± 60 B.P. (Grn-4383) to 12,300 ± 400 B.P. (Gif-358). It occurs in a late glacial tundra setting. The site is one of a series of similar small artifact scatters that are found at various stratigraphic levels within the area. The occupation is comprised of concentrations of lithic artifacts and reindeer bones around three aligned hearths (Figure 2).

Figure 2. Pincevent habitation no. 1. Reproduced from *Gallia Préhistoire.*

The excavators of the site, Leroi-Gourhan and Brézillon, have suggested that each hearth occurred within a hut of skin and poles (Figure 3a) and that the three huts overlapped to form a single larger tent with a common central gallery and multiple entrances (Figure 3b). Skin tents are common among mobile hunters of the Arctic and Subarctic and would not be unexpected at Pincevent. On the other hand, Binford (1983:156–160) has identified Hearths 2 and 3 as men's outdoor hearths, with a tent possibly having existed over Hearth 1. Hearths 2 and 3 are thought to have been made and used sequentially in response to a change in wind direction during a single occupation. Thus Binford disagrees with Leroi-Gourhan and Brézillon at the basic level of identification, concerned with developing facts.

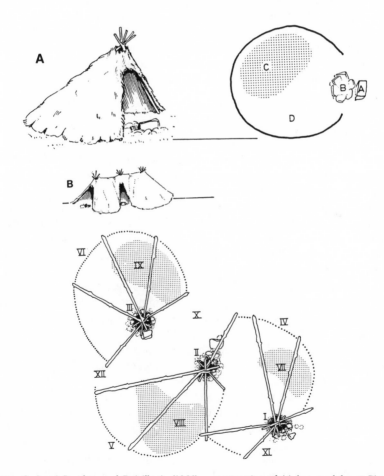

Figure 3. Leroi-Gourhan and Brézillon's (1966) reconstruction of (a) hut modules at Pincevent habitation no. 1 and (b) their integration into a common tent structure. Reproduced from *Gallia Préhistoire*.

The difference between the behavioral meanings assigned to the hearths and artifact scatters by these researchers is significant. It directly affects higher level identifications and facts. For example, estimates of site population, based on hut floor area, are affected by the meaning assigned to the hearths. When combined with seasonality and faunal kill information, their meaning also influences estimates of the duration of site occupation (Carr 1985b:385–391) and assessments of whether the site was a logistic camp or residential camp. Whereas Leroi-Gourhan and Brézillon conclude the site to be a residential base camp, Binford apparently identifies it as a logistic camp (Binford 1978:357).

The approaches used by Leroi-Gourhan and Brézillon and Binford to understand habitation no. 1 are very different. Leroi-Gourhan and Brézillon used a broad variety of contextual data and multiple models—some implicit, some explicit. The flow of their logic is generally inductive and abductive. Each of these characteristics reflects an attitude similar to CEDA. In contrast, Binford used one explicit model and a narrow range of data pertinent to it. The flow of his logic is deductive. Each of these traits define an approach similar to confirmatory statistics. Both approaches have deficiencies, and, as shall be seen, a synthesis of their strengths is preferable.

6.2. A Model-Focused Approach

First let us look at Binford's reconstruction. The model that Binford used describes the expectable distribution of debris around a men's outside hearth (Figure 4). Such hearths are said to be identifiable by two concentric arcs of debris concentration: an inner drop zone and an outer toss zone (Binford 1978:345, 355; 1983:149–156). A drop zone is composed primarily of small waste items that result from activities performed by a group of men who are seated in a circle around a fire. The items drop around each man or fall between his legs as he works (Binford 1978:349). Because the items are small, they are not bothersome to further work and are left in place. Examples of items include small impact chips created during stone-tool knapping or small fragments of bone created during marrow cracking. In contrast, a toss zone is composed of larger debris that would disrupt further work or make it impossible to sit down later if the debris were allowed to accumulate in the immediate work area. The debris are tossed behind the men or across the fire in front of them. Examples of larger debris are the intact articulator ends of long bones, the shafts of which have been crushed for marrow. The model also stipulates the spacing and dimensions of toss and drop zones (see later discussion). These parameters are based on the characteristics of men's outside hearths at a Nunamuit Eskimo hunting stand, the Mask site (Binford 1978).

Binford overlayed a scaled version of the Nunamiut model of drop and toss zones over the distribution of stone chipping debris at Pincevent habitation no.1

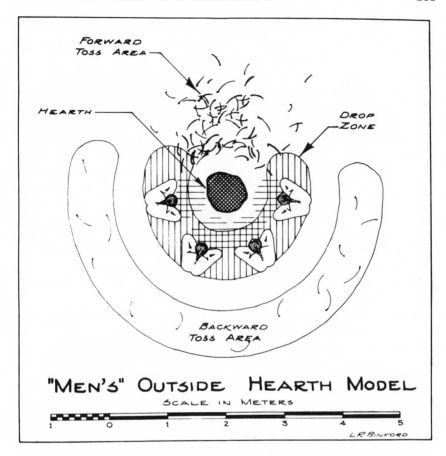

Figure 4. Binford's (1978) model of a men's outside hearth. Reproduced with permission from Lewis R. Binford.

(Figure 5). He (Binford 1983:158) concluded that the distribution at Pincevent "fits exactly" with the drop zone in the Nunamuit model. The fit does appear reasonable. The Nunamiut drop zones illustrated by Binford range from 0 to 1.2 m away from a hearth. At Pincevent, most of the chipping debris that ring the hearths lie 0 to .75 m away. (This is a correction of data previously reported by Carr [1985b:388].) However, there are also arcs of chipping debris at greater distances from the hearths that require identification (see later discussion).

The same model was overlayed by Binford on the total bone distribution at Pincevent, taking that distribution to represent tossed elements (Figure 6). There is no obvious resemblance between the two distributions. In part, this reflects a

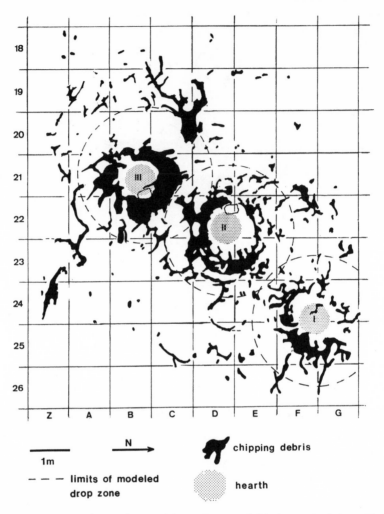

Figure 5. Distribution of stone chipping debris at Pincevent habitation no. 1 relative to Binford's (1978) model of a drop zone around a men's outside hearth.

poor choice of data. The total bone distribution is composed not only of large bones that could have been tossed but also small bones such as splinters, phalanges, and metapodials, which are less likely to have been tossed.

However, even considering and correcting for this problem by examining the individual distributions of specific kinds of faunal elements that could have been tossed, rather than a composite distribution of all bones, the fit of the model to the data is ambiguous. Table 1 shows the number of potentially tossed elements

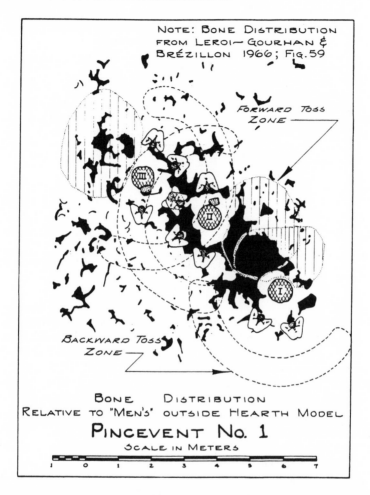

Figure 6. Distribution of all bone debris at Pincevent habitation no. 1 relative to Binford's (1978) model of toss zones around a men's outside hearth. Reproduced with permission from Lewis R. Binford.

(tibia, humeri, femurs, and ribs) that fall within sectors of the modeled drop zones and backward toss zones that do and do not overlap with each other. The data are based on Figures 7 through 10 and are a correction of data presented in Carr (1985b). Several things are clear. First, the data are ambiguous: one-third of the items occur within areas of overlap of the two kinds of zones and cannot be used to support or refute the identification. Depending on how one classifies areas as drop zones or backward toss zones, it is possible to support or refute the fit of the

Table 1.   Distribution of Potentially Tossed Items among Modeled Drop and Toss
Zones at Pincevent Habitation No. 1

Faunal element	Number of items in just drop zones[a]	Number of items in just toss zones[b]	Number of items in areas of overlap of drop and toss zones or between them	Number of items beyond both zones	Total
Tibia	7	7	10	8	32
Humeri	4	6	8	4	22
Femurs	9	8	14	2	33
Ribs	50	29	42	8	129
Total	70	50	74	22	216

[a]A drop zone is defined as 0–1.2 m from a hearth's edge, based on Binford's data from the Mask site.
[b]A toss zone is defined as 1.5–2.5 m from a hearth's edge, based on Binford's data from the Mask site.

model to the data. Second, considering only areas where drop zones and backward toss zones do not overlap, potentially tossed items fall more frequently
within the modeled drop zones than the backward toss zones. This unpredicted
pattern might be taken to suggest that the model fits poorly to the data on faunal
distribution. However, it may also relate again to the ambiguity of the data.
Forward toss zones can occur within potential drop zones. Depending on how
one classifies areas as drop zones or forward toss zones, the data can be made to
strongly support or refute the fit of the model to them. Thus the faunal distributional data cannot be used to support the identification of toss zones and the
hearths as men's outside hearths.

The distribution of ribs (Figure 10) is especially interesting. Ribs are numerous, and some of them form rings around the hearths. As potentially tossed
items, one might consider the rings to represent backward toss zones. However,
given the dimensions of the human body and the spatial geometry of men seated
around a hearth, these rings are too close to the hearths to be backward toss
zones. Some elements are as close as .1 m away. In contrast, the Nunamuit
backward toss zones reported by Binford (1978) range from 1.5 to 2.5 m away.

Other model-specified aspects of the distributional data are not congruent
with the model of a men's outside hearth. First, large faunal elements or lithic
debris occur immediately next to the hearths around most of their perimeters
(Figure 2). They would have created an intolerably rough floor and lead one to
question whether the areas were, indeed, occupied by seated men. Would you
want to sit on the debris shown in Figure 11?

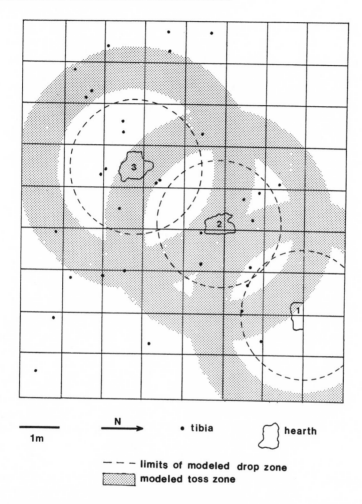

1m

N →

• tibia

⌂ hearth

– – – limits of modeled drop zone
▒▒▒ modeled toss zone

Figure 7. Distribution of reindeer tibia at Pincevent habitation no. 1 relative to Binford's (1978) model of drop and toss zones around a men's outside hearth.

Second, the nature of the borders of potential backward toss zones at Pincevent does not concord with the model. Backward toss zones, by the nature of their formation, should occur as gradients of debris density rather than sharply delimited arcs. Instead, the potentially tossed debris at Pincevent define a number of crisp borders between rings of high and low artifact density. These are seen in Figure 12, a map of most artifacts and debris of bones and stones at Pincevent. Lines 6a, 6c, and 4b correspond to strong breaks in artifact density, which if not

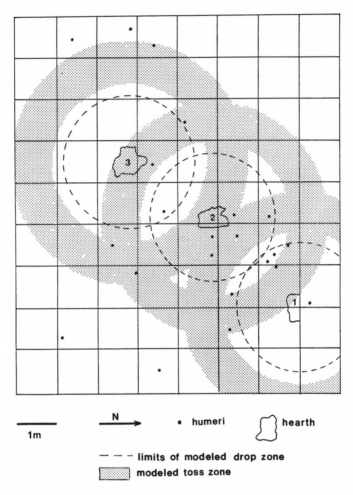

Figure 8. Distribution of reindeer humeri at Pincevent habitation no. 1 relative to Binford's (1978) model of drop and toss zones around a men's outside hearth.

crisp, might define the outer limits of backward toss zones. Lines 5a, 5b, 4a, and 4c correspond to strong density breaks, which if not crisp, might define the inner limits of backward toss zones. Thus, tossing, as described in Binford's model, does not account well for the Pincevent distributions. We shall see later that several kinds of contextual evidence suggest that these density breaks are locations where debris was moved against some now-decomposed or removed structure, such as a hut wall.

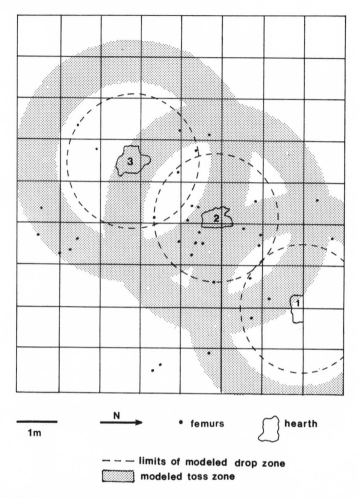

1m   N→   • femurs   ⌐ hearth

— — — limits of modeled drop zone
▒▒▒▒ modeled toss zone

Figure 9. Distribution of reindeer femurs at Pincevent habitation no. 1 relative to Binford's (1978) model of drop and toss zones around a men's outside hearth.

In sum, Binford's analysis of habitation no. 1 is good in that it involves an explicit model for identifying archaeological phenomena. Its explicitness allows one to evaluate the logic of identification. However, the analysis has several drawbacks. (1) Only one model relevant to one set of formation processes was used, rather than multiple, alternative models relevant to multiple kinds of formation processes. This was done despite the fact that Binford (1983:156–158) had built two alternative models, one for outside hearths and one for inside hearths.

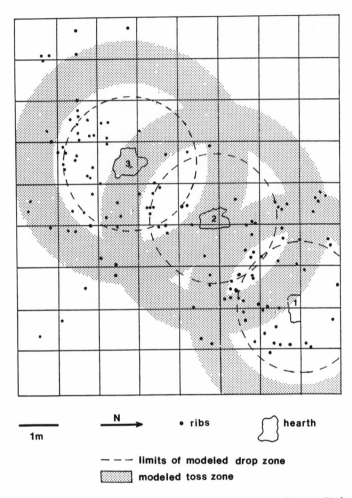

Figure 10. Distribution of reindeer ribs at Pincevent habitation no. 1 relative to Binford's (1978) model of drop and toss zones around a men's outside hearth.

As a consequence, it is difficult to assess the significance of the points of discordance between the data and his model. Had multiple models of different formation processes been used, the stronger of them would have been apparent (see later discussion). Moreover, applying the single model and noting its discordances from the data does not necessarily guide one toward any particular, more appropriate model and identification. (2) The data were handled in a deductive, confirmatory manner, apparently without the benefit of or serious con-

Figure 11. Lithic and bone debris around Hearths 3 (foreground) and 2 (background) at Pincevent habitation no. 1. Reproduced from *Gallia Préhistoire*.

sideration of prior, inductive exploration. Had the attitude of CEDA been seriously adopted, the data would have been envisioned in multiple ways, minimally by positioning arcs of toss and drop zones in various ways (i.e., varying the parameters of the men's outside hearth model). This would have revealed the ambiguity of the data shown in Table 1 and its sources already discussed. It would have suggested the need to examine other, contextual data to identify the nature of the hearths. (3) A rich amount of contextual data was overlooked (see later discussion). Considered jointly, these could have helped resolve the data ambiguities and the identity of the hearths.

In fairness to Binford, it must be said that he may have envisioned Pincevent's formation more holistically in private. However, this is not reflected in the published rendition of his procedure for identification (Binford 1983). Also, his analysis is presented in a book that is intended to be more thought provoking than substantive and in a chapter that is aimed at introducing the reader to identifying models, rather than in a research publication where a fuller treatment might have been given. At the same time, one must question the image of science and analysis that is presented and the manner in which the data are handled, for each of the reasons just given.

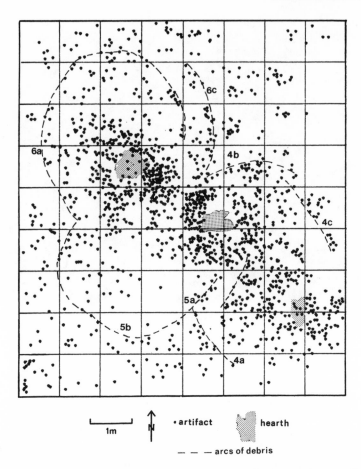

Figure 12. Crisp-bordered arcs of artifacts and debris within the distribution of most artifacts and debris at Pincevent habitation no. 1.

6.3. A Context-Sensitive Approach

Now let us look at Leroi-Gourhan and Brézillon's (1966) approach to understanding habitation no. 1. In a more traditional style of identifying observations/patterning, they use implicit models that are assumed to be understood by the profession at large. Some site-specific lines of reasoning are unstated, as well. These are the primary drawbacks of the study. To the good, multiple, diverse kinds of data are presented, each providing a context for the other. Mutually reinforcing patterns among the data were sought in an inductive, exploratory manner in order to define a coherent system of facts and to develop an integrated picture of the site's formation and use. Multiple alternative formation processes were explicitly considered and tested when identifying some aspects of the site. However, reconstructions alternative to the occurrence of three contemporaneous huts were not explicitly proposed or evaluated.

A number of converging lines support Leroi-Gourhan and Brézillon's conclusion that three huts were built at habitation no. 1, that the hearths were interior ones, and that they were used simultaneously rather than sequentially. Most of these are site-specific and constitute contextual data that would be bypassed by applications of general models for hearth identification. Some of the data are presented by Leroi-Gourhan and Brézillon in explicit support of their reconstruction. Others are simply documented as part of their general description of the site and have been used by me (Carr 1985b and here) to further support their argument.

First, as mentioned, there are arcs of artifacts and debris that have sharp borders in places and that do not correspond well with the expectable nature of toss zones. The arcs are distinguishable in the composite distribution of most artifacts and debris (Figure 12) and in the individual distributions of more frequent artifact classes, such as chipping debris (Figure 13). They were identified by Leroi-Gourhan and Brézillon (1966:332–336, 361) as places where rubbish, which was generated by activities in more central parts of the structure, was swept to its sides, forming a sharply bounded distribution. The empty spaces between the arcs and the hearths were identified as generalized work and sleeping areas that were kept clean and that were the sources of materials moved to the sides of the huts. Both the crispness of the arcs and the complementary arc-void structure support this interpretation.

Similar depositional processes and patterns, involving the build-up of secondary refuse along the walls of structures and the cleaning of central activity areas, have been recorded for the tents of gold rush prospectors in the southwest Yukon (Stevenson 1987), longhouses at Ozette, Washington (Samuels 1983), houses of Guarijo Mexicans (Dodd 1984), and multiroom dwellings at Nawthis Village (Stevenson 1985). These studies add credibility to Leroi-Gourhan and Brézillon's interpretation that huts surrounded the Pincevent hearths.

Stevenson (personal communication) has documented that refuse build-up along the walls of dwellings can result not only from sweeping but simply from persons forgetting where items were placed and from their loss in poorly lighted zones away from central light sources. A Pangnirtungmuit informant at the historic site of Kekerten, Cumberland Sound, Baffin Island, told Stevenson this, and he substantiated it through the excavation of a number of double-walled skin houses. Placing, forgetting, and losing thus may be processes that were responsible for the development of the arcs at Pincevent. Their role, however, would have been at most only partial. The spatial patterns of artifact joins and red ocher soil

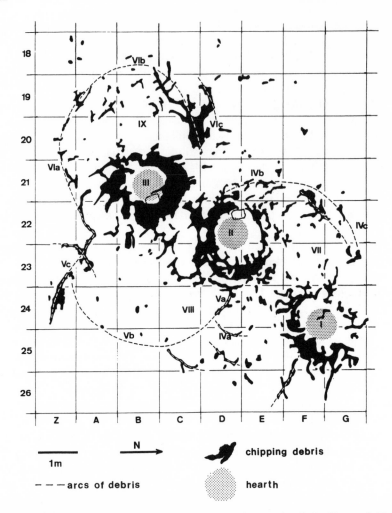

Figure 13. Distribution of chipping debris relative to distribution of arcs of artifacts and debris at Pincevent habitation no. 1. Adapted from Leroi-Gourhan and Brézillon (1966:Figure 56).

stains described later indicate the mechanical effects of sweeping and redeposition and that these processes also formed the arcs of refuse. In either case, the reconstruction of huts around the Pincevent hearths is supported.

At Pincevent, the area delimited by the arcs corresponds well with the limits of red ocher soil stains (Figure 14). A thin sprinkling of ocher underlaid the artifacts within the bounds of the hypothesized structure and helped to define it (Leroi-Gourhan and Brézillon 1966:330–332). The rationale for spreading red

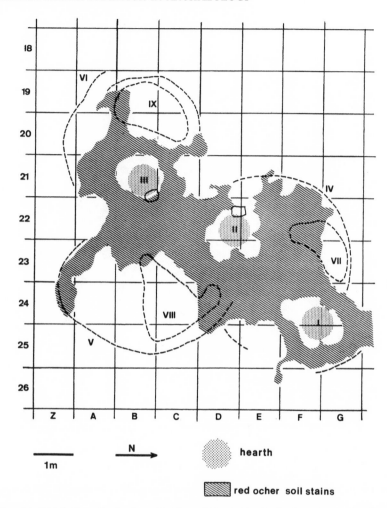

Figure 14. Distribution of red ocher soil stains relative to the distribution of arcs of artifacts and debris at Pincevent habitation no. 1. Adapted from Leroi-Gourhan and Brézillon (1966:Figure 55).

ocher over this portion of the occupation floor prior to its use is unclear. However, one is struck by the correspondence between the edges of the distribution of ocher and the arcs of debris. Also, the supposedly swept areas, indicated by low densities of debris, fall for the most part within areas lacking ocher. This is expectable if sweeping did occur. Finally, if the huts did not exist, one must wonder why the ocher was spread over only the portion of the occupation floor around the hearths rather than all work areas.

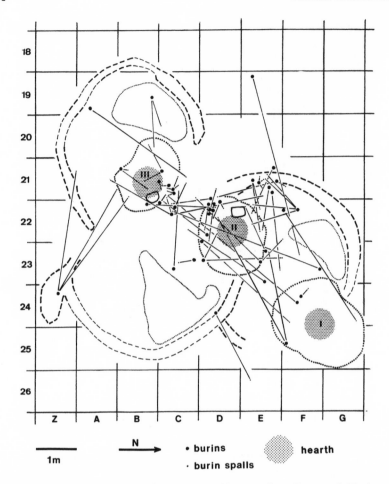

Figure 15. Distribution of joins of refitted burins and burin spalls at Pincevent habitation no. 1. Adapted from Leroi-Gourhan and Brézillon (1966:Figure 65).

Second, refitting studies of burins and burin spalls, cores and core debitage, broken scrapers, and snapped blades indicate an extensive network of conjoined pieces among the hearths and their surroundings (Leroi-Gourhan and Brézillon 1966:337, 341–345, 349–350, 364). Figures 15 and 16 provide examples. Importantly, for each of the artifact classes, some of the refitted pieces fall within the arcs of debris, which have been defined in other ways and are linked to pieces in work areas around the hearths. One possible meaning of this pattern is that some debris generated around the hearths was swept to the sides of the presumed huts during floor cleaning. This assessment of the refitting patterns is consistent with

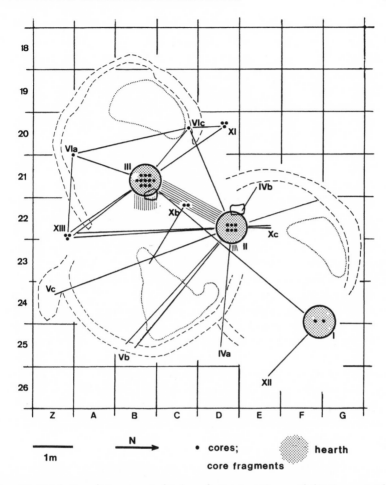

Figure 16. Distribution of joins among refitted core fragments at Pincevent habitation no. 1. Adapted from Leroi-Gourhan and Brézillon (1966:Figure 63).

the identification of the arcs, themselves, and their crisp borders. Both phenomena can be seen as the products of the same cleaning process.

Another interesting pattern is that different refitted tool and debris classes link the central work areas to different portions of the debris. Refitted burins and burin spalls fall within arc segments 6b, 5c, 5a, and 4b. Cores and core debitage fall within arc segments 6c, 6a, 5c, 5b, 4b, and perhaps 4a. Snapped blade refits fall within only segments 6c and 4c. This pattern might be taken to indicate separate episodes of different kinds of activities in work areas around the hearths, followed by sweeping in different directions. The pattern does not strengthen or weaken Leroi-Gourhan and Brézillon's identification of the hearths.

Finally, the patterns of refits can be used to suggest the contemporary use of all three hearths and the proposed hut modules. Some of the joins link items around a hearth of one proposed hut to items against the walls of another proposed hut. This pattern would have been generated if work around one hut's hearth had been followed by the sweeping of the resulting debris against the walls of another hut, which would have had been standing at the same time. The pattern is found for core and core debitage refits and burin and burin spall refits. For both, the refits relate Huts 2 and 3 and Huts 2 and 1.

Taken alone, this pattern is ambiguous. The joins that link the work and depositional areas within the different huts could be the product of mining, recycling, and redeposition of lithic material (Ascher 1968) rather than hearth and hut contemporaneity. Cahen and Keeley (1980) have provided a convincing example of this kind of situation for the Belgian Epipaleolithic site of Meer II. Considered with other contextual data discussed in this section, however, the pattern can be evoked as one of a number of mutually reinforcing patterns that identify three contemporaneous hut cells.

Third, the orientation of items within the arcs of debris also suggests that the arcs represent debris swept up against the walls of some structure. The composite artifact and debris map from Pincevent (Leroi-Gourhan and Brézillon 1966:fold-out) shows that the long axes of many larger bone and lithic items (greater than *ca.* 5 cm long) parallel the directions of curvature of the arcs that they form. This pattern in orientation is what one would expect mechanically for debris swept up against a barrier. It has also been found ethnographically to characterize the distribution of larger items along the walls of the Pangnirtungmuit skin houses mentioned before (Stevenson, personal communication). Again, the pattern does not allow one to determine whether placing and loss or sweeping are responsible for it, but does suggest the existence of the huts.

Fourth, along one arc of debris, 4b, there is a hummock of soil several centimeters thick, with large flint nodules on top. Other large nodules are spaced with some regularity along the arc. These could represent a position at which a tent pole was anchored and places where a tent skirt was weighted down (Leroi-Gourhan and Brézillon 1966:327, 362). The features occur on the prevailing, upwind (west) side of the proposed structure, where they would have been needed most. A similar criterion has been used by Campbell (1977:73–75) to identify hearths as interior ones at the LUP site of Hengistbury Head. The Lack of more frequent pole and skirt anchors of rocks or dirt at habitation no. 1 may relate to the use of the site during cold seasons (see later discussion), when the ground was frozen and snow was available for these purposes (Gordon 1988).

Fifth, information on the local weather conditions and the seasons of occupation of habitation no. 1 also are pertinent to assessing whether huts existed there. Two episodes of occupation were reconstructed by the original faunal analysts, Guillien and Perpere (1966:377): a longer period represented by winter kills and a shorter period in late spring. The methodological and sample limitations of their analyses have been discussed elsewhere (Carr 1985b:389). More recent and methodologically sensitive analyses by Gordon (1988), using the cementum of reindeer teeth, generally support the reconstructed seasons of occupation but do not reflect whether the period was discontinuous or continuous. Of seven examined teeth, three indicated late winter kills and four indicated spring kills. Other debris scatters at Pincevent (M-89, E-74, G-65, V-105), which are similar in arrangement to habitation no. 1, were found by Gordon to have early winter, late winter, and/or spring kills, in various combinations.

Winter occupation of habitation no. 1 would have been rigorous. The site was used during the Bølling or Allerød period, at the end of the second cold maximum of the Würm glacial. Winters in northern France at that time are thought to have been colder and drier than at present (Butzer 1971:274–286; see also Planchais 1976). The vicinity of Pincevent is relatively flat and can be windy, as its name, "pinching or biting wind," indicates.

In these conditions, one would expect most work to occur indoors when possible—especially tasks involving finer finger manipulations. In contrast, refuse deposition would not be expected to be spatially constrained in this way. Looking at the distribution of tools, alone, at habitation no. 1, one does find that nearly all of them occur within the limits of the proposed huts rather than outside. Also, bone debris are more ubiquitously scattered. These data are consistent with the interpretation that all three hearths were enclosed in huts. Additionally, if the hearths were not, one must ask why the tools are constrained to the areas that they are, rather than dispersed among a wider set of work areas.

Sixth, the stratigraphy of the hearths is most parsimoniously understood if all three were used simultaneously rather than sequentially. Each is similar in having two carbonaceous deposits separated by a thin lens of sediment. It would appear that there were two periods of use of all three hearths, separated by a brief period of site abandonment and water washing. This contrasts with Binford's reconstruction of the singular and sequential use of Hearths 2 and 3 in response to a change in wind direction.

The hearth stratigraphy concords with Guillien and Perpere's assessment, using independent faunal data, that habitation no. 1 was occupied discontinuously during two seasons, in winter and late spring. It is neither discordant with nor reinforced by Gordon's findings of winter and spring kills.[1] The stratigraphic data do not bear on the question of whether the hearths were outdoor or indoor features.

---

[1]It is not currently possible to conclude from faunal analyses whether the two periods of occupation of habitation no. 1, evidenced by all three hearths' stratigraphy, were shorter periods in different seasons (winter, late spring) of the same or different years, or longer periods of winter through spring in two different years.

Seventh, the deposits in each hearth are physically contained and reasonably compact, rather than unconstrained and broadly scattered. These are criteria that Binford (1983:158) attributes to indoor hearths. The deposits occur in round basins, approximately 20 cm deep, as opposed to on ground level where they might have been more easily strewn. Their diameters are about 50 cm.

Eighth, the three hearths are aligned and are approximately equally spaced (*ca.* 3 m, center to center). Also, the distances between them are such that their respective debris scatters do overlap, which probably would not be the case if the hearths had been used sequentially and placed so as to occupy fresh work space (Yellen 1974; Binford 1978; Hayden 1979; O'Connell 1979). All three characteristics point toward the simultaneous use of an integrated living space. However, they do not bear directly on whether the hearths were exterior or interior features.[2]

Thus a wide diversity of contextual data converge on the identification of the hearths at Pincevent habitation no. 1 as indoor hearths that were used simultaneously. Leroi-Gourhan and Brézillon's use of these data is good in several ways. First, many of the data are strong but would probably have been overlooked had general models for identifying hearths and model-specified data been focused upon. Second, by using many kinds of data and looking for mutually reinforcing identifying patterns, some patterns that by themselves are only moderately suggestive of past formation processes could be assigned meanings with higher probabilities of accuracy. This would not have been possible had the process of identification proceeded on each pattern individually. Third, by taking an inductive, exploratory approach and looking for mutually reinforcing patterns, the

---

[2]In particular, the equal spacing of the hearths at habitation no. 1 does not suggest whether they were outdoor or indoor features. Gamble (1986:258–263) has suggested that equispacing of hearths at approximately 3 meter distances, like the toss-and-drop pattern, can help to identify them as multiuser outside hearths. In Binford's model, he attributes the 3-meter regularity to the "size of the human body and the spatial geometry that multiple users of a common facility . . . produce when engaged in the commonplace social activities of conversation, eating, passing the time and throwing things away" (p. 258). In support of this, he cites several ethnographic examples of hunter–gatherer camps. However, there are both substantive and logical problems with Gamble's "3-m spacing principle." First, the ethnographic examples he cites include not only Nunamuit (Binford 1968) and Aborigine (Hayden 1979) camps that lack huts, but also !Kung camps (Wiessner 1974; Yellen 1977) that have huts with doorway hearths. Huts of the !Kung are individually very similar to the Pincevent hut modules (Figure 3a) and are sometimes built in groups similar to the Pincevent hut group (Figure 3b; Yellen 1977). One cannot logically support a principle that links 3-m hearth spacing to exterior hearths with ethnographic data on exterior and interior hearths. Second, the ethnographic data that Gamble cites include sleeping arrangements (Hayden 1979:Ngayuwa and Tapatapa's camp) in addition to multiuser outside hearths. Both Binford (1983:160–163) and Gamble (1986:262–263) consider interhearth spacings different (smaller) in sleeping arrangements than in multiuser outside hearths. Again, irrelevant ethnographic data are cited in support of the principle. Finally, it is not clear that the spacings, and some of the factors contributing to the spacings, of multiuser outside hearths do not also pertain to doorway or central interior hearths.

different kinds of data were used as a holistic system of observations, and it was possible to develop a consistent system of facts. Leroi-Gourhan's and Brézillon's and my own reconstruction of the huts at Pincevent involved the development or use of facts about primary artifact deposition, secondary deposition, the spatial distributions of different activities, site seasonality, site reoccupation, weather (wind direction and temperature), and architectural design. Fourth, the diversity of data that were used and that became internally consistent provide the reconstruction greater plausibility, in Hemple's sense (1966:34).

At the same time, Leroi-Gourhan and Brézillon's analysis suffers from its lack of fully explicit argumentation. Middle-range propositions that associate the characteristics of archaeological remains with their identity via formation processes were often left implicit, as assumed professional knowledge (Leroi-Gourhan and Brézillon 1966:especially 325–371). Also, the roles of some kinds of data in the inferential process were not explicitly defined. I have tried to correct some of these problems here.

The drawbacks of implicit argumentation in archaeology and more generally in science are well known (Binford 1968, 1977; Watson *et al.* 1971; Carr 1985a:40–41). In particular, archaeological knowledge has not been formalized to the point where bridging propositions are well tested and can be left unstated. Only by stating such propositions and the data pertinent to them can they be criticized, can logical discordances among them be found, and can advances in theory be made in a systematic fashion.

Finally, like Binford, Leroi-Gourhan and Brézillon did not evoke and evaluate alternative models for their relative degrees of fit to the data. Only the occurrence of three contemporaneous huts was explicitly proposed and evaluated (although alternative processes of formation of various individual features and relationships were considered).

6.4. Combining Models and Contextual Data

Binford's and Leroi-Gourhan and Brézillon's methods of reconstruction are complementary in their use of models and contextual data and inductive exploratory and deductive confirmatory strategies. It is not hard to envision a very plausible argument about the nature of the hearths at habitation no. 1 that would use both the explicit models of formation processes and the diverse contextual data cited above to weigh the two alternative identifications. Also, analytic processes could have been used whereby both inductive exploratory and deductive confirmatory logic, models, and techniques are combined in a stepwise, cyclical manner to investigate data. These are well known in outline (Carr 1985a; Kemeny 1959; Williams *et al.* 1973:215–237) and becoming better operationalized (Tukey 1977, 1980; Carr 1985b:316–328; Read 1985). I will not elaborate on them here. An example of their use to identify depositional sets of artifacts at Pincevent has been presented elsewhere (Carr 1985b).

However, to let this critique of Binford's and Leroi-Gourhan's analyses of Pincevent rest with their mechanical integration would be to miss the dynamics and synergy of combining inductive exploratory and deductive confirmatory logic, models, and contextual data. It is through their combination that creativity in developing identifications (or explanations) is maximized. This creative logic can be called *abduction,* to extend a term of Hanson's (1972). Abduction is a conceptual *gestalt.* It is the simultaneous discovery of a pattern and its significance in suggesting a possible identity or cause. It occurs as one searches data in an exploratory mode or examines residuals in a confirmatory mode in the midst of a larger cycle of exploratory and confirmatory work. It takes the approximate form of thought, "this pattern could be explained if new hypothesis X were true," although this statement does not capture abduction's gestalt quality. Abduction involves both the perception of a previously unperceived pattern and its identification or explanation by retroduction.

One essential step for combining inductive exploratory and deductive confirmatory strategies is developing and envisioning the data from the perspective of multiple alternative models. Abduction is facilitated by this stereoscopic, higher level point of view. When multiple models are used, multiple possible identifications run through the researcher's head as the data are explored inductively or their various residuals from different models are displayed in a confirmatory mode. Common dimensions of fit of the models, directionality in their degrees of fit, or mutually reinforcing patterns, among the residuals from different models— all higher levels of patterning than that exposed by examining the data from the perspective of a single model—may suggest new identifications or interpretations. These factors are among the most critical for gaining the insights that are necessary to make an abduction.

During my initial analyses of habitation no. 1 (Carr 1985a), I examined the data in both exploratory and confirmatory modes in order to assess the contemporaneity of the hearths, whether they were interior or exterior ones, and a number of other behavioral and formation issues. In the process of simultaneously considering these multiple, alternative possibilities, a variety of reconstructions beyond those favored by Leroi-Gourhan and Brézillon and Binford were suggested to me (abductin) and partially evaluated. These are as follows:

First and second, one or two hearths might have been outside hearths and the other(s) interior hearth(s), rather than all three of the same kind. Various combinations might be considered. Binford (1983:157, Figure 93) mentions this in passing, suggesting that only Hearth 1 might have been sheltered by a hut.

There are certain differences among the hearths in their forms and in the assemblage of artifacts around them, especially between Hearth 1 and Hearths 2 and 3, that are suggestive of this. (1) The basin of Hearth 1 is filled primarily with charcoal deposits, indicating a major source of fire, whereas the basins of Hearths 2 and 3 are filled more with fire-cracked rock, which might have been used in stone boiling or indirect heating (Leroi-Gourhan and Brézillon 1966:367). (2) Areas immediately adjacent to Hearths 2 and 3 exhibit much higher frequencies of tools and debris that indicate tool manufacture, tool maintenance, and fabrication of goods than do areas around Hearth 1. These include cores, burins, burin spalls, becs, some kinds of scrapers, backed bladelets, and unbacked blades. This difference between the hearths is one of degree rather than kind (Carr 1985b:449). (3) Occurring around Hearths 2 and 3, but not 1, are large blocks of stone that would have been useful as seats. Theses are surrounded by concentrations of tools and debris in possible work areas.

At the same time, a quantitative analysis of the polythetic structuring of depositional sets at Pincevent (Carr 1985b:441–451) showed a second pattern. Areas around Hearths 1 and 2 were more similar to each other and distinguished from areas around Hearth 3 in the relative proportions and patterns of asymmetry found among artifacts in the same depostional sets. These similar or different artifact proportions and asymmetries indicate similarities and differences in the formation processes that operated around the hearths (Carr 1985b:328–373).

Third, it is possible that three huts occurred at habitation no. 1 but that the modules were not interconnected so as to form a single structure with a common gallery. This reconstruction would affect estimates of the covered floor area and site population, length of occupation, and the nature of the social unit(s) that inhabited the site. One must consider that scattered over most of the 1.5 ha of Pincevent are many hut modules that are similar to those of habitation no. 1 but that occur as single units.

Fourth, it is possible that the hearths, or some of them, were outside hearths used in some kind of specialized extraction activity, rather than men's outside hearths. One possible activity is the making of bone grease through stone boiling (Leechman 1951). Leroi-Gourhan and Brézillon (1966:367) and I (Carr 1985b:426, Table 8) have suggested that this activity occurred around the hearths, based in part on the concentration of grease-producing bones (humeri, femurs, radio-cubitals) and rocks that surround the hearths. The strong spatial association of these debris classes and their probable unity as a depositional set were indicated in a quantitative analysis that I made (Carr 1985b:426, depositional set 4). Also, there are debris-free areas, 20 to 30 cm in diameter, around each hearth. Leroi-Gourhan and Brézillon (1966:367) suggested that in these locations, there might have stood racks that supported skins for making grease or broth by stone boiling. Finally, the great density of bone and stone around the hearths, which created a very rough floor in their vicinity (Figure 11), need to be evaluated relative to the alternative activities of sitting, dropping, and dumping.

If one or two of the hearths were outside hearths used for making bone grease and the other(s) were inside habitation(s), the proximity of the hearths to each other must be considered. Making bone grease is a messy activity. Messy activities, which create much debris, obnoxious odors, or residues that attract vermin or carnivores, tend to be found at a distance from permanent habitations both ethnographically (Watanabe 1972; Yellen 1974; O'Connell 1979) and archaeologically (Brose and Scarry 1976; Carr 1977). In contrast, the Pincevent hearths are closely spaced, calling this reconstruction into question. However, one must also grant that our understanding of the distribution of messy activities in habitations is based primarily on warm climate or warm season sites rather than cold season, frozen-ground sites. Factors such as vermin, carnivores, and odors might not be as important in this context.

If all three hearths were used for making bone grease, habitation no. 1 might actually represent a reindeer kill and processing site rather than a habitation site or hunting stand. Pincevent is located on the banks of the Seine between the confluences of the Loire and Yonne rivers. This would have been a natural ice crossing for migrating reindeer herds in winter (Gordon 1988) and an optimal kill location. An analogous, well-documented game kill and processing station, where the making of bone grease did occur, is the Olsen-Chubbuck bison kill site (Wheat 1972). At the same time, habitation no. 1 might have been only the processing area of a larger processing–habitation camp, the huts of which are represented by other debris scatters within Pincevent's 1.5 ha expanse.

In a complete analysis of habitation no. 1, it would be desirable to seriously consider each of these alternative reconstructions or some combination of them and to systematically outline the data that support and refute them and the data that are ambiguous. Such data searching might, in turn, lead to the abduction of additional possibilities. In contrast, only some of the possible data relationships, upon which the preceding reconstructions focus, have been weighed and reported here and elsewhere (Carr 1985b). This task is beyond the scope of these papers. The evaluations presented in the previous two sections on Binford's and Leroi-Gourhan and Brézillon's reconstructions are the end product of this process and reflect my current position.

7. CONCLUSION

The nature of the archaeological record, philosophy of science, and recent philosophical and technical developments in statistics each suggest the importance of using contextual information when identifying archaeological observations and patterns. The archaeological record often provides ambiguous data. Single characteristics can be unreliable indicators of single processes or simultaneously reflect multiple processes. As a consequence, first, the strategy of identifying individual kinds of archaeological observations in separation from each other is often less successful than one where multiple kinds of observations are analyzed simultaneously as a coherent system for their mutually reinforcing patterns. Second, using multiple models to explore the observations inductively from several different perspectives, rather than a single model in a deductive confirmatory mode, is often necessary for finding mutually reinforcing identifying relationships or unanticipated, critical ones. Those who have used factor analysis or other multivariate, model-variable search techniques are well aware of both of these constraints on archaeological analysis and inference. Implicit in both constraints is the fact that observations often need to be analyzed and identified in their own contexts of relevant observations, of varying scope, if identification is to be successful.

That contextual data can be critical to the identification process is also apparent from the philosophy of science. The plausibility of an identification in part depends on the diversity of the data that are evoked. A contextual-sensitive approach to identification draws on more kinds of observations than a model-focused one.

Finally, the general philosophy and techniques of EDA and CEDA encourage one to use contextual data in order to find unanticipated or case-specific identifying patterns. Emphasis is placed on inductive data exploration and on using multiple models to view the data from different perspectives. These tactics can reveal context-specific identifying patterns that might be overlooked when using a single model in a deductive, confirmatory mode.

Building, testing, and applying models is essential to the growth of archaeological theory and to our knowledge of prehistory. However, the process of applying a model to data in confirmatory mode in order to identify a phenomenon is usually only the final step in a longer sequence and cycle of analytic tasks that are necessary for identification; model application should not be confounded with these. The analysis that leads to an identification often requires using diverse contextual data as well as explicit models and model-specified data. And it requires data exploration as well as model confirmation. It is with this understanding that statistics has shifted from deductive hypothesis testing and modeling to a synthesis of exploratory and deductive strategies over the past decade. It is hoped that this chapter encourages a similar synthesis in archaeology and a revitalized status for contextual data.

ACKNOWLEDGMENTS

I wish to thank Brian C. Gordon for generously sharing his faunal analysis and interpretation of Pincevent habitation no. 1 with me. Marc Stevenson provided me with ethnographic references and his own information on the accumulation of artifacts near walls of tents, for which I am very appreciative. Michael Schiffer offered a number of helpful comments on a previous version of this chapter.

8. REFERENCES

Ascher, R., 1968, Time's Arrow and the Archaeology of a Contemporary Community. In *Settlement Archaeology* (K. C. Chang, ed.), National Press Books, Palo Alto, pp. 47–79.

Binford, L. R., 1968, Archaeological Perspectives. In *New Perspectives in Archaeology* (S. R. Binford and L. R. Binford, eds.), Adeline, Chicago, pp. 5–32.

Binford, L. R., 1977, General Introduction. In *For Theory Building in Archaeology* (L. R. Binford, ed.), Academic Press, New York, pp. 1–10.

Binford, L. R., 1978, Dimensional Analysis of Behavior and Site Structure: Learning from an Eskimo Hunting Stand, *American Antiquity* 43(3):330–361.

Binford, L. R., 1980, Willow Smoke and Dogs' Tails: Hunter–Gatherer Settlement Systems and Archaeological Site Formation, *American Antiquity* 45(1):4–20.

Binford, L. R., 1983, *In Pursuit of the Past: Decoding the Archaeological Record*, Thames and Hudson, New York.

Brose, D. S., and Scarry, J. R., 1976, The Boston Ledges Shelter: Comparative Spatial Analysis of Early Late Woodland Occupations in Summit County, Ohio, *Midcontinental Journal of Archaeology* 1(2):179–228.

Butzer, K. W., 1971, *Environmental Archaeology* (2nd ed.), Aldine, Chicago.

Butzer, K. W., 1982, *Archaeology as Human Ecology*, Cambridge University Press, Cambridge.

Cahen, D., and Keeley, L. H., 1980, Not Less than Two, Not More than Three, *World Archaeology* 12(2):165–180.

Campbell, J. B., 1977, *The Upper Paleolithic of Britain*, Oxford University Press, Oxford.

Carr, C., 1977, *The Internal Structure of a Middle Woodland Site and the Nature of the Archaeological Record*, Preliminary Examination Paper, Department of Anthropology, University of Michigan, Ann Arbor.

Carr, C., 1982, *Handbook on Soil Resistivity Surveying*, Chapter 5, Center for American Archaeology, Evanston, Illinois.

Carr, C., 1984, The Nature of Organization of Intrasite Archaeological Records and Spatial Analytic Approaches to Their Investigation. In *Advances in Archaeological Method and Theory, Volume 7* (M. B. Schiffer, ed.), Academic Press, New York, pp. 103–222.

Carr, C., 1985a, Getting into Data: Philosophy and Tactics for the Analysis of Complex Data Structures. In *For Concordance in Archaeological Analysis: Bridging Data Structure, Quantitative Technique, and Theory* (C. Carr, ed.), Westport Press, Kansas City, pp. 18–44.

Carr, C. 1985b, Alternative Models, Alternative Techniques: Variable Approaches to Intrasite Spatial Analysis. In *For Concordance in Archaeological Analysis: Bridging Data Structure, Quantitative Technique, and Theory* (C. Carr, ed.), Westport Press, Kansas City, pp. 302–473.

Clarke, D. L., 1968, *Analytical Archaeology*, Methuen, London.

Dodd, W. A., 1984, *The Use of Domestic Space by Sedentary Households: Some Organizing Principles*, Paper presented at the annual meetings of the Society for American Archaeology, Portland.

Gamble, C., 1986, *The Paleolithic Settlement of Europe*, Cambridge University Press, Cambridge.

Goodenough, W., 1965, Rethinking "Status" and "Role": Toward a General Model of the Cultural Organization of Social Relationships. In *The Relevance of Models for Social Anthropology* (M. Gluckman and F. Eggan, eds.), Association of Social Anthropologists of the Commonwealth, Monograph 1, pp. 1–24.

Gordon, B. C., 1988, Of Men and Reindeer Herds in French Magdalenian Prehistory, *British Archaeological Reports, International Series*, 390. British Archaeological Reports, Oxford.

Guillien, Y., and Perpere, M., 1966, Maxillaires de Rennes et Saisons de Chasse (habitation 1 de Pincevent). In *L'habitation Magdalénienne no. 1 de Pincevent près Montereau (Seine-et-Marne)* (A. Leroi-Gourhan and M. Brézillon, eds.), *Gallia Préhistoire* 9(2):373–377.

Hanson, N. R., 1972, *Patterns of discovery*, Chapter 4, Cambridge University Press, Cambridge.
Hayden, B., 1979, *Paleolithic Reflections*. Institute of Aboriginal Studies, Canberra, Australia.
Hartwig, F., and Dearing, B. E., 1979, *Exploratory Data Analysis*, Sage Publications, Beverly Hills.
Hemple, C. G., 1966, *Philosophy of Natural Science*, Prentice-Hall, Englewood Cliffs, New Jersey.
Hodder, I., 1982, Theoretical Archaeology: A Reactionary View. In *Symbolic and Structural Archaeology* (I. Hodder, ed.), Cambridge University Press, Cambridge, pp. 1–16.
Keeley, L. H., 1977, The Functions of Paleolithic Flint Tools, *Scientific American* 237:108–126.
Kemeny, J. G., 1959, *A Philosopher Looks at Science*, Van Nostrand-Reinholt, New York.
Leechman, D., 1951, Bone Grease, *American Antiquity* 16:355–356.
Leroi-Gourhan, A., and Brézillon, M., 1966, L'Habitation Magdalénienne no. 1 de Pincevent prés Montereau (Seine-et-Marne), *Gallia Préhistoire* 9(2):263–385.
O'Connell, J., 1979, *Site Structures and Dynamics among Modern Alyawara Hunters*, Paper presented at the annual meetings of the Society for American Archaeology, Vancouver.
Planchais, N., 1976, La Végétation au Pléistocène Suprieur et au Début de L'Holocène dans le Bassin de Paris et les Plaines de la Loire Moyenne. In *La Préhistoire Française* (Henry de Lumley, ed.), Éditions du Centre National de la Recherche Scientifique, Paris, pp. 534–538.
Read, D., 1985, The Substance of Archaeological Analysis and the Mold of Statistical Method: Enlightenment Out of Discordance? In *For Condordance in Archaeological Analysis: Bridging Data Structure, Quantitative Technique, and Theory* (C. Carr, ed.), Westport Press, Kansas City, pp. 45–86.
Sackett, J. R., 1982, Approaches to Style in Lithic Archaeology. *Journal of Anthropological Archaeology* 1:59–112.
Salmon, M. H., and Salmon, W. C., 1979, Alternative Models of Scientific Explanation, *American Anthropologist* 81:61–73.
Samuels, S. R., 1983, *Spatial Patterns and Cultural Processes in Three Northwest Coast Longhouse Floor Middens from Ozette*. Ph.D. Dissertation, Department of Anthropology, Washington State University, Pullman.
Schiffer, M. B., 1972, Archaeological Context and Systemic Context, *American Antiquity* 37(2):156–165.
Schiffer, M. B., 1976, *Behavioral Archaeology*, Academic Press, New York.
Schiffer, M. B., 1983, Toward the Identification of Formation Processes, *American Antiquity* 48(4):675–706.
Stevenson, M. G., 1985, The Formation of Artifact Assemblages at Workshop/Habitation Sites: Models from Peace Point in Northern Alberta, *American Antiquity* 50:63–81.
Stevenson, M. G., 1987, *What Now! Beyond the Formation of Hearth Associated Artifact Assemblages*. Paper presented at the annual meetings of the Society for American Archaeology, Toronto.
Taylor, W., 1948, *A Study of Archaeology*. Southern Illinois University Press, Carbondale.
Tukey, J., 1977, *Exploratory Data Analysis*, Addison-Wesley, Reading, Massachusetts.
Tukey, J., 1979, Comments to "Nonparametric Statistical Data Modeling," *Journal of the American Statistical Association* 74:121–122.
Tukey, J., 1980, We Need Both Exploratory and Confirmatory, *American Statistician* 34(1):23–25.
Tukey, J. W., and Wilk, M. B., 1970, Data Analysis and Statistics: Techniques and Approaches. In *The Quantitative Analysis of Social Problems* (E. R. Tufte, ed.), Addison-Wesley, Reading, Massachusetts, pp. 370–390.
Watanabe, H., 1972, *The Ainu Ecosystem*, University of Washington Press, Seattle.
Watson, P. J., Le Blanc, S. A., and Redman, C. L., 1971, *Explanation in Archaeology*, Columbia University Press, New York.
Wheat, J. B., 1972, *The Olsen-Chubbuck Site: A Paleo-Indian Bison Kill*, Society for American Archaeology, Memoirs 26.
Wiessner, P., 1974, A Functional Estimator of Population from Floor Area, *American Antiquity* 39:343–350.

Williams, L., Thomas, D. H., and Bettinger, R., 1973. Notions to Numbers: Great Basin Settlements as Polythetic Sets. In *Research and Theory in Current Archaeology* (C. L. Redman, ed.), John Wiley, New York, pp. 215–237.

Wood, W. R., and Johnson, D. L., 1978, A Survey of Disturbance Processes in Archaeological Site Formation. In *Advances in Archaeological Method and Theory, Volume 4*, (M. B. Schiffer, ed.), Academic Press, New York, pp. 315–381.

Yellen, J. E., 1974, *The !Kung Settlement Pattern: An Archaeological Perspective*, Ph.D. Dissertation, Harvard University, Cambridge.

Yellen, J. E., 1977, *Archaeological Approaches to the Present: Models for Reconstructing the Past*, Academic Press, New York.

Chapter 8

Tool Use and Spatial Patterning
Complications and Solution

Lawrence H. Keeley

1. INTRODUCTION

The concern of this chapter is not the discovery of spatial patterns *per se* but rather their interpretation, particularly the logical arguments that link spatial patterns, however discovered, with interpretations that address the use of space in prehistoric communities. Specifically, I am concerned with how data on tool utilization can be used in spatial studies.

Data on the use of stone tools is now becoming widely available through microwear and residue studies and can be, to a limited extent, included in spatial analytical studies (Cahen *et al.* 1979; Cahen and Keeley 1980; Audouze *et al.* 1981; Bamforth 1985; Yerkes 1987). Such data have yet to be incorporated in any major, formal, spatial analytical study; applications to date have involved informal methods. The great hope was that patterns in the use of space on and between sites could be determined from the distributions of functionally identifiable artifacts. But, as more has been learned about the use of prehistoric stone tools, it has become clear that we must consider the use of tools in a much wider realm of behavior if we are to understand their intra- and intersite distributions.

The factors that affect where and when a tool will be disposed, in addition to the timing and location of its use, include:

LAWRENCE H. KEELEY • Department of Anthropology, University of Illinois at Chicago, Chicago, Illinois 60680.

1. Special disposal considerations such as the cleanup of intensely used domestic areas, immediate tossing of large or troublesome waste, etc.
2. The length of a site's occupation and the timing of an activity within the span of occupation
3. The retooling of hafted artifacts

Needless to say, all of these factors may be combined in various ways. The significance of discovering a certain "functional type" in a particular location and in association with certain other types or categories of remains is a complicated issue. In general and pretentious terms, spatial patterns, however discovered, are static distributions. Only research devoted to the recovery of dynamics can hope to interpret those distributions as the result of behavior. The study of such dynamics is much easier to prescribe than it is to accomplish.

2. COMPLICATING FACTORS

The first complicating factors that affect the spatial distribution of discarded tools are those that involve formal cleanup and casual tossing, much discussed both theoretically and practically in recent literature (Schiffer 1976; Yellen 1977; Binford, 1978; Gould 1978). There are two main points to be extracted from this literature. First, the size of a tool will affect its probability of entering the record at or near the locus of its last use. Smaller pieces are much more likely to escape cleanup and tossing, or to be lost. Such small pieces are more likely to be (1) resharpening flakes and spalls, (2) small fragments of tools broken during use, or (3) tools of small size which would usually be hafted (see later discussion). Second, cleanup is more likely to be rigorous in intensely used domestic areas such as habitation interiors, areas immediately surrounding domestic hearths, and the like. Of course, such "cleaned-up" material will accumulate in special disposal loci such as middens and rubbish pits. These loci will be located peripherally and contain a wide, and confusing, variety of tools in high densities. Larger tools are thus likely to be centrifugally distributed by these processes. The actual loci of activities are likely to be evidenced either by low-density peripheral areas of low functional variety, or, in more central areas, only by the presence of the small fragments or resharpening flakes from the tools used there.

The length of time that a site is occupied is also a complicating factor. The longer the occupation, the more likely cleanup is to affect artifact distributions. On short-term habitations, tossing may be the principal complicating factor. More cleanup will also mean a greater homogenization of functional types in middens.

The various stages of an occupation may also be associated with different use and disposal modes (Stevenson 1985 and Chapter 9, this volume). In the "establishment" phase, we should find evidence of construction activities and perhaps some gearing up; formal disposal may not be very important. During the main occupation phase, we will find evidence of tool use relevant to site function, whatever that might be, and maintenance of gear in use; formal disposal is likely to be the predominant process in the central domestic areas. The abandonment phase should be evidenced by gearing-up activities in preparation for movement and in anticipation of future activities. Formal cleanup may cease and the debris from tool-using activities will remain essentially *in situ* even in the most "domestic" areas.

The complicating factor I have been most concerned with is the retooling of hafted artifacts. Problems arise because once-hafted tools accumulate where they were replaced in hafts, not necessarily where they were used (Keeley 1982). The best example of this phenomenon is projectile points. The proximal portions of projectile points tend to accumulate in domestic refuse, either primary or secondary, even though their use is completely offsite. Given the complications mentioned, unhafted tools tend to accumulate at or closer to the loci of their last use. Hafted tools are likely to be retooled when convenient, often before exhaustion or breakage. Therefore, the discard locations of hafted tools are likely to be evidence for retooling rather than the activities evidenced by wear traces on the tools themselves.

For the purposes of spatial analysis, then, the investigation of tool use and onsite activities must be concerned with the following variables:

1. The more general context in which a tool is used must be considered, for example:
    (a) Construction of facilities involving uses like heavy woodworking or digging
    (b) Gearing-up activities such as the manufacture of clothing, snowshoes, specialized hunting and fishing equipment, etc.
    (c) Maintenance involving the repair and refurbishing of equipment, especially retooling
    (d) Tool uses directly relevant to site function such as butchery at hunting stations, "plant" cutting at harvesting sites, etc.
    In practice, gearing-up and maintenance activities are almost impossible to distinguish; the same operations on the same materials are often necessary for both. Deciding which uses are relevant to site function presupposes independent data on this point and, therefore, the analyst must be concerned with the data given by a site's location, its featural, botanical, and faunal remains.
2. The distinction between once-hafted and unhafted implements must be made. As prehension traces are rare, this is not easy, but by using all available clues, it can be done (Keeley 1982).
3. One must be concerned with distinguishing curated tools whose major use

may have occurred before arrival and abandonment at the site. Wear traces thus may not be the result of activities actually conducted at the sites where they are abandoned. Of course, hafted tools are usually but not always curated between sites, but the best clues to this pattern are refitting, exotic raw materials, and tool/debitage ratios of the various raw materials.

4.   The size of the tool or tool fragment must be considered as this affects the probability of it being abandoned and remaining at the locus of its last use.

5.   Some inferences regarding the length of a tool's use life are helpful as briefly used tools tend to be abandoned nearer the locus of their last use (Gould 1978).

Perhaps these complications seem so numerous and interlinked that any use of use–wear data in spatial analysis is impossible. But this defeatist attitude would ignore the most direct and enduring evidence of onsite activities. More importantly, the interlinkage of these variables provides opportunities for using multiple and mutually-reinforcing lines of evidence to establish interpretation (Carr, Chapter 7 this volume).

3. VERBERIE

I would now like to briefly demonstrate the points made before with an interpretation of spatial patterns at the site of Verberie. This discussion is based not only on my own data but also relies heavily on data and interpretations freely provided me by Francoise Audouze, the director of the Verberie project, and by Daniel Cahen, who did the refitting work.

Verberie is a well-preserved open-air Magdalenian site in the Paris Basin of France. Several other sites of a similar nature and date are known from this region, including the famous site of Pincevent (Audouze 1985). The site is still under excavation, but certain aspects seem clear. Its location on the low terrace of the Oise River, near a bend that could have been the location of a ford, and the almost complete dominance of the fauna by reindeer, strongly suggest the site was, at least, a reindeer-hunting station. My study here concerns only the evidence from Hearth 1 at Verberie, an area with a central slab-lined hearth surrounded by habitation debris (Figure 1). Formal spatial analysis of Verberie is being undertaken by Robert Whallon, but for the purposes of this chapter I shall divide H.1 into seven crude spatial units: (1) a western zone of low density but with many large blades, (2) the actual hearth and its immediate surroundings, (3) the concentrated remains in the squares to the northern and eastern edges of the hearth, (4) the area to the north that appears to be a general disposal zone and a midden, (5) another apparent midden area to the southeast, (6) a single unit square (F19) with many small piercers, and (7) the remaining areas with a low density of material.

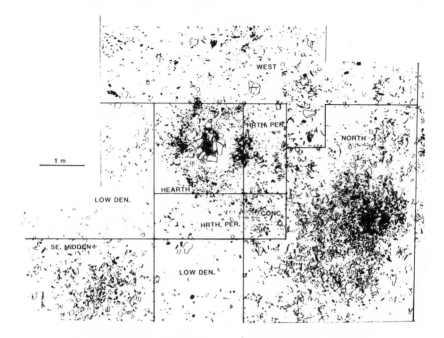

Figure 1. Plan of Hearth 1 at Verberie showing spatial units.

The data on tool use comes from a microwear analysis of a sample of 1,100 artifacts taken from the H.1 assemblage. The sample contains all of the retouched pieces and a stratified random sample of the unretouched artifacts larger than 20 mm in maximum dimension. Refitted groups, on the other hand, were selected intentionally. All refitted groups of exotic flint, all groups containing retouched tools, and a good sample of the groups of local flint without refitted tools were examined. The only sampling bias would be against a few used, unretouched blades in some refitted groups of local flint. The use traces on similar pieces suggest a slight underrepresentation of butchering knives. Of this sample, 459 implements bore traces of use; the majority of these were retouched tools or large blades.

An inspection of the proportions of different uses (counting edges, not just implements) found in the separate areas at the site shows a few differences (Table 1).

1. The western area shows slightly higher than normal percentages of elements for butchering, scraping fresh hide, "plant" cutting, and hafting.
2. The hearth area shows slightly elevated percentages of bone graving elements and projectiles.

Table 1. Percentages of Various Tool Uses by Area (counting used edges; miscellaneous and indeterminant uses excluded)

						Use							
Area	N	Woodwork	Plant cutting	Bone miscellaneous	Graving bone/antler	Light bone boring	Heavy bone boring	Butchering	Hidework (general)	Scraping fresh hide	Scraping dry hide	Projectiles	Hafted elements
West	127	1.6	4.7	3.2	15.0	2.4	11.0	35.4	5.5	8.7	2.4	7.9	2.4
Hearth	93	2.1	0	4.3	33.3	2.1	10.8	16.1	5.4	2.1	2.1	19.4	2.1
Hearth periphery	69	1.4	1.4	1.4	40.6	4.3	14.5	17.4	0	1.4	4.3	10.1	2.9
North	80	2.5	1.3	5.0	31.3	2.5	15.0	26.3	0	5.0	1.3	8.8	1.3
SE midden	28	0	0	0	28.6	0	25.0	42.9	0	0	0	3.6	0
Concentration F19	32	3.1	0	3.1	34.4	25.0	0	15.6	0	0	0	1 8.8	0
Low density	28	3.6	0	3.6	10.7	3.6	7.1	28.6	7.1	7.1	14.3	14.3	0
Average		2.0	1.8	3.3	27.4	4.2	12.0	25.8	3.0	4.4	2.8	11.6	1.8

3. The hearth periphery shows slightly elevated percentages of bone graving and haft elements.
4. The middens show high percentages of heavy bone boring elements.
5. The small concentration in unit F19 shows a very *high* percentage of light bone boring elements and a high percentage of projectile armatures.
6. The low density zones show high percentages of hide-scraping elements and a moderately high percentage of butchering traces.

The questions remain—in which of the areas did the activities actually take place, or were the tools disposed away from the place(s) of use? The data on refitting, raw material, and prehension can be used to calculate an index of the probability that an implement was not discarded at its locus of use. Because the codes I used for these variables were all significantly positively correlated, a principal component analysis was done and the first component, which explained about half the variability, provides the needed index. A high score indicates a strong probability that the tool was discarded at or very near its locus of use—that is, tools of local flint without traces of hafting and which refit into large groups. A low score indicates the opposite situation. To exclude the latter category of implements from the analysis, I removed all pieces with a principal component score below zero. A much clearer picture emerges (see Table 2) and what follows:

1. The western area is dominated by elements used for butchering, fresh hide scraping, and heavy bone boring, as well as for some other enigmatic uses on bone and for "plant" cutting. I believe all of these diverse uses are related to the same general activity that is the primary processing of reindeer. (a) Butchery and fresh hide processing are obvious, but the link with the uses on bones and plants requires further explanation. The linkage beetween butchery and heavy bone boring is provided by the implements themselves, as the majority of pieces with boring-use wear on the tip show traces from cutting soft animal tissue along one of the lateral edges. "Heavy bone boring" is merely a convenient label as the traces themselves indicate contact with bone, relatively deep penetration and some, but not necessarily full, rotation during contact. The exact use is not clear but may have something to do with disarticulation or, perhaps, marrow extraction—I am open to suggestions. The other uses on bone are either enigmatic tool actions or brief scraping episodes. Occasionally these traces are seen on pieces with meat-cutting polish on other edges; these uses may only be the result of incidental contacts with bone during butchery. (b) The evidence of plant cutting is more prob- lematic. The microwear polish itself is not "classic" soft plant polish; it resembles polishes obtained from the cutting of very dry grass or, less closely, some polishes obtained from the cutting of very wet hide (Gyssels and Cahen 1982). Bamforth (1985) argues that plant cutting is spatially associated with butchering at Lubbock Lake because the area was being cleared of some vegetation and/or to create "beds" to keep the meat clean. This is very plausible but, in this instance, use on fresh wet hide, perhaps from reindeer taken in the river, is perhaps the simpler hypothesis.

Table 2. Percentages of Uses by Area: Implements Probably Used *in Situ* (Principal components scores >1; counting used edges; miscellaneous and indeterminant uses excluded)

Area	N	Woodwork	Plant cutting	Bone miscellaneous	Graving bone/antler	Light bone boring	Heavy bone boring	Butchering	Hidework (general)	Scraping fresh hide	Scraping dry hide	Projectiles	Hafted elements
West	77	0	7.8	5.2	7.8	0	13.0	48.1	5.2	11.7	1.3	0	0
Hearth	36	2.8	0	5.6	33.3	5.6	25.0	22.2	5.6	0	0	0	0
Hearth periphery	19	5.3	5.3	5.3	15.8	5.3	10.5	47.4	0	5.3	0	0	0
North	40	2.5	0	10.0	15.0	0	22.5	45.0	0	2.5	2.5	0	0
SE midden	14	0	0	0	7.1	0	14.3	78.6	0	0	0	0	0
Concentration F19	14	7.1	0	7.1	14.3	50.0	0	21.4	0	0	0	0	0
Low density	16	6.3	0	0	12.5	6.3	0	50.0	0	6.3	18.8	0	0
Average		2.3	3.2	5.6	14.8	5.1	14.8	43.5	2.8	5.1	2.8	0	0

2. The hearth area shows a high percentage of bone/antler graving and heavy bone boring.
3. The hearth periphery was not apparently the scene of much *in situ* activity, except possibly some graving but was mainly a zone of rejection from the hearth.
4. The northern area was the scene of some butchery, heavy bone boring, and general bone work.
5. The smaller, southeastern midden was the scene of some butchery activities.
6. The small F19 concentration, as expected, is dominated by light bone boring, perhaps a single, brief episode. All these micropiercers have been reassembled into a single block.
7. The low density areas have over half of the evidence for dry hide scraping, apparently a very rare activity.

This analysis indicates that graving was a relatively unimportant activity compared to animal processing and suggests that perhaps as much as 75% of the burins found at H.1 might not have been used there but were only abandoned as a consequence of retooling.

We can further verify these conclusions by examining the size-sorting effects of disposal and loss. As I noted, resharpening spalls because of their size are much more likely to remain at the locus of a tool-using activity than the tool itself. The resharpening of burins, used almost exclusively for graving bone/antler, produces burin spalls, whereas the resharpening of the tip of heavy bone borers, mostly becs, produces small, easily recognizable pieces known as *chamfreins* that are really a peculiar form of transverse burin spall. We should find high proportions of spalls to tools where these tools were actually used. The spall-to-tool ratios for the different areas are given in Table 3.

From these figures we can conclude that burins were used around the hearth and in the hearth periphery with a few examples in the low density areas. These data indicate that heavy bone borers were used especially around the hearth, in the hearth periphery, and in the western butchering area. The hearth periphery

Table 3.   Spall-to-Tool Ratios in Different Areas at Verberie

Area	Spall/burin	Tip/bec
West	.59 (10/17)	1.22 (11/9)
Hearth	1.03 (29/28)	2.67 (8/3)
Hearth periphery	1.06 (18/17)	1.67 (5/3)
North	.58 (14/24)	.10 (1/10)
SE midden	.125 (1/8)	0 (0/5)
Concentration F19	.66 (6/9)	—
Low density	1.00 (2/2)	—

was an area of activity. This also shows that the northern area was not a site of heavy bone boring but only an area to which the becs themselves were removed from around the hearth. These results agree very well with the previous analyses, although they are based on different data.

We can search for retooling areas by using the artifacts rejected from the first analysis on the basis of their low principal components scores. The abandoned projectile armatures (*lamelle á dos*) are especially useful for the purpose because of their small size. Because burins seem predominantly to be hafted tools at Verberie, above-average percentages of these in an area may also indicate retooling or the disposal of retooling debris. The (percentages of gravers (burins) and used projectiles (*lamelle á dos*) with low PRIN1 scores in the various areas are shown in Table 4.

Most of the gravers ended up in rejection zones with the exception of the small F19 concentration, which also exhibits one of the highest percentages of used projectile armatures. These figures indicate that the principle location for retooling was, as expected, around the hearth. The small F19 concentration also fits the expectations for a retooling locus where burins and composite antler points were repaired, probably in a single episode involving the use of micro-piercers.

The interpretations for each of the use areas at Verberie are summarized in Table 5. As for the timing of various activities during the occupation, there is no space here to develop the various arguments that provide clues to this problem. But my findings and those of my colleagues suggest to me that something like the following occurred: arrival, possibly some gearing up, hunting and repair of projectiles, carcass processing with expediently produced and used tools, extensive retooling of burins and replacement of other tools, departure. The argu-

Table 4. Percentages of Tool Types Probably Not Used *in Situ* in Specific Areas at Verberie

Area	N^a	% gravers	% projectiles
West	50	26.00	20.00
Hearth	57	33.33	31.58
Hearth periphery	50	50.00	14.00
North	40	47.50	17.50
SE midden	14	50.00	7.14
Concentration F19	18	50.00	33.33
Low density	12	8.33	33.33
Average		38.60	22.00

[a]Number of pieces with principal components scores < 0 (i.e., tools unlikely to have been used *in situ*).

Table 5.   Summary of Activities in Various Areas around the Verberie Hearth

Area	Activities
West	Butchery, heavy bone "boring," miscellaneous bone work, fresh hide scraping, "plant" cutting
Hearth	Bone/antler graving, heavy bone "boring," retooling
Hearth periphery	Graving, heavy bone "boring"
North	Some butchery, miscellaneous bone work, disposal
Southeast midden	Butchery, disposal
Concentration F19	Light bone boring, retooling of hafted burins and backed blade lets
Low density	Dry hide scraping

ments for this scenario are intricate and problematic so, happily, I will leave them for another time.

4. CONCLUSIONS

The use of space on prehistoric living floors is not a simple problem to solve, even at sites like Verberie and Pincevent, which represent relatively brief episodes of occupation and show clear patterns of spatial distribution. Many factors complicate the interpretation of spatial patterning, but it is the careful choice of relevant variables for analysis that opens a path through the thicket. Several of these variables have been the focus of this study: artifact size, hafting, and raw material. These variables are as important as the actual uses of tools in deciphering the kind and location of onsite activities. If we are interested in what happened in the past, then the examination of all such details is essential. For the successful spatial analysis of prehistoric sites, I think we are better off as the tortoise than as the hare.

ACKNOWLEDGMENTS

I have already mentioned my indebetedness to my colleagues, Françoise Audouze and Daniel Cahen, but my gratitude for their open-handed policies regarding data and hospitality deserve more formal thanks. Real cooperative research is rather rare, and I was lucky to find it with them over Verberie. I also want to thank James L. Phillips and Lawrence Kimball for their stimulating discussions of the topic of this chapter. But—this is not just an obligatory disclaimer—none of the previously mentioned necessarily agree with the interpretations or principles outlined in this chapter, and, as a whole, they remain my responsibility. The research reported here was funded by a grant from the National Science Foundation (BNS-8218557), and it was partially funded by a fellowship from the French Ministère de la Recherche Scientifique et Technique.

5. REFERENCES

Audouze, F., 1985, *The Paris Basin in Magdalenian Times*. Paper read at Society for American Archaeology, 50th Annual Meeting, Denver, Colorado, May 2, 1985.

Audouze, F., Cahen, D., Keeley, L., and Schmider, B., 1981, Le Site Magdalénien du Buisson Campin à Verberie (Oise), *Gallia Préhistoire* 24:99–143.

Bamforth, D., 1985, The Technological Organization of Paleo-Indian Small-Group Bison Hunting on the Llano Estacado, *Plains Anthropologist* 30:243–258.

Binford, L., 1978, Dimensional Analysis of Behavior and Site Structure: Learning From an Eskimo Hunting Stand, *American Antiquity* 443:330–361.

Cahen, D., and Keeley, L. H., 1980, Not Less than Two, Not More than Three, *World Archaeology* 12:166–180.

Cahen, D., Keeley, L. H., and Van Noten, F., 1979, Stone Tools, Tool Kits and Human Behavior in Prehistory, *Current Anthropology 20:661–683.*

Gould, R., 1978, The Anthropology of Human Residues, *American Anthropologist* 80:815–835.

Gyssels, J., and Cahen, D., 1982 Le Lustre des Faucilles et les Autre Traces d'Usure des Outils en Silex, *Bulletin de la Société Préhistoire Française* 79:221–224.

Keeley, L. H., 1982, Hafting and Retooling: Effects on the Archaeological Record, *American Antiquity* 47:798–809.

Schiffer, M., 1976, *Behavioral Archaeology*, Academic Press, New York.

Stevenson, M., 1985, The Formation of Artifact Assemblages at Workshop/Habitation Sites: Models From Peace Point, *American Antiquity* 50:63–81.

Yellen, J., 1977, *Archaeological Approaches to the Present*, Academic Press, New York.

Yerkes, R., 1987, *Prehistoric Life on the Mississippi Floodplain*, University of Chicago Press, Chicago.

Chapter 9

Beyond the Formation of Hearth-Associated Artifact Assemblages

MARC G. STEVENSON

1. INTRODUCTION

Ethnoarchaeological investigations have recently shown that cultural formation processes contribute significantly to the structure of modern hunter–gatherer campsites. One of the more important findings of this research has been the discovery that the sorting of artifacts according to size determines, to a large extent, their final spatial distribution around hut and hearth. Given the variety of ethnographic settings (e.g., Binford 1978, 1983; O'Connell 1979, 1987; Meehan 1982; Yellen 1977; Jarvenpa and Brumbach 1983; Gifford and Brehensmeyer 1977) and experimental studies (e.g., Gifford-Gonzalez *et al.* 1985; Stockton 1973; Courtin and Villa 1982; Villa and Courtin 1983) in which size-dependent sorting by human activity has been documented there is little reason to believe that this process was not operative in the past. Prehistoric people, after all, faced many of the same life–space problems and challenges that hunter–gatherers do today (Binford 1983). For thousands of years, refuse had to be managed and living areas maintained to minimize interference with activity performance. In short, I would submit that size sorting within domestic and intensively occupied areas

---

MARC G. STEVENSON • Department of Anthropology, University of Alberta, Edmonton, Alberta T6G 2H4, Canada.

may be one of the few recurrent phenomena we can expect to find at hunter–gatherer campsites.

Three years ago I presented a model that described the sequential formation of artifact asssemblages around exterior hearths at a deeply stratified site of uncommon integrity and resolution in northern Alberta, Canada (Stevenson 1985). The model was considered relevant for understanding the spatial and temporal formation of artifact scatters at workshop/habitation sites. However, I also felt that, because the model was derived from observations on artifact sorting in a variety of contexts, it had potential for describing the formation of hearth-associated artifact assemblages at most types of short term and seasonally occupied hunter–gatherer campsites.

In this chapter I review the model and cultural processes that tend to sort objects by size across and within occupation floors. The main intent of the chapter, however, is to explore some of the more theoretically interesting and challenging implications of the model. Specifically, if we are willing to make the fundamental assumptions that (1) size sorting and general dispersal (see later discussion) are incremental, time-sensitive processes and (2) hunter–gatherer behavior is likely to vary during the occupation of sites, I believe a door will open into a potentially fruitful line of inquiry. Before we step through this door, however, it is important to review the model and its basic assumptions. The chapter concludes with two examples of how the model can be utilized to address human activity and behavior at short-term hunter–gatherer campsites. In so doing, the chapter attempts to take some preliminary steps toward foraging some necessary links between midrange and general theory (Raab and Goodyear 1984).

2. CULTURAL SIZE SORTING AND GENERAL DISPERSAL

2.1. Size Sorting

Human activity can sort, concentrate, and disperse artifacts according to size horizontally across living surfaces as well as vertically within deposits. Regrettably, few archaeologists have recognized the three-dimensional nature of cultural size sorting processes (but see Gifford and Brehensmeyer 1977; Gifford-Gonzalez et al. 1985; Savelle 1984; Yellen 1977:103 for notable exceptions). Although a number of factors can result in the sorting of objects by size across and within living floors, other properties, for example the shape (Moeyersons 1978) and salience (DeBoer 1983) of objects, may also result in patterned and predictable distributions. Another process that may be sensitive to documenting the formation of lithic assemblages through time and space is the accumulation of edge damage on artifacts (Tringham et al. 1974; Gifford-Gonzalez et al. 1985). The sorting and dispersal of objects according to size, however, may hold the most potential in this regard.

2.2. Unintentional Size-Sorting Processes

Cultural size sorting and general dispersal—the dispersion of artifact concentrations regardless of object size (Figure 1)—can result from activity that is intentionally or unintentionally generated. I introduce the terms *intentional* and *unintentional* size sorting and dispersal here only as heuristic devices; their mutual exclusiveness is less important than their organizational utility. Unintentional size sorting occurs indirectly as a consequence of two major processes: scuffage (Stockton 1973) and trampling. *Scuffage* refers specifically to the horizontal displacement of discarded artifacts across occupation surfaces by foot traffic (Stockton 1973). Although scuffage is essentially an unintentional behavior, its effects are far from random. One can readily appreciate how compact living floors repeatedly exposed to foot traffic might eventually be cleared of larger artifacts discarded during earlier depositional events. Consequently, intensively used outdoor activity areas, such as playas or courtyards in Shipibo and highland Mayan communities, rarely contain any obtrusive or observable refuse (DeBoer and Lathrap 1979:129; Hayden and Cannon 1983). Because larger artifacts are particularly susceptible to foot traffic (Stockton 1973; Stevenson 1985), it is easy

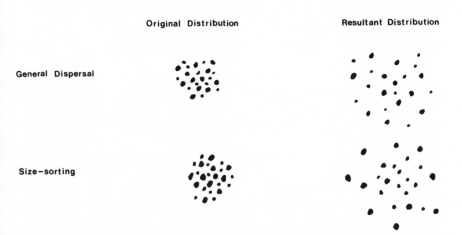

Figure 1. Schematic representation of artifact size sorting and general dispersal processes across two dimensions.

to see how they might migrate rapidly toward activity peripheries and other areas where such activity is reduced. Several researchers have found that larger objects tend to find their way to the edges of foot paths and walkways (e.g., Wilk and Schiffer 1979; DeBoer 1983; South 1979), where vegetation serves to impede further dispersal and concentrate objects (M. Schiffer, personal communication, 1987). Archaeological evidence of such traffic corridors has recently come to light at the middle prehistoric Sun River site near Great Falls, Montana (see Greiser 1984; Greiser *et al.* 1985:Figure 9). O'Connell's (1979, 1987) work among the Alyawara has clearly shown that, for objects participating in the same activity and/or deposited at the same time, larger items tend to migrate further from areas of activity than smaller ones.

Small artifacts, on the other hand, are more prone to trampling, that is, being embedded in occupation surfaces by foot traffic. Gifford-Gonzalez *et al.* (1985) have demonstrated by experimentation that, holding the intensity and duration of trampling constant, smaller artifacts penetrate deeper into occupation surfaces than larger ones. Gifford and Brehensmeyer (1977) furnish an intriguing example of this in their study of a modern Dassanetch campsite at Lake Turkana, Kenya. After abandonment, 200 bones were observed and plotted in one area of the site. Yet, excavation of the same area yielded 10 times as many pieces, most of which were less than 3 cm in length. Treadage by the camp's eight occupants appears to have driven many small pieces into the sandy ground during the three days that the site was occupied (Gifford-Gonzalez *et al.* 1985:804). Similarly, Yellen (1977:103) found that smaller objects in the vicinity of !Kung Bushmen [San] hearths were more susceptible to downward migration than were larger objects. Studies by Stockton (1973) also suggest that trampled material will sort according to size, with larger pieces occurring on or close to the ground surface and smaller items being pushed down to a depth of 10 cm or more. Experiments by Villa and Courtin (1983) clearly establish the vertical size-sorting effects of trampling.

Trampling, it should be noted, may not be the only cultural activity that vertically sorts objects according to size within deposits. Baker (1978) has suggested that scavenging and the reuse of larger (and more salient) objects by later inhabitants of sites may account for the vertical separation of objects by size within occupation floors.

Trampling studies (Stockton 1973; Courtin and Villa 1983; Gifford-Gonzalez *et al.* 1985) have shown that substrate compaction and grain size affect the downward penetration of artifacts into living floors. Not only do artifacts tend to migrate deeper into unconsolidated, sandy deposits than into more compacted substrates, but size sorting is not evident to the same degree in loose deposits. Apparently, discarded artifacts, regardless of size, circulate more freely in loose deposits during trampling (Villa and Courtin 1983; Gifford-Gonzalez *et al.* 1985). In experimental studies as well as archaeological sites, vertical distributions of trampled materials in unconsolidated sand seem to approximate a normal curve

(Gifford-Gonzalez *et al.* 1985). In extremely loose deposits of sand, however, artifact size, when related to weight (as it usually is), could exhibit different size-sorting patterns. Barton and Bergman (1982), for example, observed a positive correlation between artifact depth and weight in eolian sands at the Upper Paleolithic site of Hengistbury, England, although Gifford-Gonzalez *et al.* (1985) questioned whether this finding was due to trampling.

Objects subjected to foot traffic on loose, sandy substrates also appear to be less prone to horizontal dispersal than objects on harder substrates. Gifford-Gonzalez *et al.* (1985), for example, found that artifact assemblages tend to disperse less across unconsolidated floors than across compact surfaces. This suggested to them that the movement of artifacts exposed to foot traffic on loose substrates may be characterized more by vertical displacement than by horizontal dispersal.

Another process, which is less intentional than unavoidable, that may account for the dispersal of large objects away from activity areas is children's play. Even though the activities of children may occur virtually anywhere within settlements (e.g., Yellen 1977; Janes 1983), play is sometimes socially and logistically incompatible with the performance of domestic tasks essential to the daily operation and maintenance of groups. Consequently, in many contexts from historic Inuit settlements (Stevenson 1984a) to !Kung Bushmen [San] camps (Yellen 1977), play areas can be found on site peripheries away from domestic areas, along with other special-purpose activity areas. At the same time, because large and salient objects in provisional or final states of discard may hold special fascination for children (Hammond and Hammond 1981), they are more prone to dispersal during play than smaller, less interesting objects. Hammond and Hammond (1981) clearly demonstrated that not only were large items preferentially selected as play objects but that they were removed further from their original locus than small items. Cursory examination of Yellen's (1977:Appendix B) site plans reveal that children play a significant role in the dispersal of large items, especially, it seems, in camps occupied for less than a few days. The dispersal of discarded items by chidlren away from areas of intense activity has been observed in numerous contexts (e.g., Bonnichsen 1973; Wilk and Schiffer 1979; Hammond and Hammond 1981; Hayden and Cannon 1983).

2.3. Intentional Size-Sorting Processes

In virtually all preindustrial societies methods have evolved for coping with refuse buildup within domestic and intensively occupied areas. Even though considerable variation might be expected in the thoroughness with which areas are cleared, artifact size clearly plays a major role in determining whether an artifact will be redeposited as secondary refuse or left behind as residual primary refuse. Because small items are less visible and less obtrusive than large objects, they are more likely to be missed during refuse clearance, regardless of the diligence of the cleanup operation. Even though the intensity of cleanup, surface compaction, and other possible variables determine the size threshhold at which objects are passed over, a range of 2 cm to 9 cm has been reported in the literature (e.g., Rathje 1979; McKellar 1983; Dodd 1984), with dimensions nearer the lower extreme appearing more characteristic of intensive cleanup in sedentary communities.

This size-sorting effect has become known as the "McKellar principle." This principle has been observed in many modern settings from American university campuses (McKellar 1983) to herder camps in Greece (Murray and Chang 1981). Particularly instructive cases of this principle have been observed among the Alyawara of central Australia (O'Connell 1979, 1987) and the Nunamuit of northern Alaska (Binford 1978, 1983). The potential universality of the principle has been further supported by experimental studies. DeBoer (1983), for example, found that even after exhaustive pickups of lithic (obsidian) artifacts in defined areas, smaller objects were selectively left behind.

Intentional size sorting normally occurs directly as a result of expedient or systematic refuse disposal operations. Expedient clearing is an opportunistic, *ad hoc* activity involving little conscious thought or effort. Even though activities producing large amounts of disruptive or hazardous waste may call forth unscheduled, intensive cleanup operations (Schiffer 1987), the expedient clearing of refuse if usually linked with casual, low energy maintenance. Its goals are simply to facilitate immediate occupation or the performance of specific tasks within defined areas over the short term.

Intentional size sorting normally takes place horizontally across two dimensions. Infrequently, however, it can occur in all three dimensions. Savelle (1984), in his analysis of Inuit snowhouse structure, for example, found that items discarded on snow floors can be pressed downward intentionally just as easily as they can be discarded horizontally away from living areas.

Brushing debris aside by hand or foot in an area where occupation or a specific activity is intended may be the simplest, most expedient form of refuse disposal. A slightly more mentally demanding method of waste management involves the tossing of large or potentially disruptive debris away from activity centers. This latter form of refuse disposal, first described by Binford (1978, 1983) for the Nunamuit Eskimo, has been observed among hunter–gatherers in a number of modern settings from Australia (O'Connell 1979, 1987) to northern Canada (Jarvenpa and Brumbach 1983).

Both types of expedient refuse clearing would be expected to produce zones of debris just outside the perimeter of the "drop zone" (Binford 1978, 1983) or the area of most intensive use and activity. However, because hand/foot sweeping is a more inclusive, less discriminating activity than the selective retrieval and tossing of discrete objects, these zones might differ. Specifically, "toss zones" (Binford 1978, 1983), in contrast to "displacement zones" (Stevenson 1985), would tend to be less dense and to contain a higher proportion of large and/or immediately disruptive items (Stevenson 1985). In addition, "toss zones" would generally occur further away from activity centers than "displacement zones." One obvious exception to this may be when downwind or little-used sides of hearths are used as "toss zones" (Stevenson 1985, 1986), as they frequently seem to be (Binford 1983; O'Connell 1987).

Unlike expedient clearing, systematic refuse disposal is a planned, often intensive, activity conducted more or less on a scheduled basis (Schiffer 1987). For example, Coxoh Mayan kitchens are swept of debris daily (Hayden and Cannon 1983:126), whereas Gidjingali Aborigine hearth areas are cleared every week or two (Meehan 1982:114). And among the Willowlake Dene of the Northwest Territories house exteriors are raked and burned of refuse every spring (Janes 1983). Although intensive clearing is normally linked to scheduled refuse disposal, the accidental production of dangerous waste materials may, again, initiate *ad hoc*, intensive cleanup operations. The regular maintenance of activity areas, it should be noted, frequently involves a number of storage and transportation steps (Schiffer 1987), with refuse often being stored temporarily in receptacles or out-of-the-way places for future disposal, or even reuse (Deal 1985).

Systematic refuse clearing often produces secondary refuse deposits (Schiffer 1972, 1976) on the periphery of intensively or repeatedly occupied activity areas. Meehan (1982:14) notes how rubbish dumped on the perimeter of Gidjingali hearth complexes—areas unimportant for use and access—eventually accumulated to form quite large banks of debris. The formation of crescent-shaped zones of refuse on the peripheries of household activity areas has also been noted among the Shipibo (DeBoer and Lathrap 1979:128), the Alyawara (O'Connell 1987), and the Hadza (O'Connell *et al.*, Chapter 3 this volume).

Secondary refuse deposits would be expected to be located at least as far from activity centers as "toss zones." In fact, in many instances, they may overlap (e.g., O'Connell 1979, 1987). O'Connell (1987), for example, observed that both large and small items were deposited as secondary refuse on Alyawara household activity peripheries. Similarly, Rapson and Todd (1987) report the co-occurrence of both large bison bone and small bone fragments from a hearth fill in a suspected dump on the periphery of the late prehistoric Bugas-Holding site in Wyoming. Depending on the thoroughness of the cleanup (e.g., sweeping or raking) operation, duration of occupation, compaction of living surfaces, and other possible factors, systematically redeposited refuse disposal zones might contain a higher percentage of smaller items than "toss zones." Pam Stephenson (1985), for example, has suggested that intensive maintenance of compact house floor interiors may account for the unexpected predominance of small items (< 2 cm) on activity peripheries at the Nawthis village site in Utah.

No matter how diligent the cleaning operation or how compact the occupation surface, it seems clear that smaller items have a greater probability of being left behind than larger objects, particularly in difficult-to-reach places. Dodd

(1985), in his study of Guarijo Mexican house structure, found considerable amounts of small trash items (averaging 1.8 cm in length or diameter) in floor depressions and along the wall margins of kitchens. In a similar vein, O'Connell (1987:82) observed that, in spite of intensive sweeping, many small items remained behind in Alyawara household activity areas, although not necessarily in the precise spot where they were discarded.

Systematic refuse clearing involving regular cleanup and disposal is expected to be more characteristic of sites occupied for greater lengths of time than short-term hunter–gatherer campsites. A cross-cultural study of cultural deposition conducted by Murray (1980) revealed that secondary refuse disposal tends to be common among sedentary and semisedentary peoples possessing habitation structures. Conversely, migratory populations were more likely to discard elements near their locations of use, particularly when occupying outdoor living spaces (Murray 1980). Even before Murray's important study the suspected relationship between occupational intensity and discard location led Schiffer (1972:162) to speculate that with "increasing intensity of occupation, there will be decreasing correspondence between use and discard locations for all elements used in activities and discarded at the site." Although most societies studied by archaeologists probably maintained their life spaces to some degree, populations who moved camp frequently may have rarely engaged in intensive refuse clearing operations. The ethnographic literature clearly suggests that expedient, unscheduled refuse disposal would have characterized most occupations (Murray 1980).

Even though most size-sorting processes may occur to varying degrees at most hunter–gatherer sites, irrespective of duration of occupation, the formation of artifact assemblages at short-term or briefly occupied campsites concerns us here. Yet what constitutes a short-term campsite, and what does not, remains unclear. More importantly, it is not the duration of occupation *per se* that is likely to be the key variable in hunter–gatherer site structure and artifact distribution but the rate of refuse production as it relates to the intensity of occupation of specific areas. Occupational intensity, in turn, is conditioned by the length of stay, size of the area occupied, number of users, types of activities carried out, and numerous other variables.

An emic definition of a short-term camp is apt to vary from one cultural context to the next. However, from an archaeological perspective, I would submit that a campsite ceases to be short-term when (1) systematic refuse disposal becomes the dominant waste management strategy and (2) secondary refuse deposits overwhelm other types of refuse deposits in area, volume, and number of elements present. In this sense, most Gidjingali (Meehan 1982), some Alyawara (O'Connell 1979, 1987), and even a few !Kung Bushmen [San] (Yellen 1977:78) camps would not be considered short-term.

3. THE MODEL

The effects of the above size-sorting and general dispersal processes can now be synthesized into a model that I believe has some utility for describing the sequential formation of hearth-associated artifact assemblages at short-term hunter–gatherer campsites. Although I limit discussion to exterior hearths only, it is evident that size sorting and general dispersal take place indoors as well as out. Although Binford (1983:157) observes that maintenance tactics within house structures may be quite different from those conducted in spaces occupied outside, concentrations of large objects along interior walls and small elements dispersed around interior hearths and kitchen areas have been observed in long-houses at Ozette, Washington (Samuels 1983), multiroom structures at Nawthis Village in Utah (Stephenson 1985), and gold rush tents in the southwest Yukon (Stevenson, personal observation). In modern settings, this pattern is particularly prevalent among the Guarijio (Dodd 1985) and Maya (Hayden and Cannon 1983; Deal 1985). The following model, however, considers only the formation of artifact assemblages around exterior hearths; they are freqently the center of social life and activity in mobile hunter–gathering societies, particularly in temperate and warm climates (e.g., Yellen 1977; O'Connell 1979, 1987). Even in cold climates, hunters may conduct a large portion of their daily activities outdoors around hearths (Binford 1978, 1980, 1983; R. Janes, personal communication, 1987).

Frequently, when mobile groups of hunter–gatherers select a site deemed suitable for habitation, huts, hearths, and other facilities necessary for comfort and survival during occupation are constructed (e.g., Yellen 1977; Irimoto 1979). These features, unless others are added later, normally provide the skeleton around which camp activities are organized and conducted (Binford 1983:145). At first, routine daily activities carried out beside exterior hearths would generate concentrations of refuse resulting from food preparation, tool manufacturing, and other individual and communal processing and maintenance tasks. Assuming that occupation occurs on a sufficiently compact living surface, this refuse would be subject to a number of size-sorting and general dispersal processes over time. Specifically, scuffage would displace larger objects away from intensively occupied areas adjacent to hearths, as might the activities of children. Trampling, on the other hand, would quickly bury smaller artifacts in "drop zone" areas. (Both processes might be expected to occur concurrently on fluvial and other sufficiently compact substrates with high silt and clay fractions.) Large items and other potentially disruptive refuse dropped or discarded near hearths may be selectively retrieved and tossed to activity peripheries or to little-used sides of hearths. Alternatively, refuse allowed to accumulate beside hearths may be periodically displaced by hand or foot toward the perimeters of intensive use and activity. Figure 2 shows a schematic representation of this flow of refuse across two dimensions.

As occupation proceeds, both newly produced and earlier deposits of refuse would continue to undergo size sorting and general dispersal by expedient clearing, trampling, scuffage, and children's play. With repeated exposure to foot traffic, smaller artifacts in "displacement zones" may now become susceptible to trampling, whereas larger objects would continue to be displaced horizontally by scuffage. (The latter process, in fact, may account for the positive correlation between outer ring size and occupation span that Yellen [1977] observed among the !Kung [M. Schiffer, personal communication, 1987].) Dispersal by both children and scuffage may also explain why nut-cracking stones (some of the most common large artifacts recorded by Yellen) were found to be so weakly associated with nut shells—an explanation that Gregg *et al.* (Chapter 5 this volume) failed to consider. Constant exposure of artifacts to foot traffic on depositional surfaces might begin to result in the breakage of smaller objects and the incremental formation of edge damage on larger objects (Tringham *et al.* 1974; Gifford-Gonzalez *et al.* 1985). Secondary refuse deposits may even begin to form on the periphery of activity areas, as more systematic methods of refuse disposal, such as tossing and sweeping, are pressed into service to cope with the continuous production of refuse around hearths.

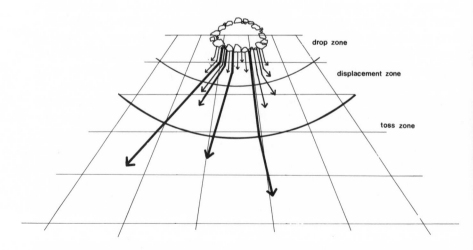

Figure 2. Model of flow of refuse produced in the vicinity of exterior hearths according to size sorting and general dispersal principles outlined in text. Note: Line weight is positively correlated with object size.

With the onset of abandonment, however, refuse would no longer be subject to the same degree of size sorting and general dispersal as earlier episodes of occupation. With the need to maintain living spaces dramatically reduced, newly discarded items, regardless of size or disruptive potential, would tend to remain clustered around hearths. This would result in one of the most noticeable differences in site structure between earlier and later episodes of occupations. Smaller artifacts would tend to remain intact and on their depositional surfaces, whereas comparatively little trampling damage on large artifacts would be expected. In addition, if return was planned, still functional or valuable artifacts might be cached in protective locations away from hearths for future use (Baker 1975; Stevenson 1982). A cross-section of a hearth area showing the hypothesized horizontal and vertical distribution of refuse upon site abandonment is presented in Figure 3. Of course, with the placement of other hearths nearby, this pattern would take on added complexity.

The formation of horizontal distributions of refuse consistent with expectations derived from the model have been recorded in ethnographic contexts by Binford (1978, 1983), O'Connell (1979, 1987), and Jarvenpa and Brumbach (1983), among others. The occurrence of small items in concentrations around hearths and large objects in more dispersed arrangements away from hearths has also been observed in numerous archaeological settings (e.g., Leroi-Gourhan and Brézillon 1966; Madsen 1982; Greiser 1984; Stevenson 1985, 1986; Rapson and Todd 1987). This pattern seems to be particularly well developed in several levels of the 1981 block excavation at the Peace Point site in northern Alberta, Canada (Figures 4, 5, and 6), and is clearly evident around several hearths at the Bugas–Holding site in Wyoming (Rapson and Todd 1987). (Regrettably, no attempt was made to record or assess the vertical separation of large and small items within occupation floors during the Peace Point excavation.)

We may now examine the significance of the model in light of broader theoretical concerns. First and foremost, adoption of the perspective advocated by the model suggests that we no longer need to view the cultural formation of such

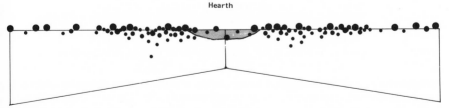

Hearth

Figure 3. Schematic cross-section of abandoned hearth area showing the horizontal and vertical distributions of three size classes of objects according to size sorting and general dispersal principles discussed in text.

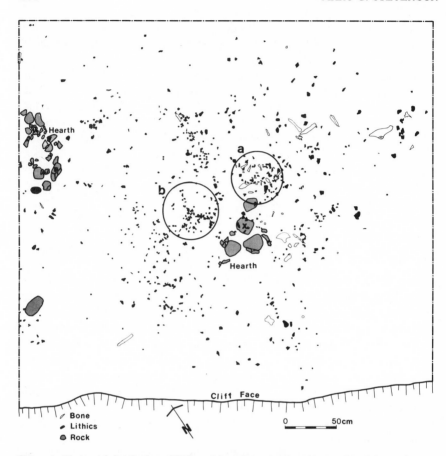

Figure 4. Horizontal distribution of lithic and faunal remains found in Level 1 of the 1981 Peace Point block excavation. Note conformity with expectations derived from model. Circle "a" defines a dense concentration of broken bone, whereas "b" encircles a concentration of refuse that may or may not represent the exact distribution of debitage and expedient tools as they fell between an individual's legs. [14]C dates suggest that this deposit formed about 2,200 years ago. Figure redrawn from Stevenson (1986:49, Figure 17) with permission of Environment Canada, Parks.

assemblages as static. We can now begin to partition the archaeological record of short-term hunter–gatherer campsites into units of some potential behavioral significance. For example, other things being equal, large or disruptive items concentrated on the surface of "drop zones" should be traceable to activities that occurred later than those that produced comparable refuse dispersed within "toss zone" areas. Similarly, objects embedded in "displacement zones" should be related to activities that occurred prior to those that produced equivalently sized

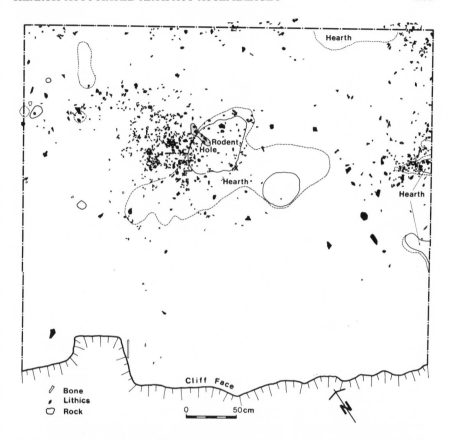

Figure 5. Horizontal distribution of lithic and faunal remains found in Level 5 of the 1981 Peace Point site block excavation. Solid lines indicate hearth centers or maximum vertical and horizontal deposits of ash and red/black soil staining. Dotted lines indicate approximate horizontal extent of ash and soil staining. Estimated age of deposit is about 2000 years B.P. Figure redrawn from Stevenson (1986:64, Figure 22) with permission of Environment Canada, Parks.

refuse concentrated on the surface of "drop zone" areas (Stevenson 1985). Holding size constant, embedded artifacts, irrespective of zone, probably relate to activities that took place prior to those that resulted in the discard of artifacts found on depositional surfaces. In a similar vein, the more dispersed an artifact assemblage is, and the more breakage and edge damage it exhibits, the greater the likelihood that it was produced during activities earlier than those producing less damaged and less dispersed assemblages.

The proposition that we might be able to trace the sequential formation of hearth-associated artifact assemblages at short-term hunter–gatherer campsites

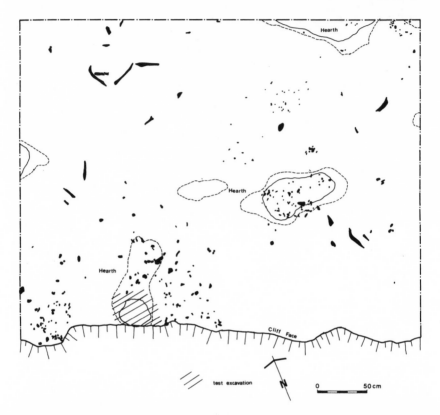

Figure 6. Horizontal distribution of remains found in Level 6 of the 1981 Peace Point block excavation. Note that both faunal elements and lithics are shaded in black.[14]C dates place the age of this level at about 1400 years B.P. Figure redrawn from Stevenson (1986:68, Figure 26) with permission of Environment Canada, Parks.

is an exciting one (see Keeley, Chapter 8 this volume). Few archaeologists, I believe, would dispute the claim that activity and behavior is likely to change during the occupation of such sites. At the most basic level, three separate, though overlapping, periods of activity differing in kind, intensity, and duration might be expected. These include (1) a brief settling-in phase in which site preparation activities would predominate; (2) a longer occupational phase characterized by procurement, processing, and maintenance tasks; and (3) a short abandonment phase in which activities indicative of increasing awareness of projected needs at future locations, and decreasing concern for present living conditions, would rule (Stevenson 1985). In many contexts, behavioral differences between Phases 2 and 3 should be evident in the content and structure of hearth-associated artifact asemblages. For example, at Peace Point, I have recorded several dense accumulations of lithic artifacts beside hearths. Their content is suggests that they relate more to later, than earlier, episodes of occupation. For a more thorough discussion of the anticipated archaeological and behavioral expressions of these phases, as applied to lithic workshop/habitation sites, see Stevenson (1985).

It follows from previous discussion that the spatial distribution of objects around exterior hearths at short-term hunter–gatherer campsites might map changes over time in resource exploitation strategies, food processing techniques, and social relations. It is at this point that the real potential of this site formation model comes to the fore. In the following two examples, I explore the potential of the model to document and illuminate certain aspects of hunter–gatherer activity and behavior at short-term hunter–gatherer campsites.

4. EXAMPLE 1: SITE STRUCTURE AND RESOURCE STRESS

It is not unreasonable to expect the kinds and quantities of resources exploited during earlier periods of occupation to differ from those of later episodes. Specifically, the larger, more abundant, more easily procured, that is, more desirable, resources would be harvested before others. This proposition is consistent not only with ethnographic observation (e.g., Yellen 1977) but with the marginal value theorem of optimal foraging theory (Charnov 1976; Winterhalder and Smith 1981) and the concept of r- and K-selection as it pertains to human foraging strategies (e.g., Hayden 1981). At the same time, the progressive depletion of resources in the area around a settlement would be expected to be met by an increase in the efficiency with which food is processed, especially if there were social (e.g., the obligation to live with kinsmen) or other incentives (e.g., considerable investments in site facilities) not to move on. (These propositions do not ignore the economic importance of small game systematically and unsystematically gathered by women and children throughout the entire occupation of settlements. Rather, if the hunting of large, mobile animals was a criterion in site selection, basic strategies of procurement and processing for such species may be expected to change during occupational episodes. Shifts toward harvesting less favored resources by women and children would be expected only in settlements of considerable duration.) The preceding propositions can be evaluated with evidence from the Peace Point site in northern Alberta, Canada (Stevenson 1985, 1986) and the Bugas–Holding site in northwestern Wyoming (Rapson and Todd 1987).

If the manufacture of bone grease/soup accounts for the fine breakage of large mammal bone, as many archaeologists believe (e.g., Leechman 1951; Vehik 1977; Binford 1981a), a shift in food processing strategies appears evident in the spatial organization of faunal refuse in Level 1 of the 1981 Peace Point block excavation. Adjacent to the central hearth feature an accumulation of broken mammal bones was found (Figure 4a). The fragmented nature of these remains indicates a food-processing technique more intensive than that responsible for the larger, more complete bones dispersed in "toss zone" areas, whereas their concentration within a "drop zone" suggests that they were produced during a later episode of occupation. The possibility that these bones were deposited later in the occupation of this feature is also suggested by the fact they exhibited a lesser degree of weathering (cracking, flaking, and pitting) than larger bones found in "drop zones" (Stevenson, personal observation). Differences in the size of these bones, however, could just as easily account for the differential weathering of individual faunal elements in these areas (see Rapson and Todd 1987).

In the same level, primary cores/core fragments and scrapers occur largely in "toss zone" areas (see Stevenson 1986:Figure 19). Similarly, cores, scrapers, and biface preforms in Level 5 are generally found dispersed in areas away from hearths (see Stevenson 1986:Figure 23). Alternatively, edge-modified flakes, prepared cores/core fragments, and later-stage reduction debitage in both levels are concentrated near hearths. Interestingly, a dense pattern of lithic artifacts in Level 1, which may or may not delineate the exact arrangement of items as they fell between the legs of an individual (Figure 4b), contained flake tools unlike any others found in the level (Stevenson 1986). Level 6 produced similar, albeit less conclusive, evidence of a possible shift in resource utilization at Peace Point. Large artiodactyl (bison and moose) rib fragments in this level were strongly disassociated with hearths and other remains in this level (Figure 6). Freshwater mollusc fragments, on the other hand, were found concentrated exclusively beside and in hearths. Whereas this evidence might suggest changes over time in resource utilization, it is important to point out that both artiodactyl and mollusc remains simply might have been deposited at the same time but subjected to different size-sorting processes because of their size. Although more tantalizing than conclusive, the spatial distributions of hearth-associated artifact assemblages at Peace Point are suggestive of changing resource utilization strategies over time.

Interpretive problems that arise from confusion over simultaneously deposited items subject to differential dispersal because of size, and remains produced at different times during occupation, appear to be minimized at the Bugas–Holding site, a late prehistoric campsite of uncommon integrity along the front range of the Rocky Mountains in northwestern Wyoming. Here, Rapson and Todd (1987) recovered more conclusive contextual evidence of a shift in resource use over time. Refitting of faunal elements revealed that not only were bison bone refits significantly more dispersed than bighorn sheep bone refits—faunal elements that arguably would have posed similar problems to site inhabitants upon discard—but the latter tended to be localized around individual hearths. Rapson and Todd (1987) interpret this finding as the result of either multiple occupation or *differential organizational "trajectories" of introduction, use, and disposal of the two species during a single occupation*. In the latter regard, it is perhaps significant that a higher percentage of bison bone was weathered; only 30% of the bighorn sheep bone demonstrated any evidence of weathering. Although Rapson and Todd (1987) attribute this finding primarily to the fact that large bone tends to weather more readily than small bone, it is instructive that the larger and more heavily weathered faunal elements, i.e., bison bones, were found several meters away from hearths (i.e., on hearth peripheries) where the absolute frequency of bone was lowest.

The Peace Point and Bugas–Holding data tend to support the propositions that (1) there will be a general shift during the occupation of some short-term and seasonally occupied hunter–gatherer campsites toward harvesting less desirable, smaller, more labor-intensive resources and (2) this shift should be readily detectable in the spatial organization of refuse at such sites. This perspective has, among other things, important implications for refining nutritional optimization models in archaeology. Reidhead (1980), for example, compared faunal remains from the Late Woodland occupation at the Haag site in Indiana with an idealized list of species based on 10 different nutrients, as well as procurement and processing costs. Yet, virtually no agreement was found between the observed and predicted rankings. Had Reidhead viewed the composition and provenience of his faunal assemblage as the product of dynamic, but patterned, depositional and behavioral processes, and modified his data collection methods accordingly, I cannot help but think that his results would have been different. In short, had he divided his assemblage into units representative of different stages of procurement or strategies of processing, rather than viewing it *a priori* as a homogeneous behavioral unit, a tighter fit might have resulted. Reidhead's findings alert us to the fact that we can no longer view the archaeological record as a product of synchronic behavior or static depositional histories.

In many mobile hunter–gatherer societies, food scarcity seems to be a major, if not the overriding, factor influencing the decision to move camp (e.g., see Yellen 1977:Appendix B). This is not to ignore noneconomic factors. Clearly, social tensions, the desire to live with relatives, tradition, and the like motivate hunter–gatherers to move camps in many settings (e.g., Lee and DeVore 1976; Yellen 1977). Nonetheless, for most mobile hunting and gathering groups, particularly those who exploit resources on the basis of their encounter frequency (Binford 1982), the promise of better food sources elsewhere may be the major incentive to move on.

Resource stress and social tension in hunting and gathering societies are frequently related. In many settings, social stress, particularly as it bears on the social relations of production, may be a major consequence of resource depletion. The relationship between site structure and social stress among men and women in northern hunting societies and its implications for the archaeological study of gender constitute our second example.

5. EXAMPLE 2: SITE STRUCTURE AND SOCIAL STRESS

One corollary of the model presented for recognizing the sequential formation of artifact assemblages is that a large part of the structural integrity of habitually and intensively occupied spaces within short-term hunter–gatherer campsites may be the product of later and/or abandonment episodes of occupation (Stevenson 1982, 1985). I do not mean to suggest that this will be the case for all or even most sites; one can envision many situations, for example, overnight stops, where the abandonment phase may be so brief as to play an inconsequential role in structuring the final distributions and associations of artifacts at a site. Nonetheless, where occupational intensity and/or duration is greater, and abandonment is gradual and planned (Stevenson 1982), artifact arrangements and associations are likely to have been produced or at least last effected, in part, by activity and behavior different than that which occurred previously (see previous discussion). Figure 7 depicts this relationship for a hypothetical campsite occupied for 10 days. The term *life history* may best summarize conceptually the process of assemblage formation I am attempting to describe here. It thus may be justifiable to speak of the life history of hearth-associated artifact assemblages in much the same way as Schiffer (1972) uses "life history" to refer to the manufacture, use, maintenance, and discard of artifacts (C. Carr, personal communication, 1987).

Note that this perspective is consistent with Ascher's (1968) view that the record of a living community is constantly in the process of destroying and renewing itself. Clear arrangements and associations of artifacts produced during earlier episodes of the same occupation are apt to become "smeared and blended" by subsequent occupational activities. Thus we may be on particularly shaky ground if we extend behavioral inferences derived from the structure of a settlement to include the occupation as a whole. A case in point is the archaeological study of gender relations in northern hunting societies.

Among all ethnographically recorded northern hunter–gatherers (e.g., Giffen 1930; Wantanabe 1968; Sharp 1981, among others), and even among some equatorial ones (O'Connell *et al.*, Chapter 3 this volume), differences between men and women in their roles and activities are pronounced. While men generally hunt and trap a variety of large, mobile, dispersed mammals away from camp, women usually forage for plant foods and small game in the vicinity of camps. Women also contribute to group comfort and survival by rearing children, processing food, manufacturing clothing, and maintaining shelters and other facilities. Gender-related differences in tool abundance, type, diversity, and technolog-

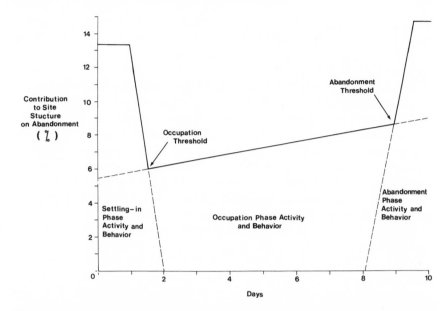

Figure 7. Relationship between occupational duration and relative contribution of various activities and behaviors to the structure of a short-term camp upon abandonment. Note that about 10% of the resultant site structure has not been accounted for. I have done this to include the variety of environmental formation processes that refuse would likely be subject to during occupation. Only rarely would the preceding scenario obtain in the real world; scavenging, dispersal by natural agencies, and other postoccupational disturbance processes would likely play a much larger role in shaping site structure upon discovery by an archaeologist. Therefore, the relative contribution of each phase of activity to the overall structure of a site would likely be considerably less than that depicted here. Note that under rapid and/or unplanned abandonment conditions, abandonment phase activities would play a negligible role in the resultant structure of a site (Stevenson 1982).

ical sophistication would be expected as a result of this division of labor (Stevenson 1984b, 1986; Janes and Stevenson 1984). Differences in the tasks carried out by each sex would also predict different gender-related activity areas (Janes and Stevenson 1984). In addition, as activities may become more repetitive and organized through time during the occupation of sites (Yellen 1977; Stevenson 1984b, 1986), and as women in most northern hunting societies (e.g., Giffen 1930; Wantanabe 1968; Savashinski 1971) are less mobile and spend more time in camps than men, their tasks may become more localized to specific areas. Conversely, men, being more mobile and less tied to specific activity patterns within settlements than women, may produce activity areas somewhat larger and more randomly distributed than those of women. I am not inferring here that male and famale activities in northern cultures do not overlap in time and space;

this is often the case in domestic or household contexts where social status is frequently less important than the maintenance and reproduction of the family unit. However, in communal and public settings the differential use of space by men and women is expected to hold generally (compare this statement with a similar observation made by O'Connell *et al.*, Chapter 3 this volume).

In many northern hunting cultures the organization of space appears to basesd, in part, on age and gender differentiation (e.g., Tanner 1979; Wenzel 1983). Although this may be due primarily to social and functional–logistic considerations, Tanner (1979) observes that the ritual organization of private (interior) and public (exterior) space along age and sex lines among the Mistassini Cree serves to structure social relations and underpin their hunting mode of production. The same may be said of the Inuit, particularly in regards to public space (e.g., Wenzel 1983). The ritual organization of space among northern hunters would predict that men and women will carry out their respective activities in different areas.

The differential status of men and women in most Arctic and Subarctic cultures may also contribute to differences in the location and size of their activity areas, particularly in public and communal situations. Although men and women in northern hunting societies participate in different spheres of prestige (Janes and Stevenson 1984), etic interpretations of their ideology, religious (e.g., Oosten 1976; Tanner 1979) or otherwise, view the societal position of men as superior to that of women. Anthropological opinion is mixed about whether the lower status of women in such societies is based on their economic contribution, child-rearing roles, or both (see Dahlberg 1981). Alternatively, I would submit that women may not enjoy the same status or participate in the same prestige areas as men simply because, being more restricted to campsite locales, they perform tasks that after a while can offer comparatively little or new economic or social information. Conversely, men ranging over much larger areas have a greater opportunity to acquire and contribute information beneficial to present and future living conditions in northern environments where big game forms the majority of the diet (Stevenson 1984b). The crucial variable, I believe, for understanding differential status in northern hunting societies is not economic contribution, but information, and specifically its acquisition, dispensation, and control (Stevenson 1984b; Janes and Stevenson 1984).

Artifact distributions and associations explainable with reference to the model of gender-related differences proposed have been reported for a number of carefully excavated prehistoric sites (e.g., Cahen *et al.* 1979; McGhee 1979; Pokatylo 1983; Stevenson 1984b, 1986). Level 7 in the 1981 Peace Point block excavation, for example, although less than 12 m^2, produced two hearth areas differing markedly in tool type, diversity, and abundance as well as artifact density (Table 1, Figure 8; also see Stevenson [1986:72–76]). Differential occupational intensity of these areas is also suggested by the fact that size sorting appears less evident around the hypothesized male hearth than the female hearth (Figure 8).

Table 1.   Gender-Related Artifacts and Remains Associated with Hypothesized Male and Female Hearth Areas in Level 7 of the 1981 Peace Point Block Excavation. Data from Stevenson (1986)

	Hypothesized male hearth area	Hypothesized female hearth area
Bifaces	0	1
Scrapers	1	5
Multipurpose flake tools (multiple retouch or utilization)	0	7
Biface trimming flakes	38	6
Splintered bone (marrow extraction)	Present	Present
Mashed and calcined bone (bone grease-soup production)	Absent	Present

The Epipaleolithic campsite of Meer II in Belgium (Cahen *et al.* 1979) and a late prehistoric hunting stand excavated by David Pokatylo (1983) in the southern interior of British Columbia have yielded similar evidence in support of the model. Both sites produced two major artifact concentrations which have been shown by refitting to have been deposited at about the same time. Cahen *et al.* (1979) interpreted one concentration at Meer II as a multipurpose domestic activity area in which hide working predominated. The other they interpreted as an area where specialized bone and antler tool manufacturing took place. The fact that the former area produced a more diversified, less specialized, more abundant inventory of tools than the latter area conforms well with expectations derived from the model. Pokatylo's (1983:13) hilltop hunting camp produced nearly identical evidence; the area offering the best view of the surrounding country yielded an artifact assemblage indicative of weapons' manufacture and repair, whereas the lower, less exposed area produced a variety of utility implements used in "activities necessary to maintain the camp and process the products of the hunt." McGhee's (1979) findings at the Cold site at Port Refuge, Devon Island, in the High Arctic are particularly fascinating. The halves of several early Paleo-Eskimo houses produced marked gender-related differences in tool abundance, diversity, specialization, and artifact density (see also Stevenson 1986:110–114). (It is perhaps interesting that the strict division of interior space along gender lines at Port Refuge appears to be more characteristic of the organization of space within domestic dwellings of northern Algonkian-speaking Indians [e.g., see Tanner 1979] than ethnographic and prehistoric Inuit groups.)

The preceding model of gender-related differentiation in northern hunting

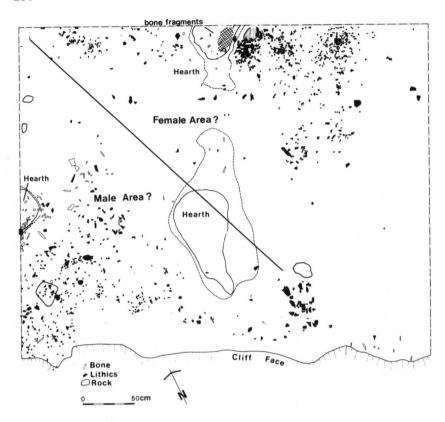

Figure 8. Hypothesized male and female hearth areas in Level 7 of the 1981 Peace Point site block excavation. Note differences in size sorting and artifact density between north (hypothesized female) and west (hypothesized male) wall hearths. Figure redrawn from Stevenson (1986:72, Figure 28) with permission of Environment Canada, Parks.

societies was constructed, in part, to account for observed differences between men and women in ethnographic settings (i.e., contexts that may not be entirely representative of all northern hunting societies at all times). In other words, the model may mask the variability in gender roles and regulations that might be expected under different or changing social, cultural, historical, demographic, and environmental conditions.

Perhaps more importantly, in view of the life-history concept advanced previously, archaeological evaluations of the model might be subject to the fallacy of affirming the consequent. Not only may the final spatial organization of artifacts map activities be unrepresentative of the occupation as a whole, but gender inequality and stress may be uncharacteristically intensified during later episodes of occupation. Specifically, as a consequence of resource stress during terminal phases of occupation, men and women would not be able to fulfill their mutually dependent socioeconomic roles. A certain amount of social tension between men and women appears to be adaptive in northern settings, in that its major method of resolution, male mobility (Savishinski 1971), is crucial to economic survival (Stevenson 1984b). Yet, task, role, and status differences would likely be exaggerated during the later stages of occupation as male mobility, and the social mechanism promoting it, social tension, would intensify to offset the decreasing availability of resources. Ultimately, however, this feedback system would fail, resulting in site abandonment.

In addition, the ritual organization of space along age and sex lines would be expected to be most pronounced under conditions of resource stress. Such use of space during times of scarcity would be needed, too, as a way of maintaining gender roles, societal order, and the hunting mode of production. In this vein, I believe it is no coincidence that the most elaborate religious ceremonies of the Inuit, which serve to give spiritual meaning to and reaffirm the social order of the Inuit world (see Boas 1964; Oosten 1976), take place in late fall when travel and hunting are virtually impossible. (In light of this suggestion, recall the strict division of space along gender lines within Paleo-Eskimo dwellings at Port Refuge.)

Given that artifact arrangements and associations within intensively utilized spaces may result largely from later episodes of occupation and that gender differences are likely to be uncharacteristically intensified during this time, the uncritical use of these data to examine gender relations in northern hunting societies is cautioned against. Such use denies exploration of the variability we might expect in gender relations during earlier episodes of occupation when women played a greater role in the acquisition and contribution of information and favored resources, and probably decision making. Stated another way, during earlier stages of occupation when gender roles could be easily fulfilled, women may have enjoyed more control over how they conducted their affairs. (This proposition developed out of a discussion with one of my elderly Inuit informants on Baffin Island in the Canadian Arctic. Qatsook Eevic told me that her biggest concern after her husband died was that she would no longer have any skins to sew [Stevenson, personal communication, 1986]. In other words, with her husband gone, she felt that she would no longer be able to fulfill her societal role or have any control over her own destiny. As it turned out, she was well provided for by her sons.)

The preceding discussion instructs us to develop archaeological methods and theories that would allow us to isolate and examine the remains of earlier behaviors and depositional events. For example, accounting for size, do subsurface horizontal distributions of hypothesized female artifacts embedded by trampling differ from or approximate those found on depositional surfaces? Alternatively, do analyses of edge-damaged lithic artifacts, weathered bone, and other data sensitive to occupational intensity and/or duration reveal greater mixing of gender-related artifacts and activities during earlier occupational episodes?

Because task, role, and status differences between men and women in northern hunting societies are among the most pronounced in the nonindustrial world, their study may help to build a theory of gender relations that is applicable to all societies. Yet, where much evidence on the evolution of gender differences lies in the ground, the indiscriminate use of data whose content, structure, and behavioral antecedents may be uncharacteristic of occupations as a whole must be abandoned.

6. CONCLUDING REMARKS

Artifact assemblages within intensively occupied areas at short-term camp-sites are not fossilized records of the operation of extinct societies (Binford 1964:425). Nor are they distorted reflections of the operation of past behavioral systems (Schiffer 1976:12). They only reflect unambiguously the operation of a past behavioral system as it continually modifies, rearranges, depletes, and destroys matter it has created (Binford 1981b). Artifact patterns and associations relating to earlier occupational events may thus be difficult, if not virtually impossible, to detect with any degree of confidence. Indeed, it is sobering to acknowledge this and the possibility that the final content and structure of such deposits as well as the behaviors and activities that produced them may be uncharacteristic of depositional and behavioral site histories. However, if we are ever to realize the potential of archaeology's contribution to the study of the human condition, we must come to grips with what the archaeological record is and what it is not. This chapter has attempted to do this.

Artifact distributions conforming to expectations of the assemblage formation model advanced here may be anticipated at many types of short-term hunter–gatherer campsites. However, unanticipated patterns failing to support the predictions of the model may be as, if not, more informative. For example, a Protohistoric level at Peace Point failed to demonstrate the degree of size sorting observed in Levels 1, 5, and 6, despite the fact that it yielded as many hearthlike features and a significantly larger artifact assemblage; over 2,350 separate items were recorded in this level, 95% of which were bones (Figure 9). Although it is well known that many societies dispose of animal bones more casually than other kinds of refuse (see Schiffer 1987 for discussion), this does not account for the lack of size sorting in this level. Alternatively, perhaps this level represents the interior of a dwelling. Yet, virtually none of the patterning that one would expect for artifact assemblages within tentlike features is present (see Carr, Chapter 7 this volume). Considering the extremely broad range of species recorded in this level (see Stevenson 1986:60–61, Table 6), there is little question that remains in this

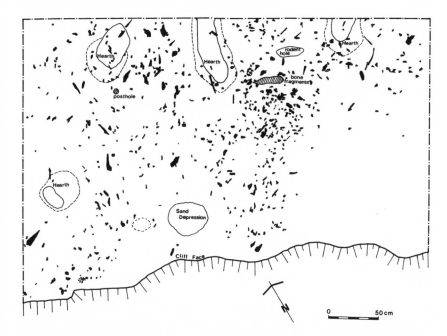

Figure 9. Level 16 of the 1981 Peace Point block excavation. Even though an occupation of considerable intensity is indicated, contrary to expectations derived from the assemblage formation model, there is a conspicuous lack of size sorting in this level. Note that both lithic and faunal remains are shaded in black. Figure redrawn from Stevenson (1986:85, Figure 38) with permission of Environment Canada, Parks.

level represent an occupation of considerable intensity and/or duration. What then accounts for the apparent lack of size sorting in this level? Carbonized spruce and pine needles found near one hearth may offer a solution. Considering this finding and other contextual information noted before, it is possible that this level was once covered with bows and that the distribution of refuse found on the floor represents the locations where objects fell or were pressed through this mat.

This chapter has presented a model that has focused almost exclusively on size sorting and general dispersal processes around exterior hearths at short-term campsites. However, hut interiors, door dumps, special-purpose activity areas, and other features should be subject to the same cultural formation processes, although their resultant structure may differ. Clearly, a more complete picture of the occupational history of short-term campsites requires the careful study and analysis of all areas.

I have studiously avoided until now consideration of the effects of natural and postabandonment processes on site structure. However, it seems obvious that before we can begin to entertain the theoretical propositions at the level presented in this chapter, the effects of natural agencies and reoccupation must be considered. How do animals, plant growth, water action, frost heave, and the like alter artifact distributions and associations in various contexts? Does nature sort and disperse artifacts in the same fashion as cultural activity? In some settings it might. For example, freeze–thaw cycles tend to expell larger objects from soil surfaces more rapidly and thoroughly than smaller objects (Wood and Johnson 1978:343). Similarly, larger bones seem to be more susceptable to scavenging and dispersal by carnivores than smaller bones. However, even though bones scattered by carnivore activity may occur in the same areas as larger bones dispersed by human activity, differential modification should distinguish the former from the latter (Rapson and Todd 1987). Although our understanding of the effects of natural formation processes on archaeological deposits is far from complete, we are continually adding to our knowledge (e.g., Wood and Johnson 1978; also see Schiffer 1983, 1987).

Reoccupation can alter the structural integrity of archaeological assemblages within campsites in the same way that later occupational episodes may "smear and blend" evidence of earlier events. Reoccupation might also produce palimpsest assemblages in which most artifact distributions and associations simply may be the accumulated result of different occupations, rather than the performance of activities during any one occupation (Binford 1982; Carr 1985). Conceivably, reoccupation may presesnt a serious hurdle to the level of theory presented in this chapter. However, some consolation may be found in (1) Ascher's (1968) observation that the products of later occupations possess greater integrity than earlier occupations; (2) the tendency of hunter–gatherers to avoid camping on the debris of previous occupations through avoidance (e.g., Yellen 1977) or refuse clearing (Schiffer 1987); and (3) the tendency for reoccupation to be less common among foragers exploiting resources on the basis of their encounter frequency than among collectors employing positioning tactics aimed at harvesting specific resource distributions (Binford 1982). Refitting has proven to be a particularly important tool in establishing the contemporaniety of spatially differentiated activity areas within archaeological sites (e.g., Cahen et al. 1979; Pokatylo 1983; Rapson and Todd 1987). Similarly, other contextual information sensitive to occupational intensity and duration, such as the formation of edge damage on lithic artifacts, the weathering of bone, and, of course, size sorting and general dispersal, hold much potential in this regard. Rapson and Todd (1987) used bone weathering particularly effectively to establish that the Bugas–Holding site was the result of a single or related occupational event rather than a series of disconnected occupations. Although we are still very far from the day when we can confidently separate the products of different and unrelated occupations from those of single or related occupations, the data and discussion presented in this chapter may hopefully move us toward that goal. At the very least, this chapter suggests that we can no longer ignore these questions when we perform analyses.

The utility of the perspective advocated here is limited only by imagination; it can profitably be employed to examine social phenomena in a variety of archaeological contexts. For example, at hunter–gatherer aggregation sites where otherwise dispersed groups came together, I would expect group identity to be exaggerated during earlier episodes of occupation (Stevenson 1989), particularly if groups were unrelated. There are selective advantages to stereotyping and the maintenance of sufficiently consistent behavior and action in such contexts; they create stages for social interaction by facilitating effective communication. That is, such behaviors enable "others to place an individual or group in some given social category, thus permitting appropriate interactive behavior" (DeVos and Romanucci-Ross 1975:374). This might result in the clustered arrangement of household areas, the creation and/or more consistent use of symbols to maintain group identity, greater standardization in ways of doing things, and other social behaviors that have implications for the archaeology of such sites (Stevenson 1989). However, over time, as social barriers break down, a more homogeneous record might result. On the other hand, if group identities were still being maintained during the later stages of occupation, other selective forces might come into play, such as the maintenance of differential distribution of power among groups (McGuire 1982), or the increased emphasis on information control and decision making that some would envision in settlements of increasing size and duration (Johnson 1982). Because this example has important implications for the emergence of ethnic processes and identity formation among mobile human populations, it may constitute a fruitful line of inquiry for Paleolithic archaeology.

To some, advocating the use of a model that describes the sequential formation of one particular type of archaeological deposit to address activity and behavior in prehistoric settings may seem perfunctory. However, the examples provided here illustrate the types of linkages that need to be forged between midrange and general theory if archaeology is ever going to advance beyond the current stage in which it finds itself. If this chapter has demonstrated anything, I hope that it would be that the search for social behaviors and culture processes in the archaeological record is not dead, only much harder than we imagined. For those willing to work at archaeology, to theorize, to build, and to continually refine models (i.e., to rigorously apply contextual approaches to archaeology), the payoffs may be just around the corner.

ACKNOWLEDGMENTS

Comments on an earlier draft of this chapter by Christopher Carr, Bob Janes, and Michael Schiffer have substantially improved the final product. The patience and editoral suggestions of Ellen Kroll and Doug Price are also appreciated. Thanks are due Kathie Graham-Stevenson and Doug Proch for the figures in this chapter. Research at Peace Point was undertaken while I was employed with Parks Canada. The support of this agency is gratefully acknowledged.

7. REFERENCES

Ascher, R., 1968, Time's Arrow and the Archaeology of a Contemporary Community. In *Settlement Archaeology* (K. C. Chang, ed.), National Press Books, Palo Alto, pp. 43–52.

Baker, C. M., 1975, Site Abandonment and the Archaeological Record: An Empirical case for Antici- pated Return, *Arkansas Academy of Science Proceedings* 29:10–11.

Baker, C. M., 1978, The Size Effect: An Explanation of Variability in Surface Artifact Assemblage Content, *American Antiquity* 43:288–293.

Barton, N. E., and Bergman, C. A., 1982, Hunters at Hengistbury: Some Evidence from Experimental Archaeology, *World Archaeology* 14:237–248.

Binford, L. R., 1964, A Consideration of Archaeology Research Design, *American Antiquity* 29:425– 4441.

Binford, L. R., 1978, Dimensional Analysis of Behavior and Site Structure: Learning from an Eskimo Hunting Stand, *American Antiquity* 43:330–361.

Binford, L. R., 1980, Willow Smoke and Dog's Tails: Hunter–Gatherer Settlement Systems and Archaeological Site Formation, *American Antiquity* 45:1–17.

Binford, L. R., 1981a, Behavioral Archaeology and the "Pompeii Premise," *Journal of Anthropological Research* 35:195–208.

Binford, L. R., 1981b, *Bones: Ancient Men and Modern Myths*, Academic Press, New York.

Binford, L. R., 1982, The Archaeology of Place, *Journal of Anthropological Archaeology* 1:5–31.

Binford, L. R., 1983, *In Pursuit of the Past: Decoding the Archaeological Record*, Thames and Hudson, London.

Boas, F., 1964, *The Central Eskimo*, The University of Nebraska Press, Lincoln.

Bonnichsen, R., 1973, Millie's Camp: An Experiment in Archaeology, *World Archaeology* 4:277–291.

Cahen, D., Keeley, L. H., and Van Noten, F. L., 1979, Stone Tools, Tool Kits, and Human Behavior in Prehistory, *Current Anthropology* 20:661–684.

Carr, C., 1985, Alternative Models, Alternative Techniques: Variable Approaches to Intrasite Spatial Analysis. In *For Concordance in Archaeological Analysis: Bridging Data Structure, Quantitative Technique, and Theory* (C. Carr, ed.), Westport Press, Kansas City, pp. 302–473.

Charnov, E. L., 1976, Optimal Foraging and the Marginal Value Theorem, *Theoretical Population Biology* 9:129–136.

Courtin, J., and Villa, P., 1982, Une Expérience de Pietinement, *Bulletin de la Société Préhistorique Française* 79:117–123.

Dahlberg, F., 1981, Introduction to *Women the Gatherer* (F. Dahlberg, ed.), Yale University Press, New Haven, pp. 1–30.

Deal, M., 1985, Household Pottery Disposal in the Mayan Highlands: An Ethnoarchaeological Inter- pretation, *Journal of Anthropological Archaeology* 4:243–291.

DeBoer, W. R., 1983, The Archaeological Record as a Preserved Death Assemblage. In *Archaeological Hammers and Theories* (J. A. Moore and A. S. Keene, eds.), Academic Press, New York, pp. 19–36.

DeBoer, W. R., and Lathrap, D. W., 1979, The Making and Breaking of Shipibo-Conibo Ceramics. In *Ethnoarchaeology: Implications for the Ethnography of Archaeology* (C. Kramer, ed.), Col- umbia University Press, New York, pp. 59–74.

DeVos, G., and Romanucci-Ross, L., 1975, Ethnicity: Vessel of Meaning and Emblem of Contrast. In *Ethnic Identity: Cultural Continuities and Change* (G. DeVos and L. Romanucci-Ross, eds.), Mayfield, Palo Alto, pp. 363–390.

Dodd, W. A., 1984, *The Use of Domestic Space by Sedentary Households: Some Organizing Principles*, Paper presented at the 49th Annual Meeting of the Society for American Archaeology, Portland, Oregon.

Giffen, N. M., 1930, *The Roles of Men and Women in Eskimo Culture*, University of Chicago Press, Chicago.

Gifford-Gonzalez, D. P., Damrosch, D. B., Damrosch, D. R., Pryor,, J., and Thunen, R. L., 1985, The Third Dimension in Site Structure: An Experiment in Trampling and Vertical Dispersal, *American Antiquity* 50:803–818.

Greiser, S. T., 1984, *Behavioral Interpretation of Floor Space Utilization in Hunter–Gatherer Campsites.* Paper Presented at the 49th Annual Meeting of the Society for American Archaeology, Portland, Oregon.

Greiser, S. T., 1984, *Behavioral Interpretation of Floor Space Utilization in Hunter–Gatherer Campsites.* Paper Presented at the 49th Annual Meeting of the Society for American Archaeology, Portland, Oregon.

Greiser, S. T., Greiser, T. W., and Vetter, S. M., 1985, Middle Prehistoric Period Adaptations and Paleoenvironment in the Northwestern Plains: The Sun River Site, *American Antiquity* 50:849–877.

Hammond, G., and Hammond, N., 1981, Child's Play: A Distorting Factor in Archaeological Distribution, *American Antiquity* 46:634–636.

Hayden, B., 1981, Research and Development in the Stone Age: Technological Transitions among Hunter–Gatherers, *Current Anthrolpology* 22:519–548.

Hayden, B., and Cannon, A., 1983, Where the Garbage Goes: Refuse Disposal in the Mayan Highlands, *Journal of Anthropological Archaeology* 2:117–163.

Irimoto, T., 1979, *Ecological Anthropology of the Caribou-Eater Chipweyan of the Wallaston Lake Region of Northern Saskatchewan* unpublished Ph.D. Dissertation, Department of Sociology and Anthropology, Simon Fraser University, Burnaby, BC.

Janes, R. R., 1983, *Archaeological Ethnography among the Mackenzie Basin Dene, Canada*, The Arctic Institute of North American Technical Paper No. 28, The Arctic Institute of North America, University of Calgary, Calgary.

Janes, R. R., and Stevenson, M. G., 1984, *Ethnoarchaeological Observations On Male/Female Activity Differentiations in Northern Hunting Societies*, Paper presented at the 17th Annual Meeting of the Canadian Archaeological Association, Victoria, BC.

Jarvenpa, R., and Brumbach, H. J., 1983, Ethnoarchaeological Perspectives on an Athapaskan Moose Kill, *Arctic* 36:174–184.

Johnson, G. A., 1982. Organizational structure and scalar stress. In *Theory and Explanation in Archaeology: The Southampton Conference* (C. Renfrew *et al.*, eds.), Academic Press, New York, pp. 389–421.

Lee, R. B., and DeVore, I., 1976, *Kalahari Hunter–Gatherers*, Harvard University Press, Cambridge.

Leechman, D., 1951, Bone Grease, *American Antiquity* 16:355–356.

Leroi-Gourhan, A., and Brézillon, M., 1966, L'habitation Magdalénienne no. 1 de Pincevent Prés de Montereau (Seine-et-Marne), *Gallia Préhistoire* 9(2)263–385.

Madsen, T., 1982, Settlement Systems of Early Agricultural Societies in East Jutland, Denmark: A Regional Study in Change, *Journal of Anthropological Archaeology* 1:197–236.

McGhee, R., 1979, *The Paleoeskimo Occupations at Port Refuge in the High Arctic, Canada*, Archaeological Survey of Canada Mercury Series, Paper No. 72, National Museum of Man, Ottawa.

McGuire, R. H., 1982, The Study of Ethnicity in Historical Archaeology, *Journal of Anthropological Archaeology* 1:159–178.

McKellar, J. A., 1983. Correlations and the Explanation of Distributions, *Atlatl, Occasional Papers* 4, Anthropology Club, University of Arizona, Tucson.

Meehan, B., 1982, *Shell Bed to Shell Midden,* Australian Institute of Aboriginal Studies, Canberra.

Moeyersons, J., 1978, The Behavior or Stones and Stone Implements Buried in Consolidating and Creeping Kalahari Sands, *Earth Surface Processes* 3:115–128.

Murray, P., 1980, Discard Location: The Ethnographic Data, *American Antiquity* 45:490–502.

Murray, P., and Chang, C., 1981, An Ethnoarchaeological Study of a Contemporary Herder's Camp, *Journal of Field Archaeology* 8:372–381.

O'Connell, J. F., 1979, *Site Structure and Dynamics among Modern Alyawara Hunters,* Paper Presented at the 44th Annual Meeting of the Society for American Archaeology, Vancouver, BC.

O'Connell, J. F., 1987, Alyawara Site Structure and Its Archaeological Implications, *American Antiquity* 52:74–108.

Oosten, J., 1976, *Theoretical Structure of the Religion of the Netsilik and Iglulik,* Special publication, Ryksuniversitit to Groningen, Groningen, Holland.

Pokatylo, D., 1983, *Blood from Stone,* Museum Note No. 11, Museum of Anthropology, University of British Columbia, Vancouver.

Rapson, D. J., and Todd, L. C., 1987, Attribute Based Spatial Analysis: An Example from a Hunter–Gatherer Site in Northwestern Wyoming, Paper Presented at the 52nd Annual Meeting of the Society for American Archaeology, Toronto, Ontario.

Rathje, W. L., 1979, Modern Material Culture Studies. In *Advances in Archaeological Method and Theory, Vol. 2,* (M. B. Schiffer, ed.), Academic Press, New York, pp. 1–37.

Reidhead, V. A., 1980, The Economics of Subsistence Change: A Test of an Optimization Model. In *Modeling Change in Prehistoric Subsistence Economics* (T. K. Earle and A. L. Christenson, eds.), Academic Press, New York, pp. 141–186.

Samuels, S. R., 1983, *Spatial Patterns and Cultural Processes in Three Northwest Coast Longhouse Floor Middens from Ozette,* unpublished Ph.D. Dissertation, Department of Anthropology, Washington State University, Pullman.

Savashinski, J. S., 1971, Mobility as an Aspect of Stress in an Arctic Community, *American Anthropologist* 73:604–618.

Savelle, J. M., 1984, Cultural and Natural Formation Processes of a Historic Inuit Snow Dwellings Site, Somerset Island, Arctic Canada, *American Antiquity* 49:508–524.

Schiffer, M. B., 1972, Archaeological Context and Systemic Context, *American Antiquity* 37:156–165.

Schiffer, M. B., 1976, *Behavioral Archaeology,* Academic Press, New York.

Schiffer, M. B., 1983, Toward the Identification of Formation Processes, *American Antiquity* 48:675–706.

Schiffer, M. B., 1987, *Formation Processes of the Archaeological Record,* University of New Mexico Press, Alburquerque.

Sharp, H. S., 1981, The Null Case: The Chippewyan. In *Woman the Gatherer* (F. Dalhberg, ed.), Yale University Press, New Haven, pp. 221–244.

South, S., 1979, Historic Site Content, Structure, and Function, *American Antiquity* 44:213–237.

Stephenson, P., 1985, *Lithic Refuse Disposal Patterns: An Archaeological Study,* Paper Presented at the 50th Annual Meeting of the Society for American Archaeology, Denver, Colorado.

Stevenson, M. G., 1982, Toward an Understanding of Site Abandonment Behavior: Evidence from Historic Mining Camps in the Southwest Yukon, *Journal of Anthropological Archaeology* 1:237–265.

Stevenson, M. G., 1984a, *Kekerten: Preliminary Archaeology of an Arctic Whaling Station,* Manuscript on Deposit, Prince of Wales Northern Heritage Centre, Yellowknife, N.W.T.

Stevenson, M. G., 1984b, *Male/Female Role and Activity Differentiation in Prehistoric Hunting Societies,* Paper Presented at the 49th Annual Meeting of the Society for American Archaeology, Portland, Oregon.

Stevenson, M. G., 1985, The Formation of Artifact Assemblages at Workshop/Habitation sites: Models from Peace Point in Northern Alberta, *American Antiquity* 50:63–81.

Stevenson, M. G., 1986, *Window on the Past: Archaeological Assessment of the Peace Point Site,*

Wood Buffalo National Park, Alberta, Studies in Archaeology, Architecture and History, National Historic Parks and Sites Branch, Parks Canada, Environment Canada, Ottawa.

Stevenson, M. G., 1989, Sourdoughs and Cheechakos: The Emergence of Identity-Signaling Groups, *Journal of Anthropological Archaeology,* 8:270–312.

Stockton, E. D., 1973, Shaw's Creek Shelter: Human Displacement of Artifacts and Its Significance, *Mankind* 9:112–117.

Tanner, A., 1979, *Bringing Home Animals: Religious Ideology and Mode of Production of the Mistassini Cree Hunters,* Social and Economic Studies No. 23, Institute of Social and Environmental Research, Memorial University of Newfoundland, St. Johns, Newfoundland.

Tringham, R., Cooper, G., Odell, G., Voytek, B., and Whitman, A., 1974, Experimentation in the Formation of Edge Damage: A New Approach to Lithic Analysis, *Journal of Field Archaeology*1:171–196.

Vehik, S., 1977, Bone Fragments and Bone Grease Manufacturing: Review of Their Archaeological Use and Potential, *Plains Anthropologist* 22:169–182.

Villa, P., and Courtin, J., 1983, The Interpretation of Stratified Sites: A View from Underground, *Journal of Archaeological Science* 10:267–281.

Wantanabe, H., 1968, Subsistence and Ecology of Northern Food Gatherers with Special Reference to the Ainu. In *Man the Hunter* (R. B. Lee and I. DeVore, eds.), Aldine, Chicago, pp. 69–77.

Wenzel, G. W., 1983, *A Survey of the Material and Social Patterning of a Recent Inuit Camp Group,* Paper Presented at the Chacmool Conference on Archaeology, University of Calgary, Calgary, Alberta.

Wilk, R., and Schiffer, M. B., 1979, The Archaeology of Vacant Lots in Tucson, Arizona, *American Antiquity* 44:530–536.

Winterhalder, B., and Smith, E. A. (eds.), 1981, *Hunter–Gatherer Foraging Strategies: Ethnographic and Archaeological Analysis,* The University of Chicago Press, Chicago.

Wood, W. R., and Johnson, D. L., 1978, A Survey of Disturbance Processes in Archaeological Site Formation. In *Advances in Archaeological Method and Theory, Vol. 1* (M. B. Schiffer, ed.), Academic Press, New York, pp. 315–381.

Yellen, J., 1977, *Archaeological Approaches to the Present: Models for Reconstructing the Past,*Academic Press, New York.

Part III

Postscript
The End of Spatial Analysis

At the beginning of this book, we outlined three phases in the study of the spatial patterning of archaeological materials: an initial period of recognition and description, followed by the development of methods, and finally the interpretation of the patterns that emerge. A brief review of these three stages reveals something about the evolution of studies of spatial patterning and perhaps something about where such investigations are headed.

Needless to say, the spatial distribution of archaeological materials today is of concern to almost every archaeologist. It is clear that such patterning, that is, the distribution and the relationships among artifacts and features in the ground, contains a great deal of important information about the past. Although this is particularly the case at Stone Age sites, it is also true of virtually any archaeological evidence. Thus recognition of the utility of such contextual information is essentially universal in the field.

A wide variety of methods for the definition of such patterns have been developed over the last 15 years. A review of spatial methods and techniques by Carr (1984) provides a useful summary of many of these. Since that time, Whallon (1984), Simek (1989), and others have suggested enhancements and improvements. It seems to be the case that the necessary statistical methods for the definition of spatial patterning are at hand. In addition, the last 5 years or so have seen the growing availability of computer software specifically for spatial analysis, developed for archaeology by archaeologists (Table 1). Suffice it to say that we now have the means to define patterns of distribution, either those obvious to the human eye or those discerned by a computer using sophisticated quantitative, analytical techniques. Such robust methods of analysis, however, are not sufficient to answer our questions. As Whallon pointed out some years ago (1978), the majority of quantitative spatial analyses to date had "produced few interpretable results and virtually no consistency. The results obtained from different kinds of analyses are usually conflicting and none are more clearly interpretable than others."

The third and final step in the study of spatial information, and the really big remaining issue then, is what do these patterns mean—how do we understand and interpret the patterns that are recognized and defined? This last step is in fact a long and difficult journey that has involved several detours and obstacles in the form of errant assumptions and concepts about the basic units of analysis (artifacts and tools) and about the kinds of patterning to be expected (e.g., tool kits and activity areas).

A number of these initial assumptions have had to be discarded. Traditional morphological types simply often do not define meaningful functional categories. Unless accurate assessment of the actual function of prehistoric implements can be made, the definition of the activities in which they were used is almost impossible. Until very recently, we simply did not know how a retouched flake or an end scraper was used.

Fortunately, studies of use residues and microwear have greatly improved our abilities to describe artifact function. The identification of organic and inorganic residues remaining on artifacts also offers an important tool for determining use (e.g., Gurfinkel and Franklin 1988; Loy 1983; Anderson-Gerfaud 1986). The analysis of microwear striations and polishes on the edges of stone tools has greatly enhanced our ability to talk about the specific functions of artifacts (e.g., Keeley 1980). Keeley's chapter in this volume is in fact a *tour de force* on how such data on tool utilization can be used in spatial studies. It is now the case that detailed studies of microwear and residues can provide critical functional information for the analysis of artifact association and patterning. We can begin to talk about the actual uses of the materials we are studying.

Other initial assumptions had to do with how artifacts came to be where they were found. Tool kits and activity areas were important concepts that arose as a part of the new archaeology (Binford and Binford 1966; Whallon 1973). "Statistical analysis of the implements found at Paleolithic sites can identify the groups of tools that were used for various kinds of jobs. These groupings suggest how early man's life was organized" (Binford and Binford 1969:70).

> We would therefore expect that the various tool types in palæolithic sites will be differentially distributed over the area of occupation and that groups of tool types will be mutually correlated in terms of their patterns of distribution, particularly in the larger and richer sites. These groups should represent functionally associated tools, or "tool kits," which were used in the same activity or activities. The distributions of these "tool kits" should, in turn, often be associated with specific cultural features or with certain types or locations of sites. (Whallon 1973:117)

The first efforts toward spatial analysis then were an attempt quantitatively define such tool kits and activity areas on prehistoric living floors. But in truth,

Table 1.   Computer Software for Display and Analysis of Spatial Archaeological Data

The Archaeologist's Analytical Toolkit—A series of computer models for data manipulation and analysis. All programs run on basic IBM PC or are compatible with 256K or more of memory. The programs use a consistent data file format and style of interactive prompts for ease of use. Some of the programs are designed for specific archaeological problems, whereas others are more general-purpose utilities. Spatial Analysis Module includes programs for converting point data to grid counts, for calculating Hodder and Okell's A and Dispersion ratios, k-means cluster analysis, Johnson's local density analysis, and nearest neighbor. (Keith Kintigh, 1988.)

Arcospace—Provides programs for a wide variety of spatial analysis, including intra- and intersite analysis, interaction analysis, and sociostructural analysis of, for example, cemeteries. It also offers opportunities for nonspatially oriented hierarchical and nonhierarchical classification. Arcospace also provides options for siumlation studies and the creation of artificial data sets and includes a number of utility programs for basic operations such as point to grid conversions, data smoothing, and file organization. Specifically Arcospace includes facilities for k-means nonhierarchical cluster analysis, unconstrained clustering, index of segregation, and index of aggregation, nearest neighbor and gravity analysis, Hodder and Okell's A-Index of Association, dimensional analysis of variance, and Morisita's index, local density analysis, Greig-Smith's variance/mean ratio and chi-square index of dispersion, and Carr's coefficient of polythetic association. (T. Douglas Price and Hans Peter Blankholm, 1988.)

GMS—A sophisticated computer mapping system which produces publication-quality maps or working documents at a fraction of the cost of conventional methods. GMS brings out the graphic, spatial component of your data so often lost in a welter of lengthy description and dull tabulation. GMS increase both both the visual impact and the interpretative potential of your data. Map coverage can range from a statewide map to an individual collection unit plan. GMS will window onto a part of the basemap and scale the window to any desired size. GMS takes data from your data base and superimposes them on a digitized basemap. GMS includes the tools to digitize and edit base maps, while your data base system provides the data base data through its report formatter. Objects and features can be mapped using different colors, symbols, line or hatch styles to identify attributes such as site type, period, species, soil type, survey intensity, features type, etc. (Ian Johnson, 1986.)

Hindsite—Is a computer tool for archaeology based on AutoCAD, C and dBase III+. The system is designed to let the computer draw composite plans for archaeology and to help the archaeologist in site interpretation by using three dimensional modeling techniques. The archaeologist first draws each deposit of the site using a digitizer and then adds stratigraphic relationships of each deposit in to a data base. It is then possible to reconstruct phase plans by recalling each deposit in turn from the bottom of the phase to the top. As each plan is called up, Hindsite "tests" each deposit, and providing that it is stratigraphically correct, will draw the deposit on the screen. The archaeologist is able to look at all or part of a trench, or indeed, more than one trench, provided that they are based on the same grid. (Brian Alvey, 1989.)

Siteplot—A statistical and graphical site analyzing program to produce artifact quantity plans by means of proportional circles. The limits of computable digging areas are 60 × 42 squares, equivalent to nine screens. The class calculation methods also include the Cziesla algorithm. Program includes: (1) Sitebase—a data recording and retrieval package (SAA standard) for archaeological sites with up to five levels of heirarchical recording structures (dBase III+/IV) compatible. Comprises general entry fields for site data as well as archaeological finds. Can be tailored to almost all customer's needs. Program can be combined with other products in the Site-series. Prints formatted data record lists as well as find labels if used on the spot, and (2) Sitemap—a 3-D program to produce surface and section plans from archaeological sites. Facilitates artifact plots, projections, and views from any angle with various symbols. Variable zooming from 10 to 3000%. Requires Hercules card. (Jörg Lindenbeck, 1989.)

quantitative spatial analyses have rarely been successful in identifying meaningful sets of tools or activity areas.

The failure of these methods is, in fact, an indictment of our basic assumptions. Ethnoarchaeological studies have played a particularly important role in challenging those initial assumptions and in suggesting new models for our consideration in the investigation of spatial patterning (e.g., Yellen 1977; O'Connell 1987, among others). As we noted earlier (p. 197), some of the conclusions from actualistic observations during the past 10 years include: (1) concentrations of functionally associated artifacts or tool kits were not regularly discarded where they were used in single-purpose activity areas; (2) hearths commonly represent a focal point for a variety of domestic, maintenance, and special-purpose activities; (3) size sorting of refuse can be an important means for distinguishing locations where refuse-producing activities actually occurred; and (4) a variety of natural processes can reorder the refuse generated by human activities.

Several chapters in this volume elaborate on the theme of postdepositional modification of distributional patterns. Carr, Keeley, and Stevenson emphasize the influence of *human* activities, either the deliberate or incidental rearranging of refuse. Rigaud and Simek focus on the impact of *natural* processes that can rearrange refuse, including the impact of nonhuman predators on distributions of bone refuse. Gregg, Kintigh, and Whallon use simulated disturbances of an ethnographically known arrangement of structures, features, and refuse to make two very important observations. They demonstrate that quantitative methods for the analysis of intrasite distributions can identify the original spatial patterns from the site. Moreover, despite significant simulated postdepositional disturbances, they demonstrate that much of the original patterning can be retrieved.

Actualistic studies are helping to reveal both prior misconceptions and to offer new concepts of great use to prehistoric research. O'Connell, Hawkes, and Blurton Jones (Chapter 3 in this volume) examine male and female activities with regard to the overall camp structure of contemporary Hadza hunter–gatherers of Tanzania and the implications for archaeological spatial analysis. Gargett and Hayden (Chapter 1 in this volume) provide eloquent evidence for the power of new models of spatial patterning. Their study examines the relationship between kinship distance and physical distance at a Pintupi encampment in the Western Desert of Australia and identifies the kinship links associated with the most pronounced spatial patterning. They argue that kinship and economic interdependence provide the best insights into the reasons for observable habitation patterning at a site. Sharing between individuals and families is a common thread in relationships that display the most predictable spatial patterning. Such studies of traditional groups offer one of the only opportunities for us to investigate directly the determinants of spatial patterning.

As the chapters in this volume attest, we stand today at the threshold of the last step in the study of spatial patterning—we are beginning to know what we do not know about the meaning of the distribution of prehistoric materials at stone age sites. In effect, we are at the end of the beginning of spatial analytical studies. We know that patterns of distribution contain important information. We have the methods necessary to define such patterns. We are now beginning to concentrate on what those patterns mean. Experimental studies of stone tool use, archaeometric analyses of residues, computer simulations of patterns of discard and of postdepositional disturbance, and ethnoarchaeological investigations offer new data and new models for understanding these patterns from past, and more importantly for deciphering human behavior in the archaeological record.

1. REFERENCES

Anderson-Gerfaud, P., 1986, A Few Comments Concerning Residue Analysis of Stone Plant-Processing Tools. In *Technical Aspects of Microwear Studies on Stone Tools* (L. Owen and G. Unrath, eds.), Early Man News, Tübingen, pp.. 69–81.

Binford, S. R., and Binford, L. R., 1966, A Preliminary Analysis of Functional Variability in the Mousterian of Levallois Facies. In *Recent Studies in Paleoanthropology* (J. D. Clarke and F. C. Howell, eds.), *American Anthropologist* 69(2,2), pp. 238–295.

Binford, S. R., and Binford, L. R., 1969, Stone Tools and Human Behavior, *Scientific American* 220(4):70–84.

Carr, C., 1984, The Nature of Organization of Intrasite Archaeological Records and Spatial Analytic Approaches to Their Investigation, *Advances in Archaeological Method and Theory* 7:103–222.

Gurfinkel, D. M., and Franklin, U. M., 1988, A Study of the Feasibility of Detecting Blood Residue on Artifacts, *Journal of Archaeological Science* 15:83–97.

Kintigh, K. W., and Ammerman, A., 1982, Heuristic Approaches to Spatial Analysis in Archaeology, *American Antiquity* 47:31–63.

Keeley, L. H., 1980, *Experimental Determination of Stone Tool Uses*, University of Chicago Press, Chicago.

Lindenbeck, J., 1989, SITEPLOT. Ein Programm zur archäologischen Mengenkartierung, *Bulletin de la Société Préhistorique Luxembourgeoise* 10:55–63.

Loy, T. H., 1983, Prehistoric Blood Residues: Detection on Tool Surfaces and Identification of the Species of Origin, *Science* 220:1269–1271.

O'Connell, J. F., 1987, Alyawara Site Structure and Its Archaeological Implications, *American Antiquity* 52:74–108.

Simek, J., 1989, Structure and Diversity in Intrasite Spatial Analysis. In *Quantifying Diversity in Archaeology*, (R. D. Leonard and G. T. Jones, eds.), Cambridge University Press, Cambridge, pp. 59–68.

Whallon, R., 1973, Spatial Analysis of Palaeolithic Occupation Areas. In *The Explanation of Culture Change: Models in Prehistory*, (C. Renfrew, ed.), University of Pittsburgh Press, Pittsburgh, pp. 115–130.

Whallon, R., 1978, The Spatial Analysis of Mesolithic Occupation Floors: A Reappraisal. In *Mesolithic Settlement in Northwest Europe*, (P. A. Mellars, ed.), Duckworth, London, pp. 27–35.

Whallon, R., 1984, Unconstrained Clustering for the Analysis of Spatial Distributions in Archaeology. In *Intrasite Spatial Analysis in Archaeology* (H. J. Hietala, ed.), Cambridge University Press, Cambridge, pp. 242–277.

Yellen, J., 1977, *Archaeological Approaches to the Present*, Academic Press, New York.

Index

Aborigine, 22, 23, 72, 248. *See also* Alyawara; Gidjingali; Pintupi; Pitjantjara
Aché, 28, 44, 72–74
Activity areas, intrasite, 1–3, 7–9, 13, 27, 30, 35, 37, 39, 41, 61, 62, 65, 66, 69–75, 96, 98, 135, 140, 150, 197, 215–217, 248, 249, 251, 259, 273, 275, 277, 278, 288, 302
  animal processing, 216, 263
  butchery, 103, 115, 118, 136, 137, 142, 174, 263
  bone tool manufacture, 263, 265, 267, 289
  grease processing, 251, 252, 283
  hide processing, 263, 265, 267, 289
  marrow extraction, 103, 115, 118, 132, 134, 137, 142, 230, 263
  communal, 65, 67–74, 92, 93, 97, 103, 104, 127, 136–138, 277, 288
  concept defined, 200
  consumption, 29, 66, 103, 108, 109, 111, 114, 115, 118, 127, 131, 132, 137, 142, 164, 216–217
  cooking, 97, 108, 109, 111, 114, 118
  household, 27, 29, 30, 65, 68, 69–74, 91–94, 97, 98, 103–105, 108–111, 114, 115, 118, 127, 131, 137–141, 151, 152, 155, 163, 174, 179, 181, 258, 259, 269, 273, 275, 276, 288, 289, 295
  maintenance, 69–71, 108, 111, 241, 244–247, 251, 277
  male/female, division, 4, 8, 67, 70, 73, 74, 223, 287–292
  plant processing, 263, 267
  sleeping, 29, 64, 66, 95, 97, 103, 108, 111, 115, 216, 241, 248
  special-purpose, 65, 68, 69, 72, 74, 97, 155, 174, 251, 258, 273, 293
  stone knapping, 29, 216, 230, 251

Activity areas (*Cont.*)
  See also Disposal areas; Hadza; Hafted tools, retooling, location of; Hearths; Kua San; !Kung San; Peace Point site; Pincevent site, habitation no. 1; Roasting pits; Site use, stages of occupation; Size sorting of refuse; Vaufrey site, Grotte XV; Verberie site, Hearth 1
Actualistic research, vii, 2–5, 7–9, 78, 197–198, 200, 304. *See also* Ethnoarchaeological research; Experimental research; Taphonomic research
Algonkian, 29, 289
Alyawara, 12–14, 22, 26, 27, 30, 43, 44, 72–74, 272, 274, 275, 276
Ammerman, A., 153
Anticipated mobility. *See* Site structure, length of occupation, anticipated
Archaeological sites
  cave, 4, 199, 201, 205
  open-air, 1, 2, 4, 8, 142, 150, 260
  rockshelter, 4
  See also Peace Point site; Pincevent site; Site types; Vaufrey site; Verberie site
Artifacts, miscellaneous, 156, 157, 162, 163, 167, 168, 170, 171, 177, 179, 180, 184, 188–192. *See also* Stone artifacts
Ascher, R., 2, 286, 294
Ashdumps, 67, 97, 106, 107, 109, 110, 125, 127, 136
Athapaskan, 29
Audouze, F., 260

Baker, C., 272
Bakgalagadi, 35, 39, 42, 53, 54
  description of spatial patterns, 36, 38–42, 44–55

Visual inspection of site plans *(Cont.)*
  See also (Cont.)
    data analysis; Quantitative methods;
    Vaufrey site, Grotte XV; Verberie site,
    Hearth 1

Whallon, R., 2–3, 8, 148, 260, 301–302, 304
Whitelaw, T., 12, 13, 16, 26–28, 30, 34, 44, 49, 72, 74
Willowlake Dene, 275

Windbreaks, 7, 13, 66, 92–94, 96, 97, 103–106, 108, 111, 112, 114–122, 125–128, 131–138, 141
  toss zone, 118
Woodburn, J., 62, 64, 68

Yellen, J., 2–3, 8, 26, 27, 43, 44, 53, 55, 72, 74, 93, 135, 136, 141, 149–155, 157, 163, 194, 195, 272, 273, 278